IMAGES
of America

MORAGA

On the Cover: The delightful smile of former longtime Moraga resident Louise Sherritt Tibbetts was captured in this photograph taken about 1940 by her husband, D. Reginald Tibbetts. Wearing a skirt and blouse purchased on a recent trip to Mexico, Louise sits in a field of mustard flowers. The eucalyptus tree in the background stood close to the intersection of Oxford Drive and Camino Pablo, when the area was relatively undeveloped. While the field of flowers has become a neighborhood of roads and houses, the backdrop of the hills of King Canyon still looks much the same today. (Photograph by D. Reginald Tibbetts.)

IMAGES of America

MORAGA

Susan K. Skilton

ARCADIA PUBLISHING

ISBN 978-1-4671-1620-6

Published by Arcadia Publishing
Charleston, South Carolina

Printed in the United States of America

Library of Congress Control Number: 2015952340

For all general information, please contact Arcadia Publishing:
Telephone 843-853-2070
Fax 843-853-0044
E-mail sales@arcadiapublishing.com
For customer service and orders:
Toll-Free 1-888-313-2665

Visit us on the Internet at www.arcadiapublishing.com

To my father, Ron, and in memory of my mother, Evelyn.

Contents

ACKNOWLEDGMENTS

In preparing this book, I had a wonderful opportunity to learn a lot about the town I live in by working in the archives at the Moraga History Center. I wish to express my gratitude to my fellow Moraga Historical Society board members and to the archives staff in the Moraga History Center who were most helpful in my endeavor to find the photographs and stories of the town of Moraga. I am especially grateful to archives director Elsie Mastick, who helped me find photographs and documents and answered my many questions. Both Elsie Mastick and Moraga Historical Society president Susan Sperry kindly reviewed the manuscript. Thanks also to my husband, John A. Kaiser, for sharing his expertise in local geology. I also wish to most sincerely thank Stuart J. Swiedler, whose website eastbayhillsproject.org and personal assistance identifying train photographs were immensely helpful in my work on the second chapter. I am also very grateful for the kind and helpful assistance of my title managers at Arcadia Publishing, Ginny Rasmussen and Sarah Gottlieb.

Two written resources were very informative as I worked on this photograph history of Moraga. The history of Moraga Rancho property is well documented by Sandy Kimball in the second edition of *Moraga's Pride: Rancho Laguna de los Palos Colorados*. Frank Draeger's manuscript "Developing the Moraga Company Ranch: 1922–1977" is written with Draeger's first-hand knowledge of people, places, and events in the development of the Moraga Valley.

Unless otherwise noted, all images appear courtesy of the Moraga Historical Society.

INTRODUCTION

While it has developed into a suburb active with community life, Moraga holds on to its historic charm of ranches and orchards, its legacy as part of a Mexican land grant, and its treasured open space. The beautiful name of the land grant originally awarded in 1835 to Moraga's namesake, Joaquin Moraga, Rancho Laguna de los Palos Colorados, takes its imagery from the tule pond (*laguna*), now filled in, at the site of the local high school, and the redwoods (*Palos Colorados*) at the southeastern end of town.

Moraga is one of three small towns and cities in the East Bay area that work together to form a sense of community and cooperation: Lafayette, Orinda, and Moraga. As a group, the cities and town are often referred to as Lamorinda. Situated between Orinda and Lafayette, Moraga is the only suburb of the three to lack a freeway entrance, which means it is just a little more isolated from commuter traffic and urban development. Moraga is just a few miles away from a bit more hustle and bustle in the neighboring towns and cities—close enough for easy access to city life, but far enough removed for its residents to feel nestled away in a quiet little valley surrounded by hills.

The first human inhabitants in the area were the Saklan Indians, who hunted, gathered, and fished. The first European settlers were the Moraga and Bernal families, who had jointly received the land grant of just over 13,000 acres, encompassing a far greater area than the land that was eventually developed into a town. These families settled in 1835. When the land that was granted to Moraga and his cousin Juan Bernal by the Mexican government came under US dominion in 1848, the two families had to prove to the new government that their grant was valid and obtain a patent. The process took many years, and while the land title was finally upheld in 1855, the final patent was only granted in 1878. In the meantime, land was lost to other settlers by various means including tract sales and forfeitures. Some early residents took up farming and ranching on land they claimed under the homesteading act, assuming that the land was in public domain. Whether they were squatters or homesteaders, they established homes, ranches, and businesses on the rancho. Some were entitled to keep their property by the Pre-Emption Law of 1841, and others found different legal means to hold onto the land where they had chosen to settle. Many of the parcels were disputed in the courts for many years. Horace Carpentier, a lawyer from New York (and sometime state assemblyman and mayor of Oakland) had visions of controlling the shipping and railway routes from the San Francisco Bay up through Northern California. Carpentier was initially involved in representing the claim of the Moraga Rancho for the family. As payment for his legal services, he acquired land and continued to obtain more as it became available. He eventually controlled most of the property. Losing interest in the potential for the railway route as economic prospects changed, he sold off his holdings.

Shortly after Moraga and Bernal settled on their rancho, they were followed by the gold rush immigrants, who had quickly increased the population and dotted the area with ranches and farms, which they owned, rented, or sharecropped, by 1850. Loggers were also attracted to the area's redwoods, and roads were soon created for the transportation of cattle and lumber. Many of the settlers came to the area from the East, and some of them had only recently landed there from Ireland and Europe. Others followed their predecessors from Mexico. Many farmers, including dairy farmers, came from the Azores. The first trains ran through the area in 1910. Moraga was a significant waypoint for both passengers and freight for many years.

Long before it became a town, Moraga (then called the Moraga Valley) developed into an early suburb as a stop on the train route. Subdivisions sprang up to serve the commuters from the small town to Oakland and San Francisco. When the trains eventually stopped carrying passengers in 1941, they had long been replaced with roads and a plan to connect Moraga to the nearby freeway. Development plans for Moraga increased during that time, but eventually the plan for a freeway entrance was abandoned due to opposition. Residents of Moraga also passed Measure A in 1986 to protect steep ridgelines from development. While development in Moraga has continued on a small scale, so has the maintenance and development of open space, which has proven to be a jewel in the crown of the town, much prized by its residents and visitors. At one time attracting the attention of construction companies for development into a model city, and at another attracting interest as a potential site for the United Nations, the town remained quietly semi-rural into the 1970s when it was incorporated, and still has its beautiful grassy rolling hills, creeks, redwoods, oaks, and wildflowers. Horses and cows have long been a common sight here. Deer wander freely from the hills into yards to munch on garden flowers. Red-tailed hawks soar overhead. Occasionally, wildcats, foxes, and raccoons are among the wildlife spotted within town boundaries.

In 2010, the population of the town was just over 16,000. Moraga's community spirit has contributed to the development of its organizations and their activities, and to the preservation of its natural beauty, all of which make the small town a lively, pretty, and stimulating environment to live in or visit.

One

HERITAGE OF THE LAND

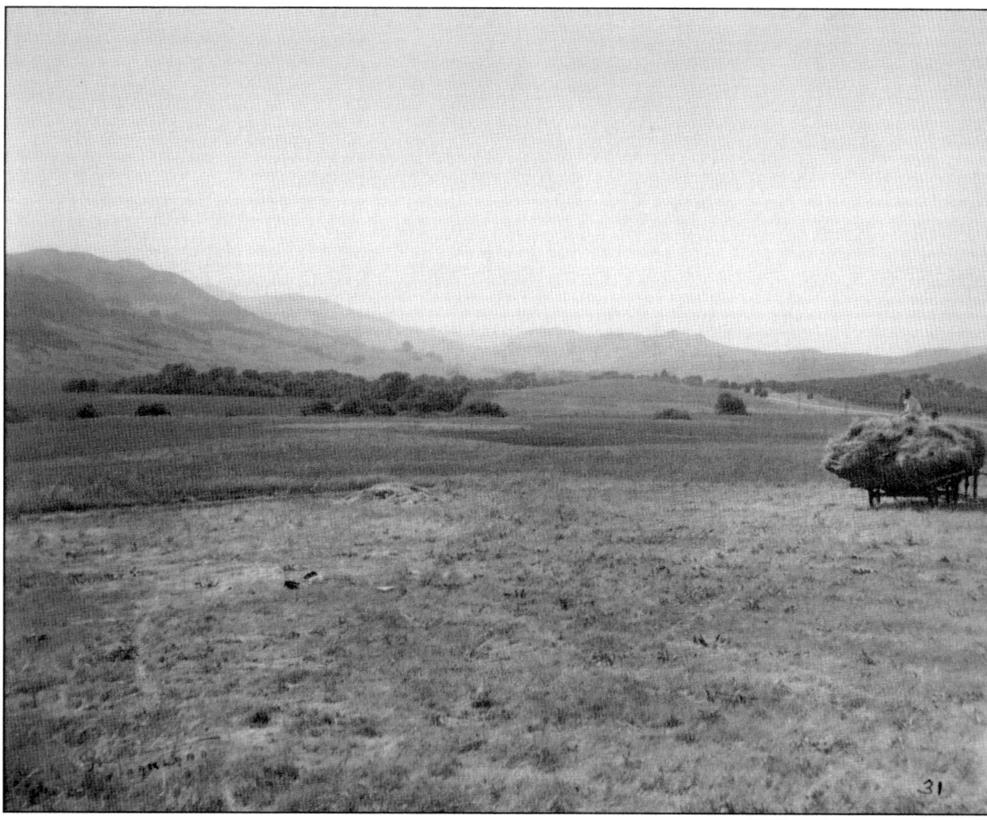

Ample water resources and a pleasant climate created a good hunting and fishing environment for the Saklan Indians who once lived in the Moraga Valley. Although current residents of the area may complain that the garden soil is thick clay that can only reluctantly be tilled, that same earth paired with a temperate climate has been well suited to ranching and agriculture since the early 1800s.

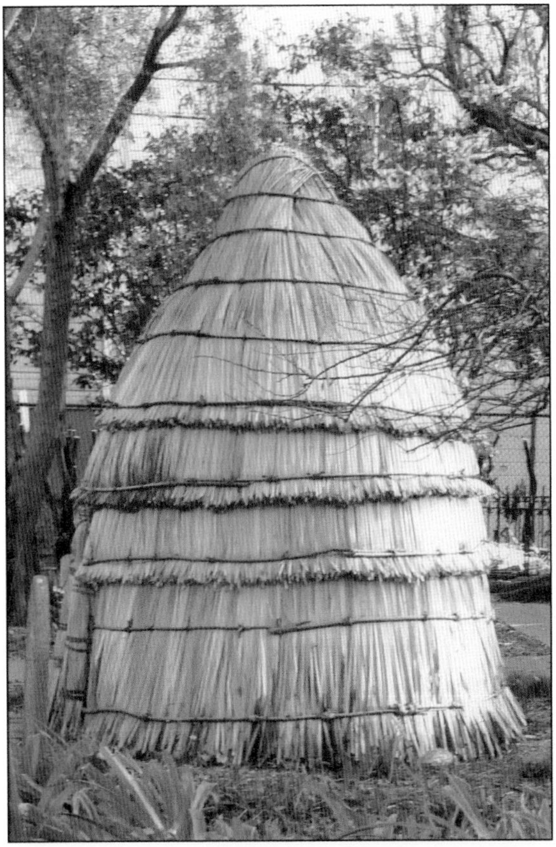

The Saklan Indians, a tribelet of the Miwok language group, lived in small bands hunting, fishing, and gathering in the grasslands area, where elk, bear, and antelope roamed. The indigenous trees were an asset, providing both food and weaponry. The Indians ground acorns from the native oaks into a mush. They threw buckeye balls into the streams to stun the fish. They traded with other tribes to the north for obsidian in order to fashion arrowheads, many of which were found during the construction of Lake La Salle on the St. Mary's College campus. The Saklan villages were temporary structures of tule reed huts that were moved when better hunting, fishing, and gathering opportunities appeared elsewhere. Like other Northern California Indians, some Saklans were drawn into mission life by the Spanish. Some escaped back to their villages, sometimes extending an authorized furlough into a permanent return to their families. Raids by the Spanish to recapture them were often unsuccessful.

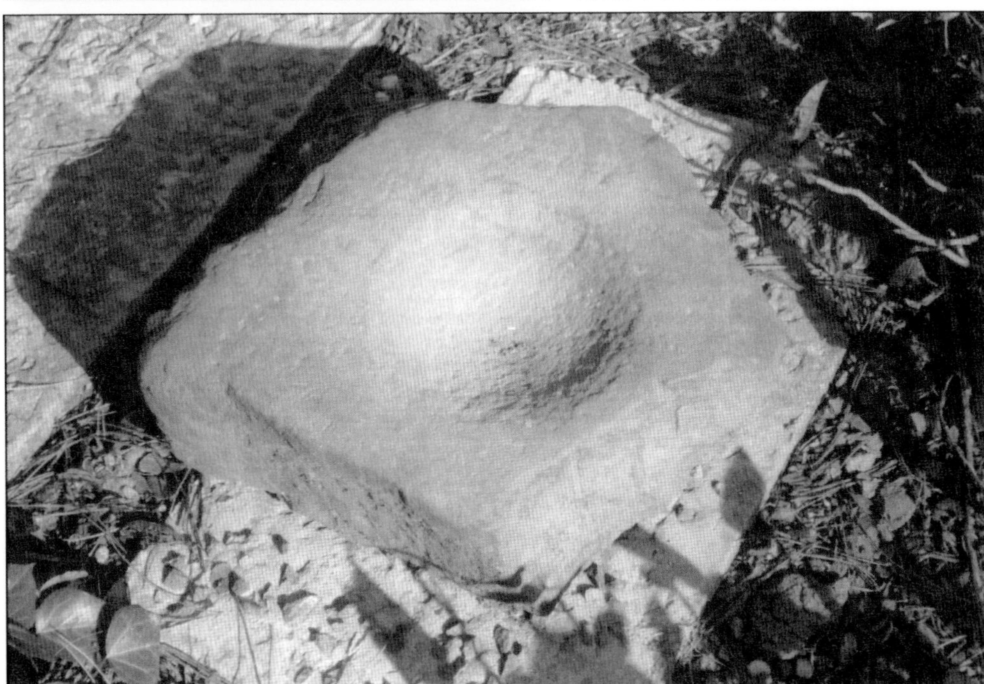

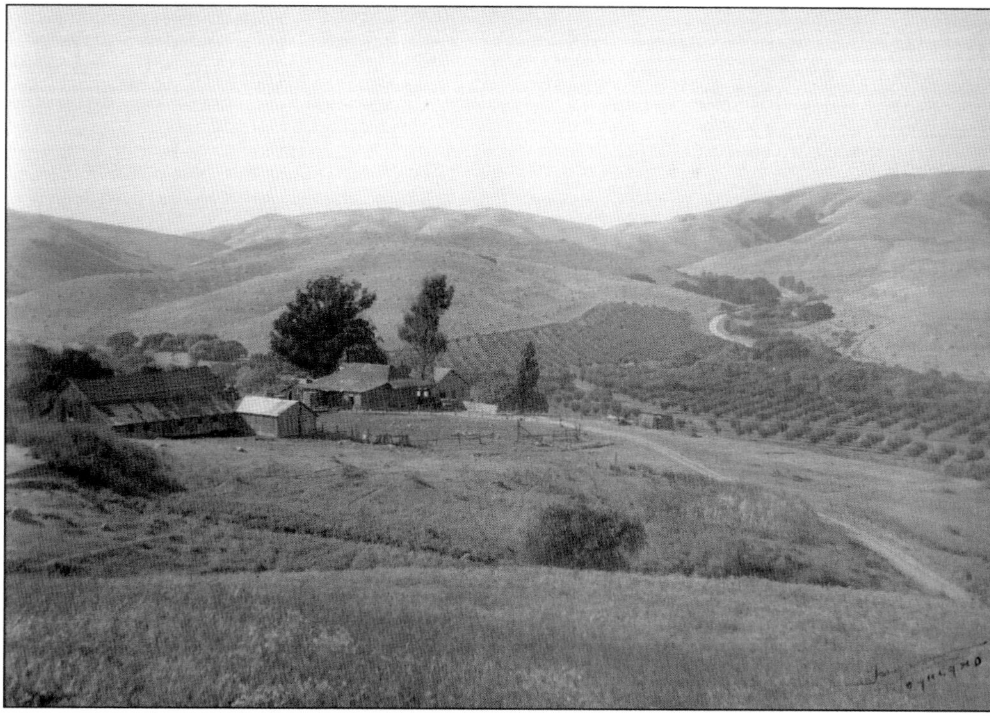

The family of Joaquin Moraga lived first in wooden structures built in the area where the Camino Woods subdivision, off of Camino Pablo, now stands. Within a few years, they built their adobe close to a spring, on a hill with a view of the nearby valley. Now falling within the borders of the neighboring town of Orinda, the adobe still retains its original adobe bricks and has been designated a heritage structure. The photograph above shows the adobe home as it appeared in 1935, surrounded by the hills and valleys. It is shown below undergoing reconstruction in 1940 under the direction of owner Katherine Irvine, wife of developer James Irvine.

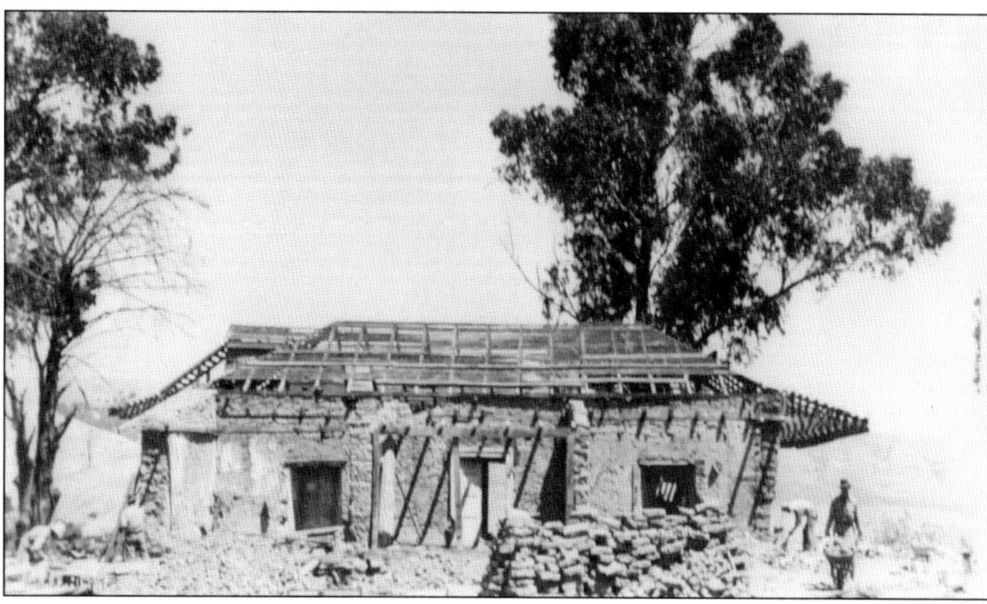

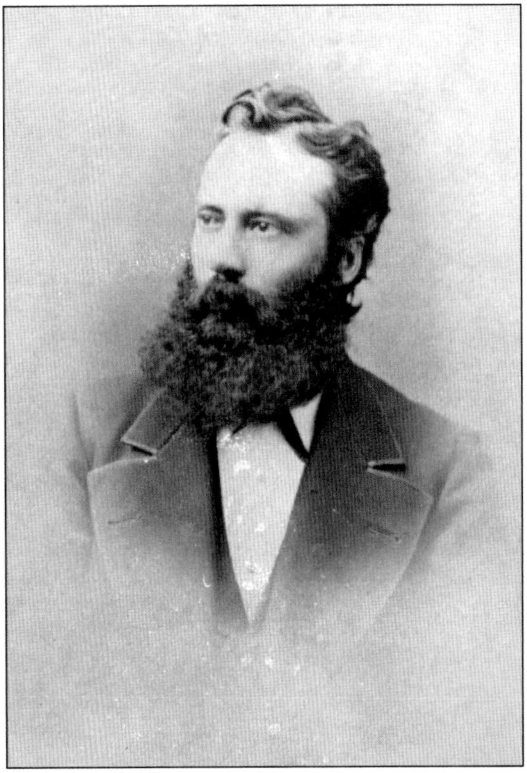

Charles A. Hooper, pictured at left, acquired 10,000 acres of the Moraga Rancho lands from Horace Carpentier in 1912 and sold the property to James Irvine soon after. Irvine (below) formed the Moraga Company in order to develop the land. He was the majority stockholder and president of the Moraga Company. Sales were conducted in the office of Sen. Arthur H. Breed in Oakland. In 1914 and 1915, the company created four subdivisions near the railway. However, the only subdivision in which lots were sold was Valle Vista, where 55 lots were sold and 20 houses were built. The Moraga Company also planted orchards and vegetable crops in the valley and developed a commercial center near the railway station. The Moraga Company built the hotel, which later became known as the "Barn" to attract interest in land sales.

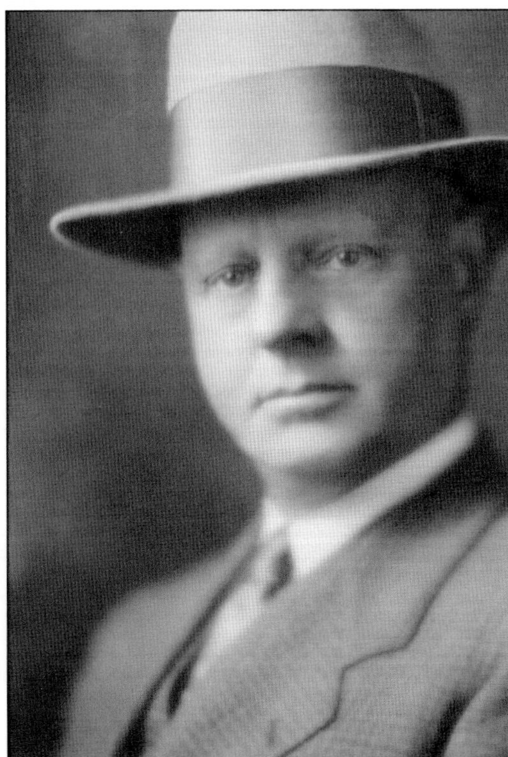

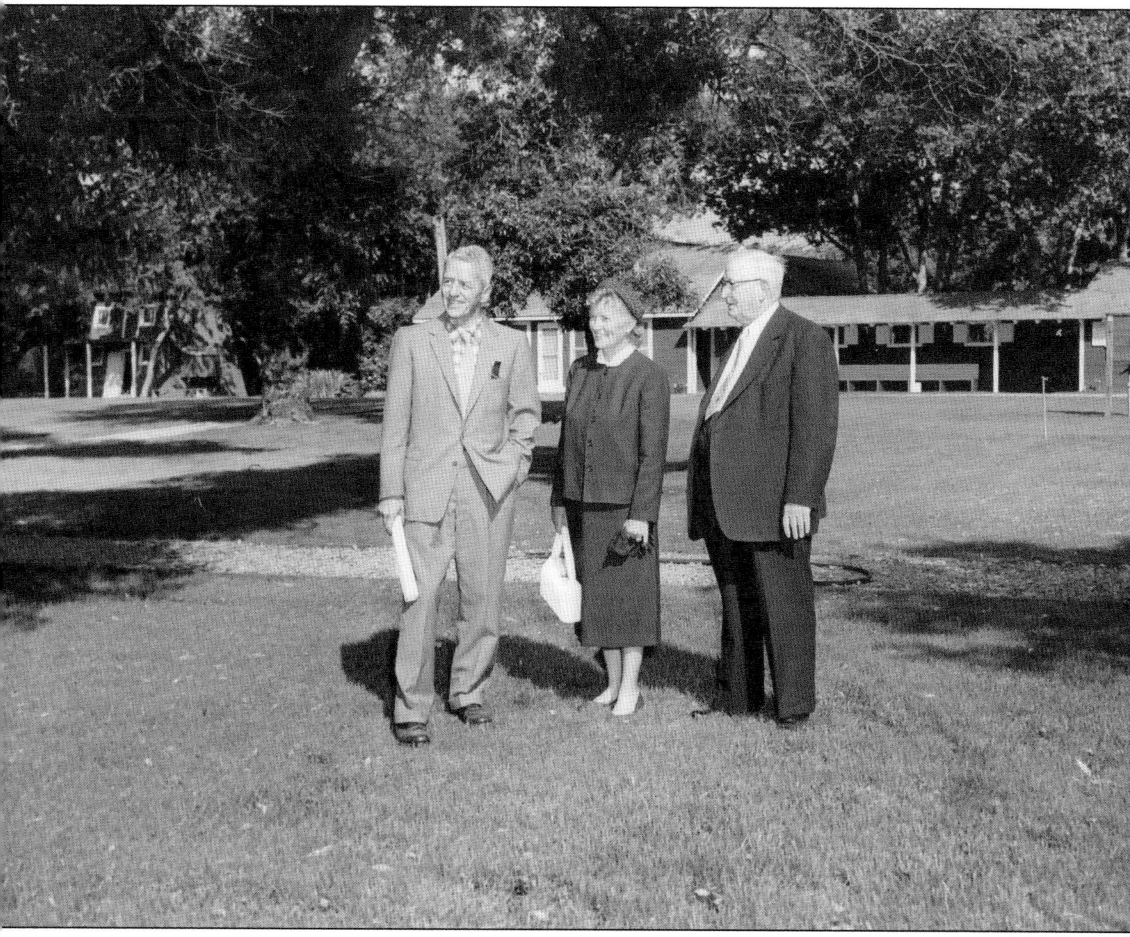

The property purchased by James Irvine from Charles A. Hooper, and then sold to Utah Construction & Mining Company, about 5,000 acres of the original Mexican land grant, was referred to as "the Ranch." At the intersection of Larch Avenue and Tia Place, hogs were raised on a piece of land called "the pig ranch" for the company cookhouse. Staff could eat and bunk in the Ranch buildings. In this 1950s photograph, from left to right, Benson Eschenbach, chief architect for the Utah Construction Company; Mrs. Harold Parker, longtime Moraga Valley resident; and Bill Barnes meet in front of the Moraga Ranch buildings. An architectural review committee of Barnes, Parker, and civil engineer Frank Draeger met each week to review the plans of the Utah Construction Company to approve the exterior design of any building before construction was begun. Eschenbach designed Moraga's first post office, which was used until 1966.

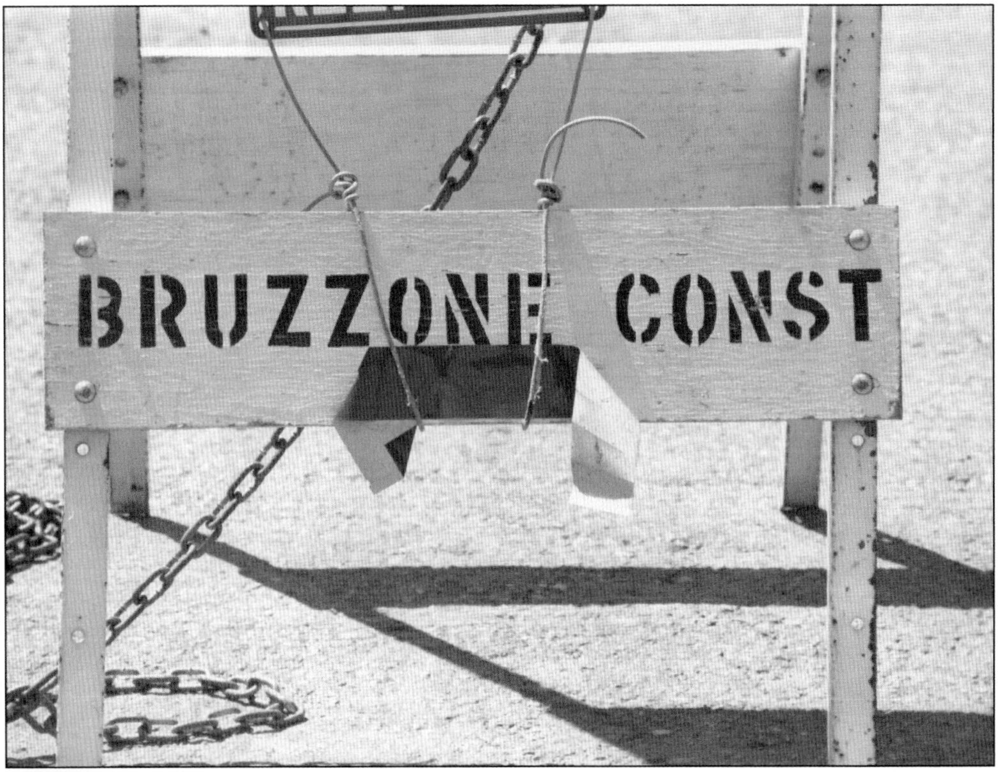

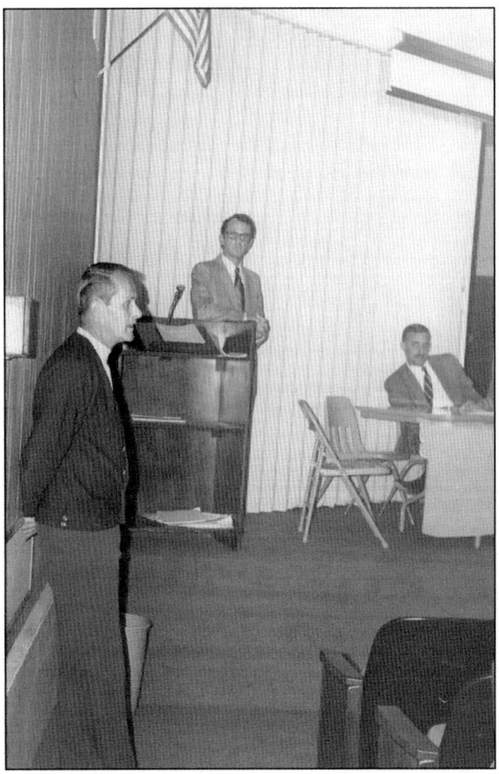

A well-known name in the Moraga area, Russell Bruzzone owned, controlled, and developed much of the land that had not previously been developed by the Moraga Company. In the 1960s, Bruzzone bought land for development from the Utah Construction Company. At that time, he already owned the Moraga Shopping Center, and had done some development on Moraga Ranch property. Bruzzone developed commercial property in and around Moraga Center and leased areas surrounding Moraga Center for residential and commercial use. Having used them previously, Bruzzone retained the Wallace Moraga Realty company as his sales representative and Wilson & Co. (where Frank Draeger, civil engineer of much of Moraga, was employed) as his engineering company. Bruzzone built many subdivisions and sold numerous lots in the Moraga area and sold raw land parcels to builders and individuals to construct their own subdivisions or housing units. In the photograph at left, he is speaking at far left. Also pictured are realtor Clark Wallace, also standing, and community member Tom Holmes, seated.

Moraga owes its name and its initial development to the Moraga family who owned and ranched the land in an area much larger than the eventual town boundaries. Joaquin Moraga and his cousin Juan Bernal had been granted over 13,000 acres by the Mexican government in 1835. José Joaquin de la Santisima Trinidad Moraga died in 1856, not long after he and his family began ranching the land. His son Joseph (also known as José) de Jesus Moraga and his wife, Maria de la Cruz Sibrian, inherited much of the property. In the cabinet photograph below, Maria wears an elegant dress. She died in 1880 at the age of 53. Her son, who was baptized as José Gabriel Marciel Moraga but went by the name Gabriel Ygnacio Moraga, is pictured at right. He and his wife, Ella Florence Olive Moraga, were the last of the family to own the adobe and some of its adjacent property.

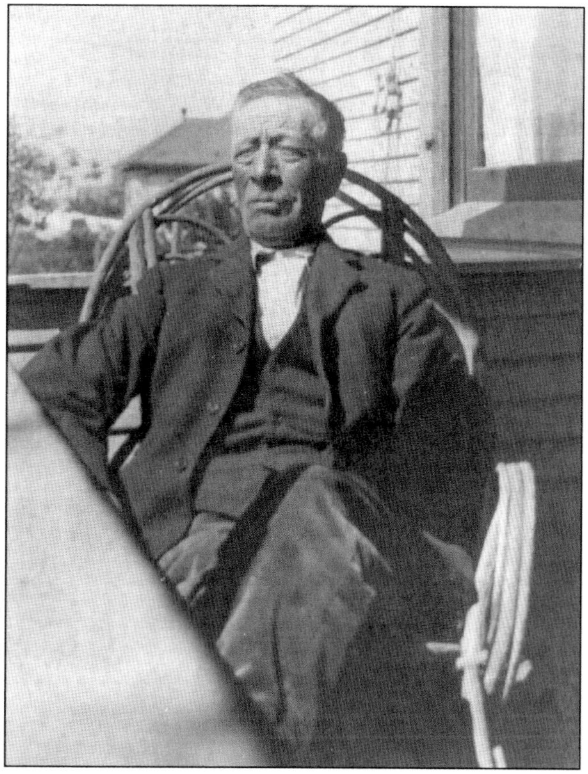

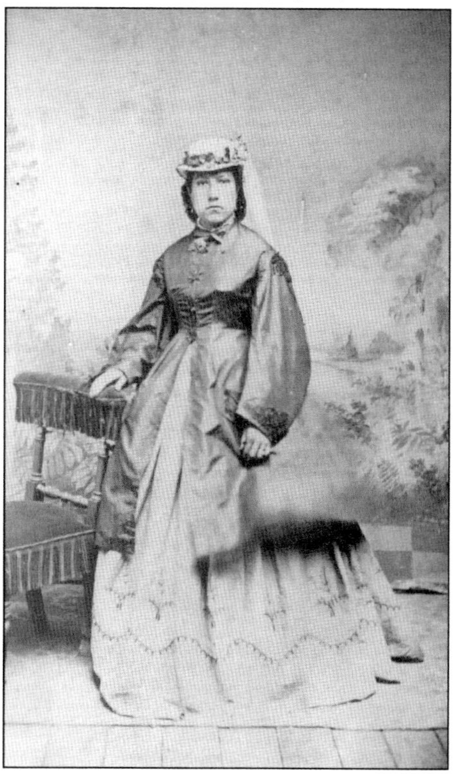

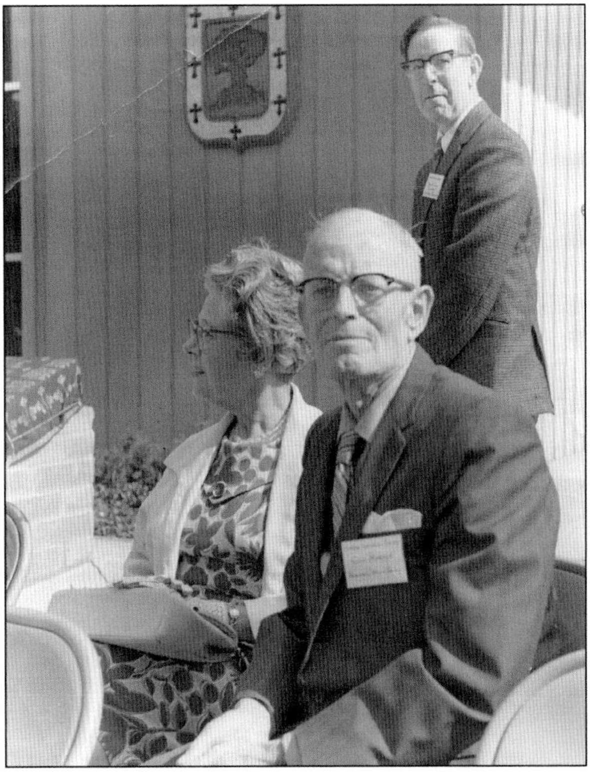

Some Moraga family descendants have preserved the family history in Moraga by donating documents and artifacts to the Moraga History Center and participating in events celebrating town history. In 1970, the Moraga Historical Society installed a plaque at the post office on School Street to commemorate the original plans made in 1894 for a townsite in the Moraga Valley. Pictured here are Moraga family descendant Eugene Winslow Moraga (front) and his wife, Lenore Boucher Moraga, with East Bay Regional Parks district manager Richard Trudeau (rear). The crest of the Moraga family can be seen in the background. The shield has a gold background with a green mulberry tree in the center. This post office operated for many years and was recently closed. The shield has been removed, leaving a shadow in its place, and the building is now empty.

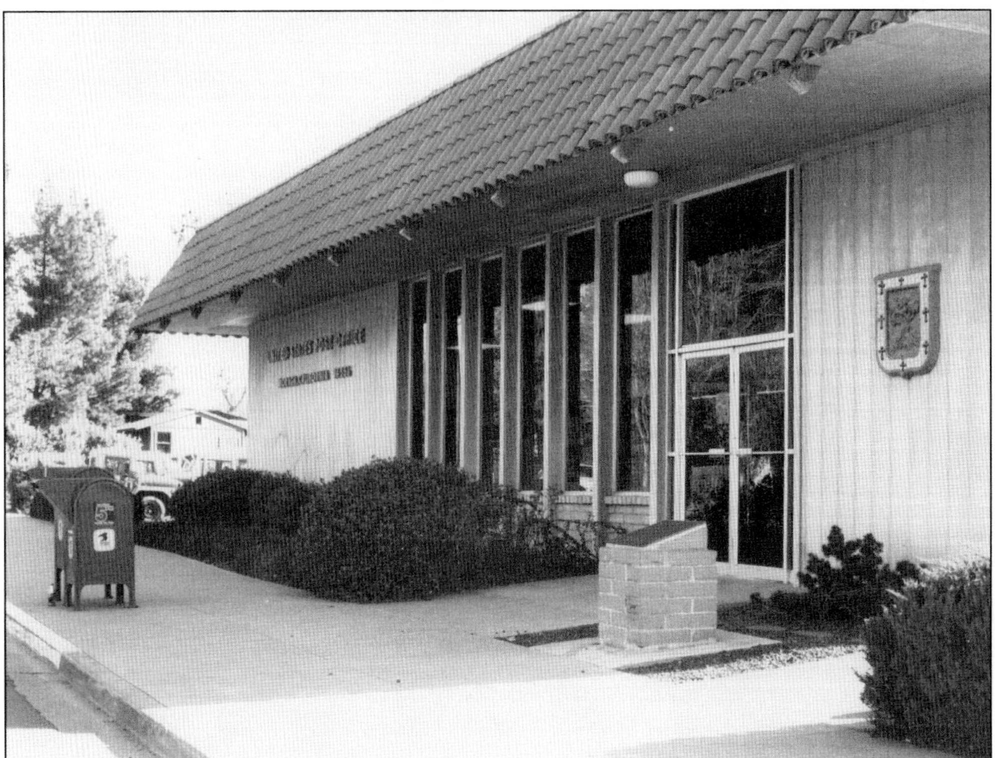

Recovered by members of the Moraga Historical Society in 1974 in the area formerly known as Redwood and now uninhabited, these US gold coins bear the date 1878. Paul Meder first located the liberty dollars using a metal detector at the site of a demolished farmhouse. The East Bay Municipal Utility District claimed them as property on land it owned by eminent domain. The public utility company then donated the gold dollars to the Oakland Museum of California. Unfortunately, the coins were then stolen from the museum.

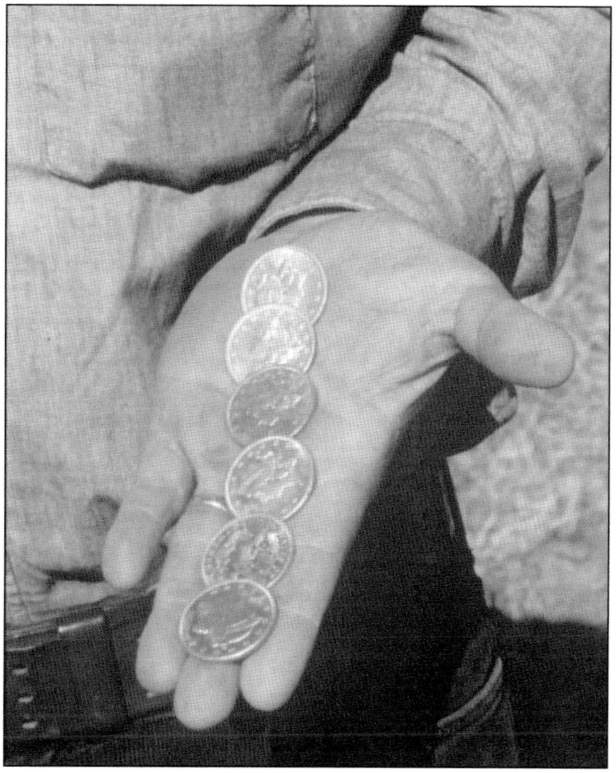

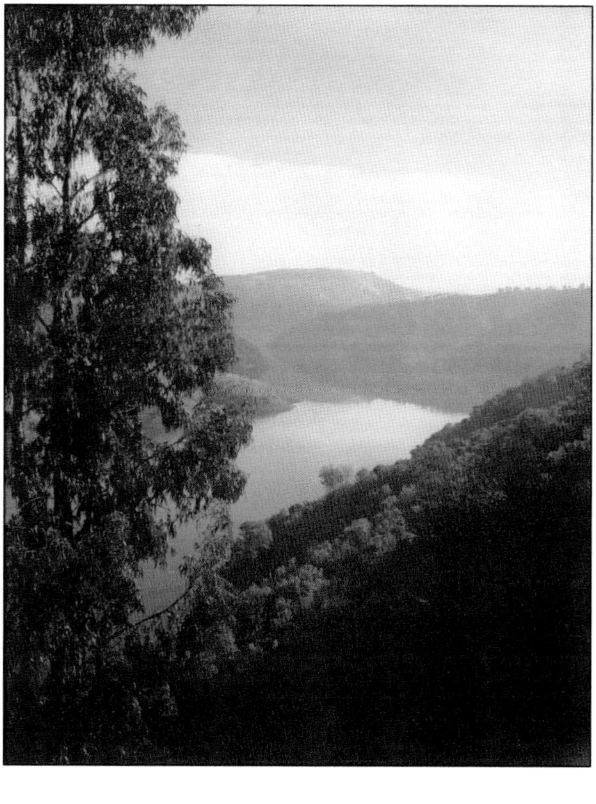

The town of Moraga borders the Upper San Leandro Reservoir, created by the damming of San Leandro Creek in 1876. Local trout still swim in its tributaries, which include Moraga creeks. In 1855, a subspecies of wild rainbow trout was identified in the local streams. When San Leandro Creek was dammed, trout were isolated in the reservoir and retained their genetic heritage because they were not interbred with other trout, as has occurred commonly elsewhere. San Leandro Creek has the distinction of being the location for the first rainbow trout hatchery in the world. In the watershed, trails along the reservoir provide beautiful views. (Photograph by Don Falconer.)

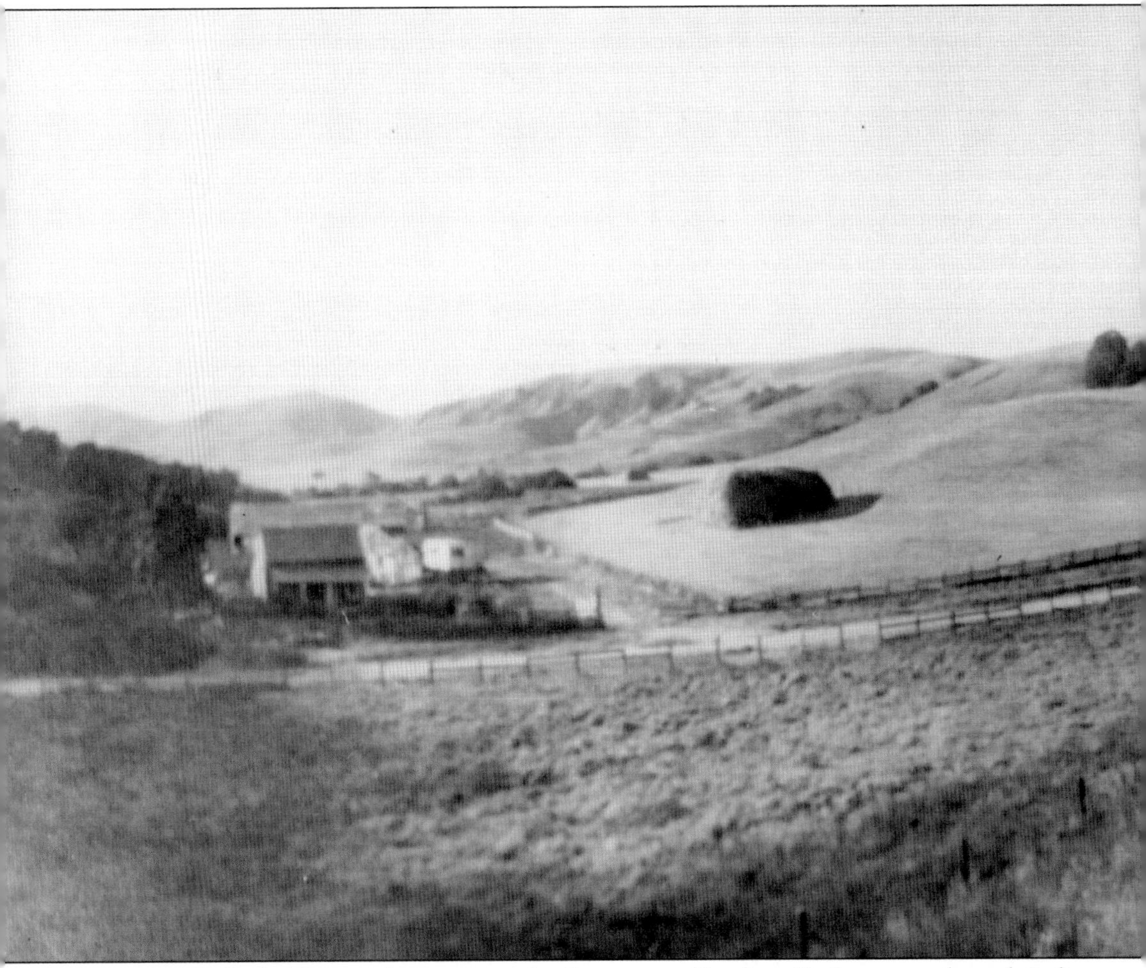

Passing the Jack Allen ranch, a train on the Sacramento Northern Railway runs through Indian Valley in 1920. The Moraga family adobe is slightly to the north. Diarist Joseph Lamson, who resided on the Jack Allen ranch in Indian Valley, rented a room from Allen and kept a store on the ranch. In his diary, Lamson recorded walking on a trail in moonlight to a fandango at the

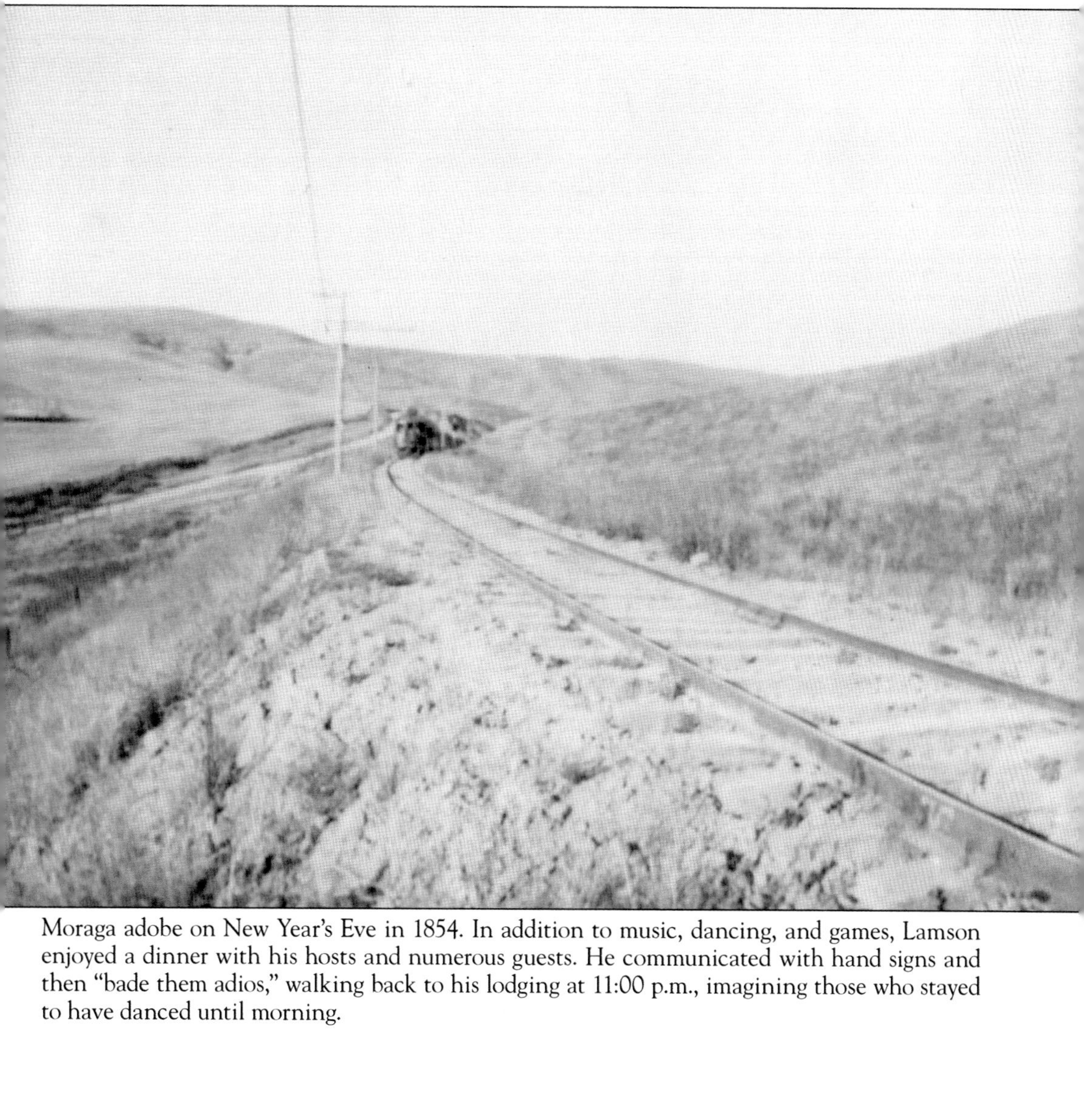

Moraga adobe on New Year's Eve in 1854. In addition to music, dancing, and games, Lamson enjoyed a dinner with his hosts and numerous guests. He communicated with hand signs and then "bade them adios," walking back to his lodging at 11:00 p.m., imagining those who stayed to have danced until morning.

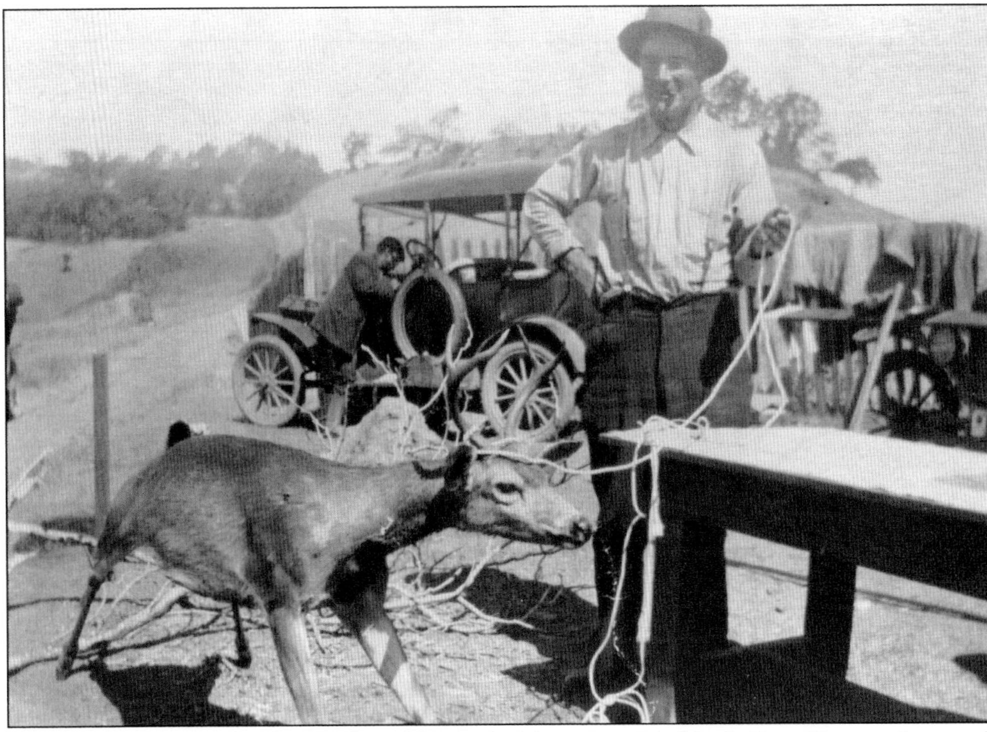

Irish Immigrants Michael Carroll and his wife, Mary Ann Maddock Carroll, owned a ranch near what is now Campolindo High School on Moraga Road, previously called Jonas Hill Road. Michael Carroll was one of the few ranchers to have bought land directly from Horace Carpentier, who owned or controlled ownership of much of the Moraga Rancho. Carroll purchased 250 acres in 1865. Mary Ann, who was born in 1855, came across the plains on the back of a mule in her mother's arms. She was still residing on the family property at the age of 83 when interviewed for a newspaper article. The ranch stayed in the hands of the Carroll family for many years. Tom Carroll, pictured above with a deer, was a longtime resident of Moraga. Part of the former ranch has since given way to a residential subdivision aptly called Carroll Ranch.

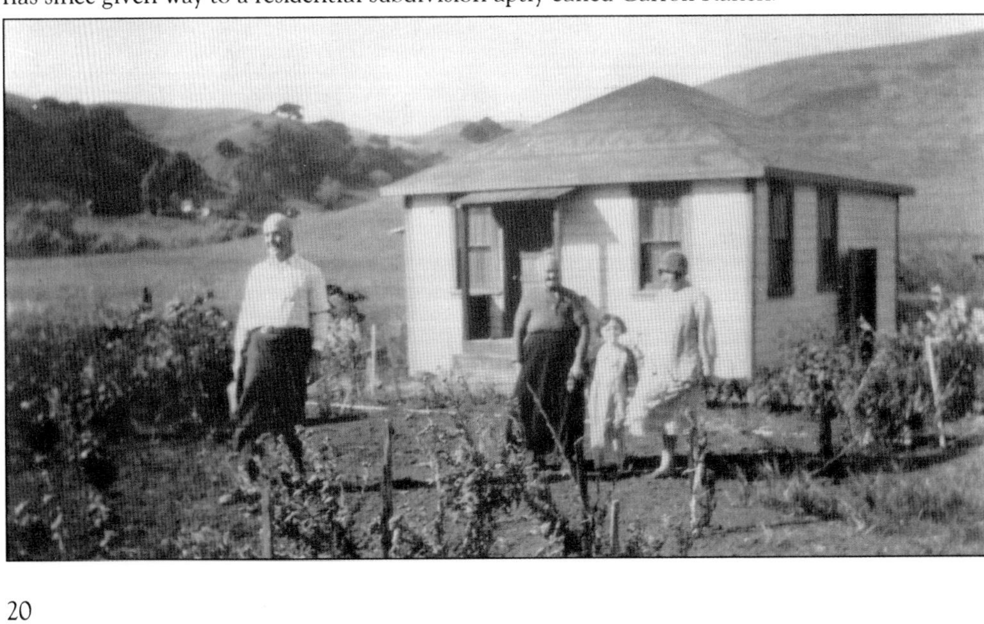

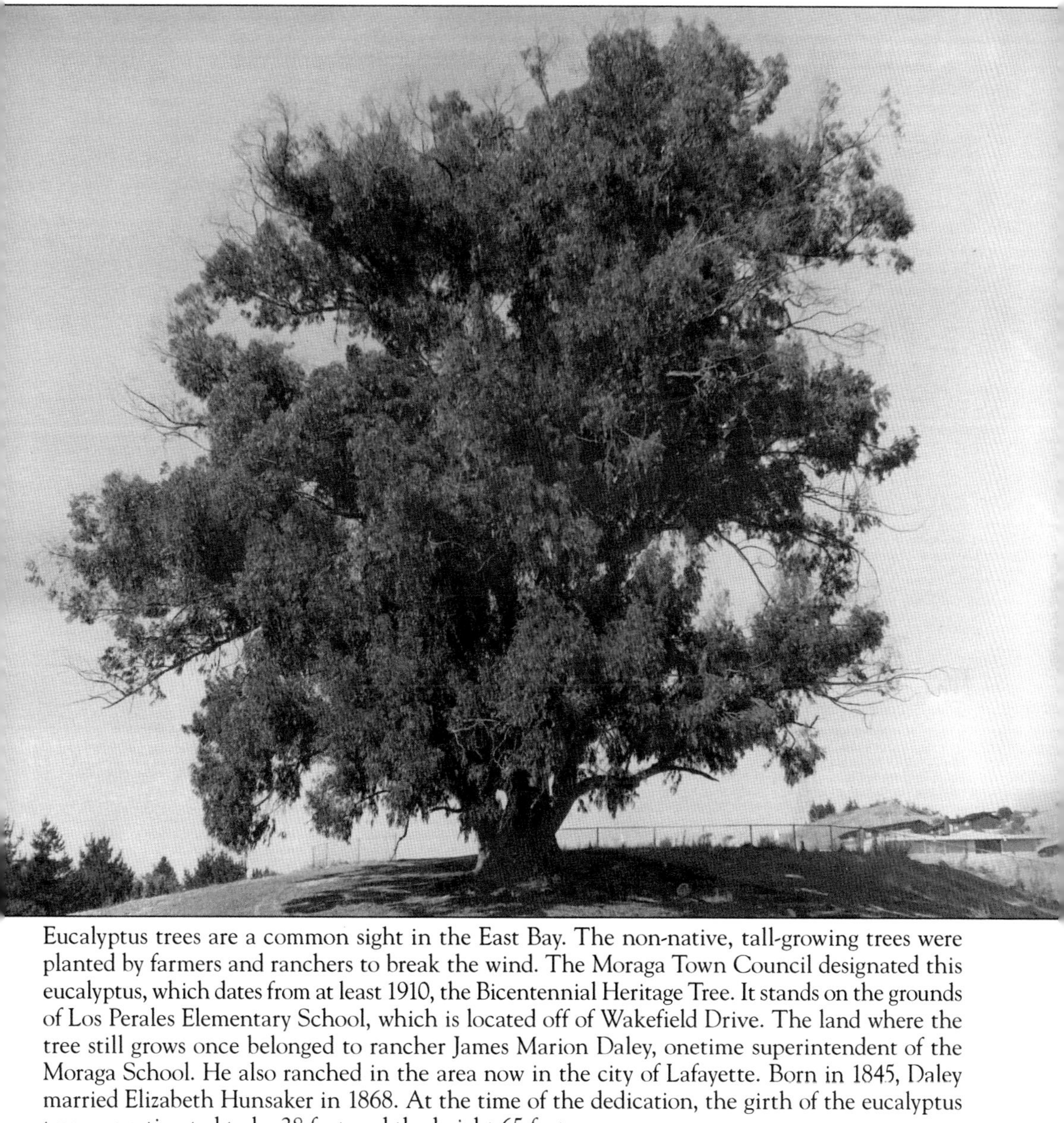

Eucalyptus trees are a common sight in the East Bay. The non-native, tall-growing trees were planted by farmers and ranchers to break the wind. The Moraga Town Council designated this eucalyptus, which dates from at least 1910, the Bicentennial Heritage Tree. It stands on the grounds of Los Perales Elementary School, which is located off of Wakefield Drive. The land where the tree still grows once belonged to rancher James Marion Daley, onetime superintendent of the Moraga School. He also ranched in the area now in the city of Lafayette. Born in 1845, Daley married Elizabeth Hunsaker in 1868. At the time of the dedication, the girth of the eucalyptus tree was estimated to be 28 feet and the height 65 feet.

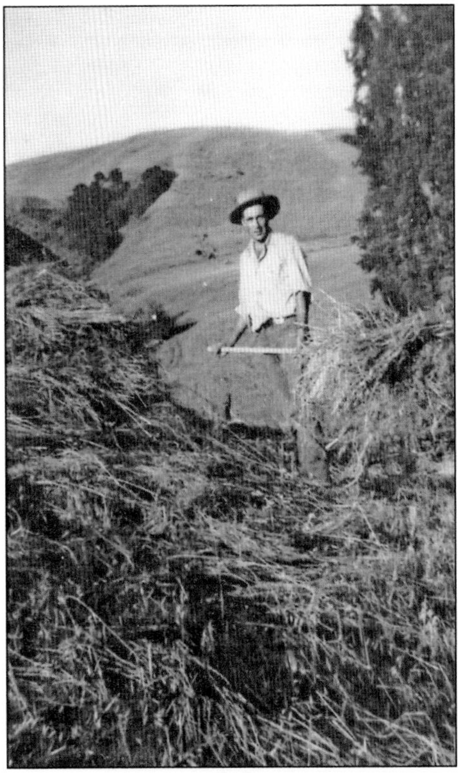

Moraga still had working ranches as it began to grown into a town. Gordon Frazell was ranching in the Bollinger Canyon area from the 1940s on. In the photograph at left, he is moving hay he had cut with a tractor. He would put it in the barn to feed cattle in the winter. The ranch, El Rancho Ynez, was named after Gordon's wife. The photograph below shows Moraga real estate in 1971, juxtaposing the old with the new. The Barn, the large white building at center, and Willow Springs School, a white building to the left with a curved front, both historical structures, are visible, while Moraga Center is actively under construction. The shopping center is starting to grow. At this time, the valley was still surrounded by orchards and open space. Moraga was an active, bustling community, only three years from incorporation. The hills and valleys had been dotted with growing subdivisions. Public schools, including a high school, were in operation, a post office had been designed and built, and land for a permanent library had been purchased. In the thriving suburb, commercial, political, and social organizations were busy keeping things interesting and planning for the future. (Left, courtesy of Susan Sperry.)

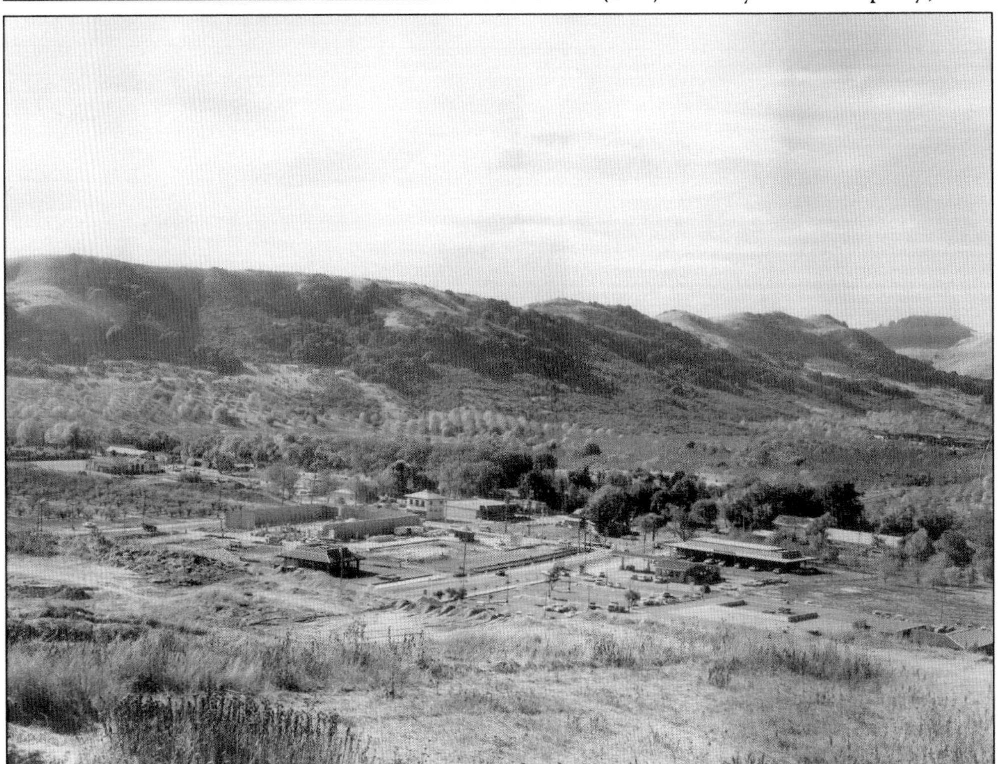

Two

Trains across the Valley

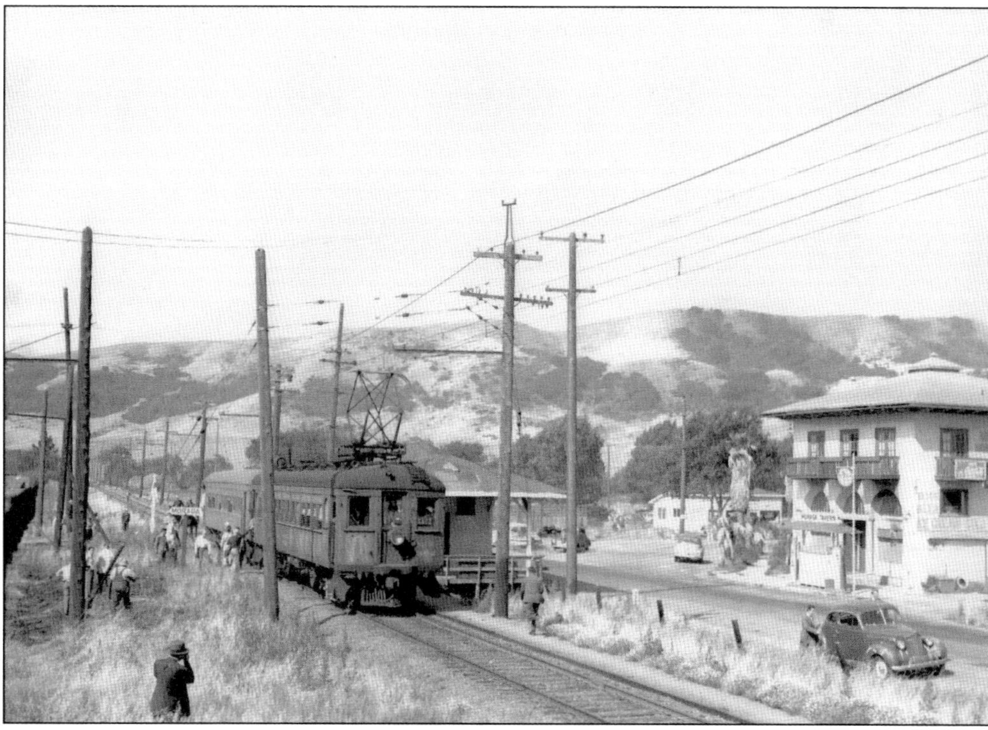

Trains began running through the Moraga Valley in the early 1900s, carrying commuters, students, and tourists to their destinations. Freight trains carried produce and livestock from local ranches, farms, and orchards to be sold in larger urban areas. The main train station for the Moraga Valley was located near the local tavern, an old landmark now known as the Moraga Barn, seen here on the right. The excursion train pictured was photographed on July 4, 1950. (Photograph by J.G. Graham, courtesy Bay Area Electric Railroad Association, Western Railway Museum archives.)

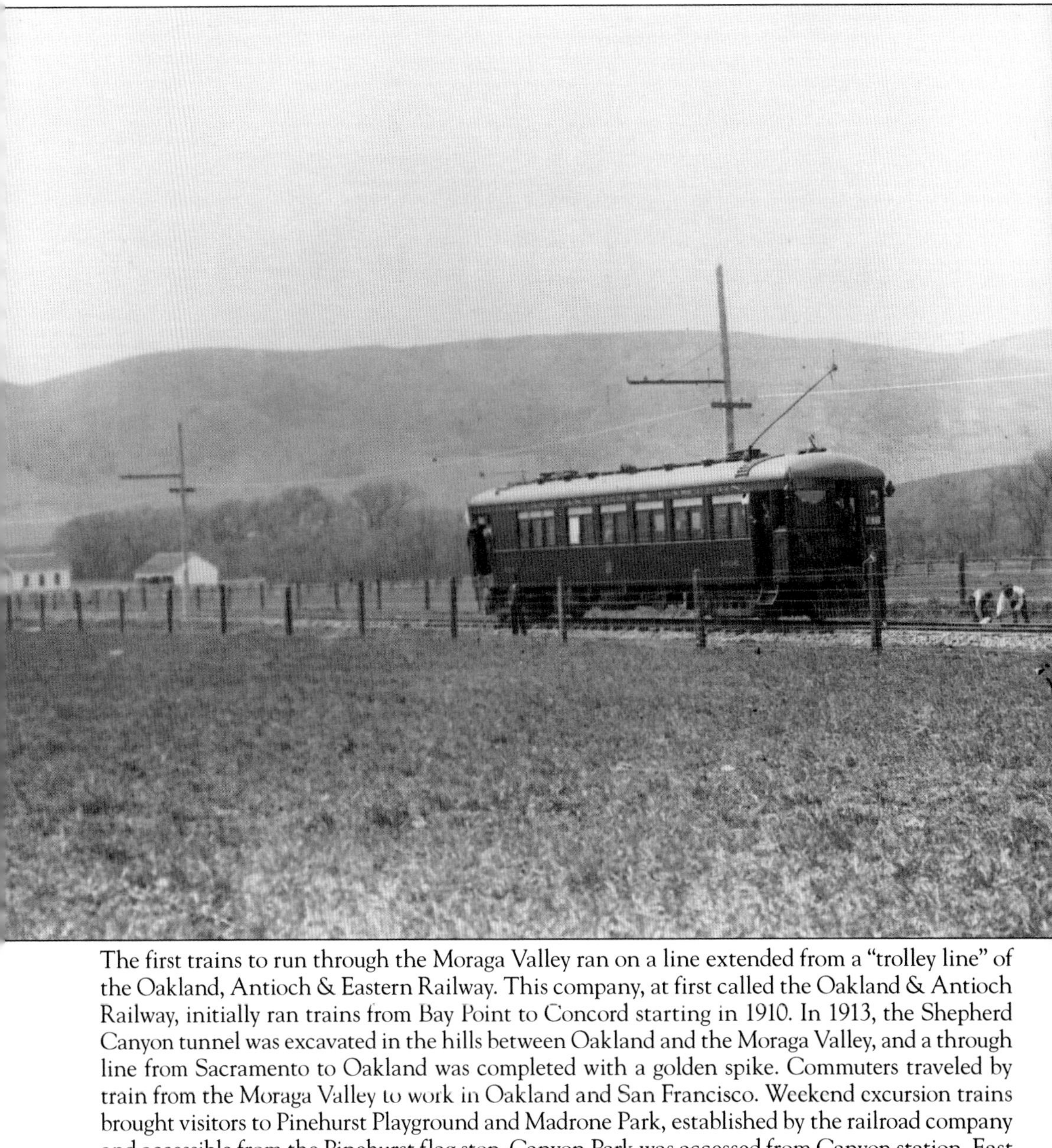

The first trains to run through the Moraga Valley ran on a line extended from a "trolley line" of the Oakland, Antioch & Eastern Railway. This company, at first called the Oakland & Antioch Railway, initially ran trains from Bay Point to Concord starting in 1910. In 1913, the Shepherd Canyon tunnel was excavated in the hills between Oakland and the Moraga Valley, and a through line from Sacramento to Oakland was completed with a golden spike. Commuters traveled by train from the Moraga Valley to work in Oakland and San Francisco. Weekend excursion trains brought visitors to Pinehurst Playground and Madrone Park, established by the railroad company and accessible from the Pinehurst flag stop. Canyon Park was accessed from Canyon station. East Bay students headed to local schools also rode the trains. Workmen are pictured repairing tracks on the Oakland, Antioch & Eastern line in the Moraga Valley in 1919.

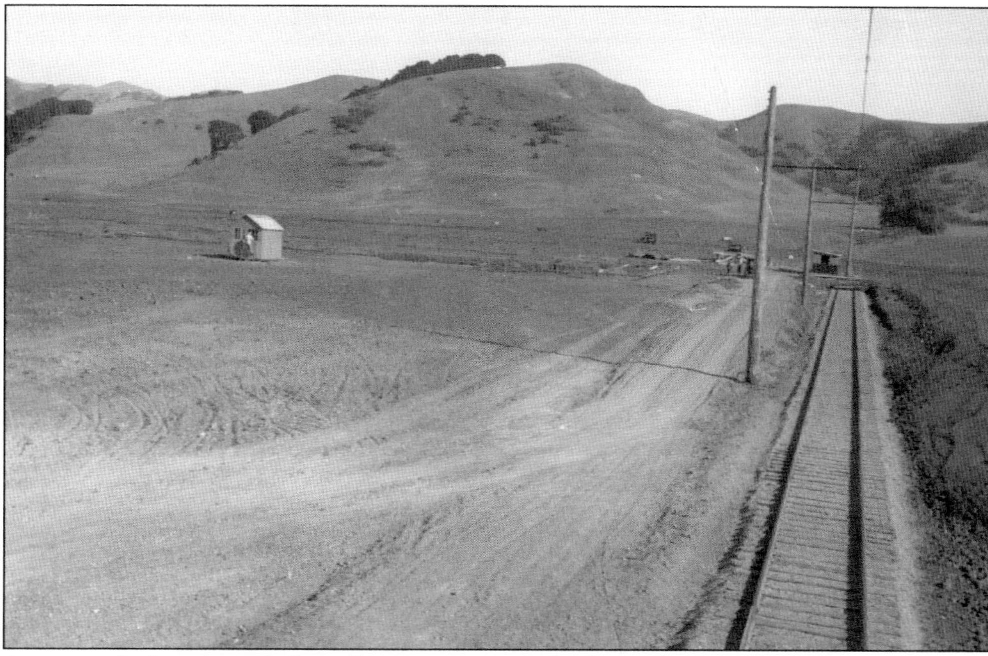

A spur on the line through the valley was constructed to bring the railroad to St. Mary's College. The college was originally founded in 1863 in San Francisco and then moved to Oakland in 1889. In 1927, the college moved again to the Moraga Valley, where it opened for classes in 1928 with an enrollment of 600, and has since flourished as an educational institution. The photograph below, taken in 1948 by Roger Heller, shows Sacramento Northern freight train No. 661 stopping at the St. Mary's College station on what appears to be a windy day, judging from the bending of the young trees at the college entrance.

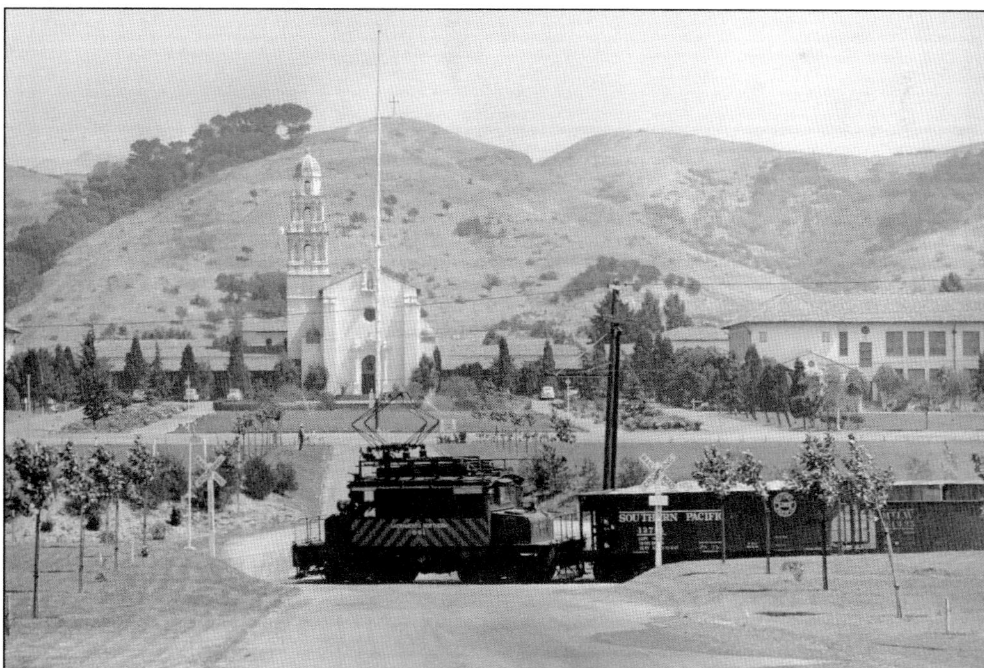

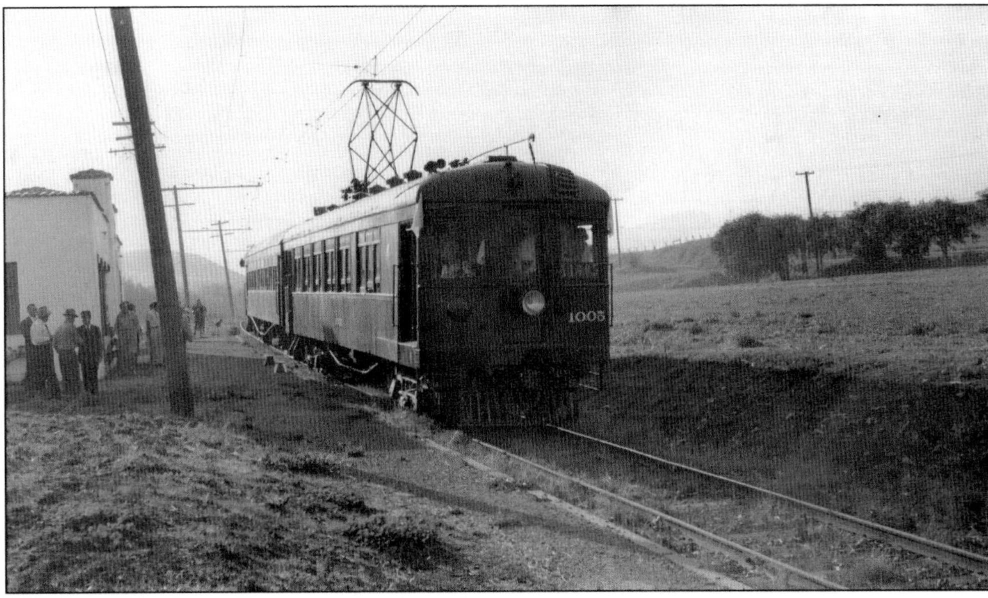

Passenger train travel ceased in the valley in 1941, but the passenger trains did not stop running entirely. Here, an excursion train of the Bay Area Electric Railroad Association, founded in 1946 by electric rail enthusiasts, stops at St. Mary's College, where there are many riders in transit. The view looks west towards Moraga. (Photograph by Marvin Maynard.)

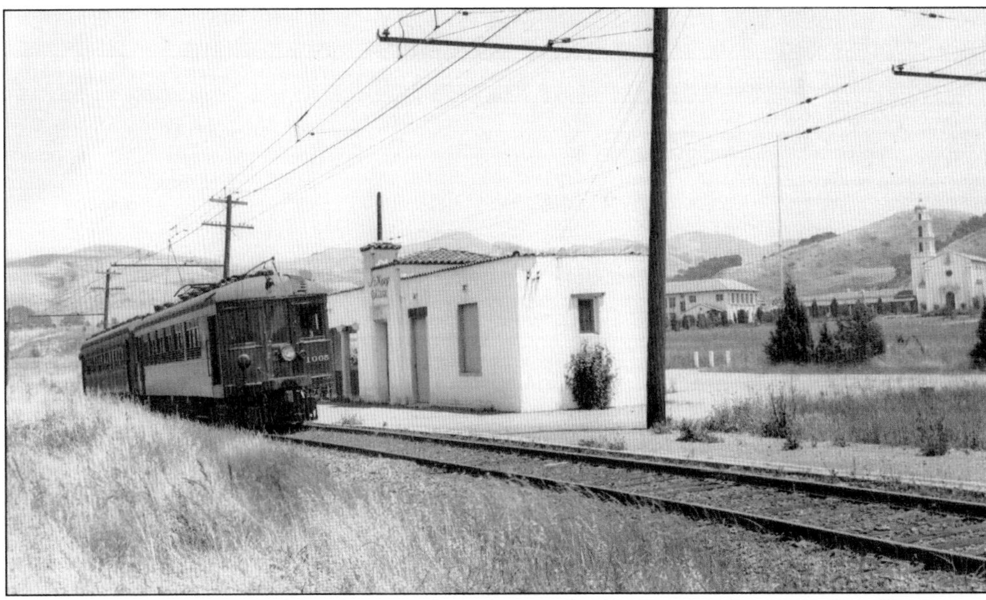

By December 1928, the Oakland, Antioch & Eastern had reorganized into the San Francisco–Sacramento Railroad and subsequently merged with the Sacramento Northern Railroad, itself reorganized from Northern Electric. The new railway, a subsidiary of the Western Pacific, had become the Sacramento Northern Railway. The Moraga Valley was now a waypoint for freight travel, commuters headed to school or work, and tourists on what was now the longest electric interurban line. Here, a Sacramento Northern train stops at St. Mary's station on June 8, 1941, en route from Pittsburgh to San Francisco. St. Mary's Chapel can be seen to the right. At that time, the entrance to St. Mary's was located farther east than today. (Photograph by Ted Wurm.)

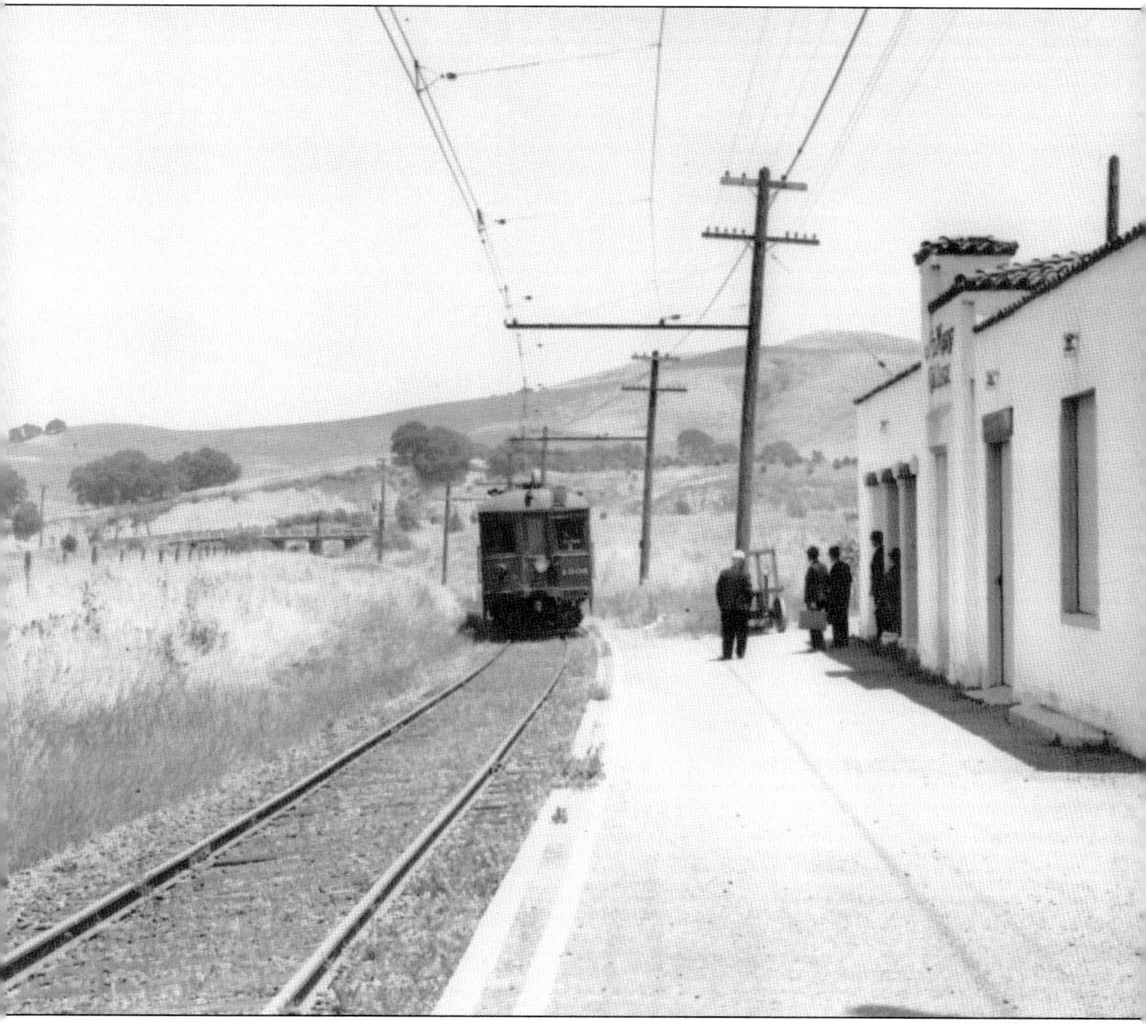

In this photograph, brothers from St. Mary's College are waiting for the train on June 8, 1941. The last passenger train ran later the same month on June 30. Although the freight window of the station is closed, freight trains were operational at the time and continued to run long after the passenger trains had stopped carrying students and faculty. The bridge in the background was removed in 1945. After the last passenger train had gone, automobile traffic naturally increased. Naval cadets arrived to the pre-flight school at St. Mary's in 1942, and the entrance to the college was adjusted to prioritize cars rather than trains. (Photograph by Ted Wurm.)

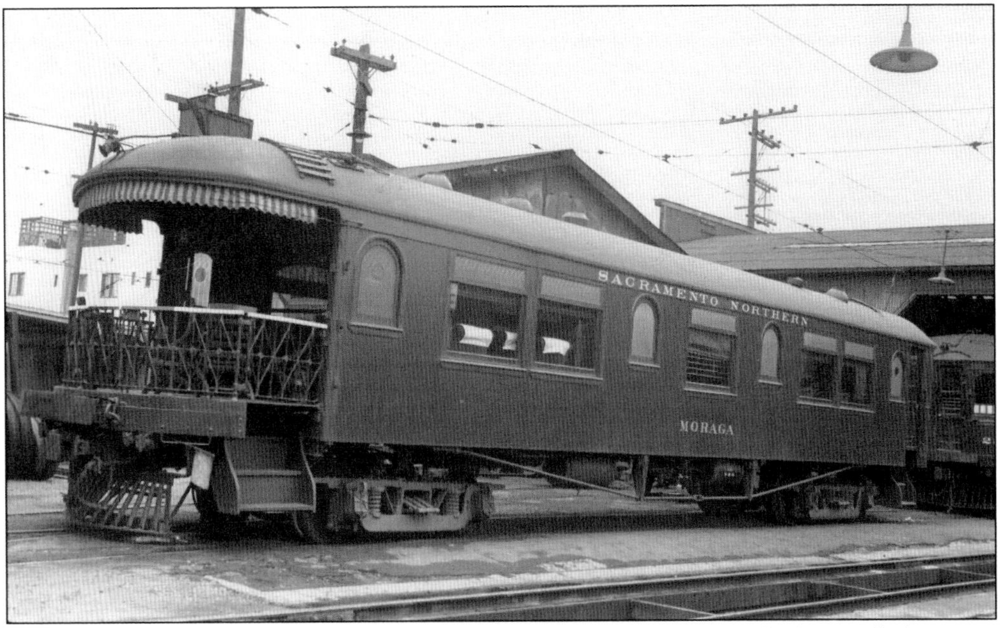

The Sacramento Northern line had an observation parlor car with dining facilities called *Moraga*, built in 1913. To ride in it, passengers needed to pay an extra quarter. Originally a powered car, the engines were removed in 1915, and the car was rebuilt in 1925 as a single-ended car. The *Moraga* car was placed on the end of the Comet train. At one time, the *Moraga* was the last car on a train that ran through the redwoods.

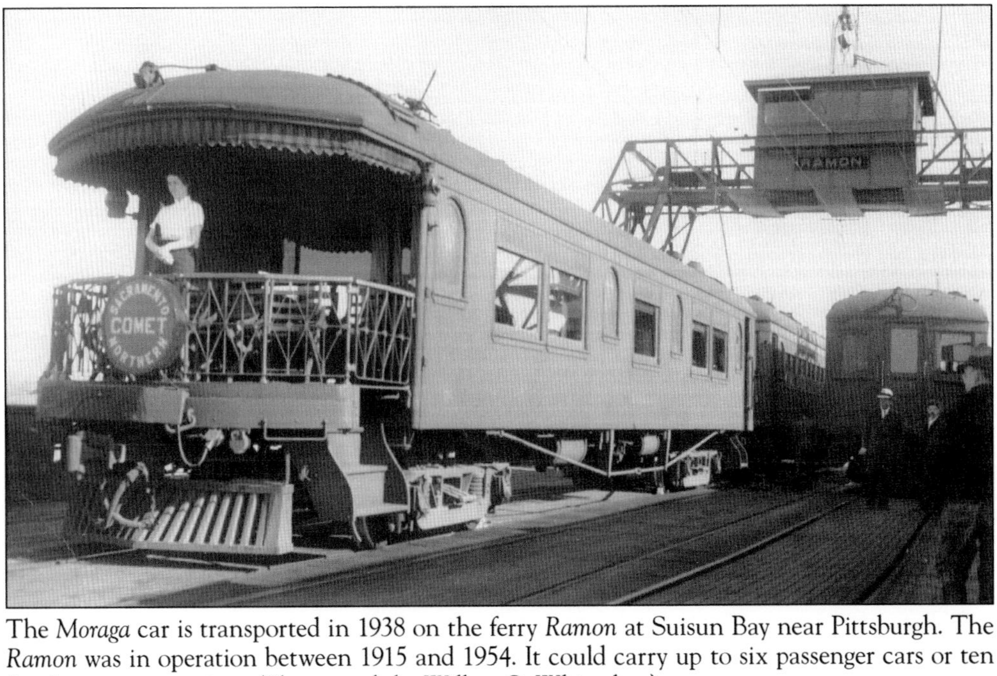

The *Moraga* car is transported in 1938 on the ferry *Ramon* at Suisun Bay near Pittsburgh. The *Ramon* was in operation between 1915 and 1954. It could carry up to six passenger cars or ten freight cars at one time. (Photograph by Wilbur C. Whittaker.)

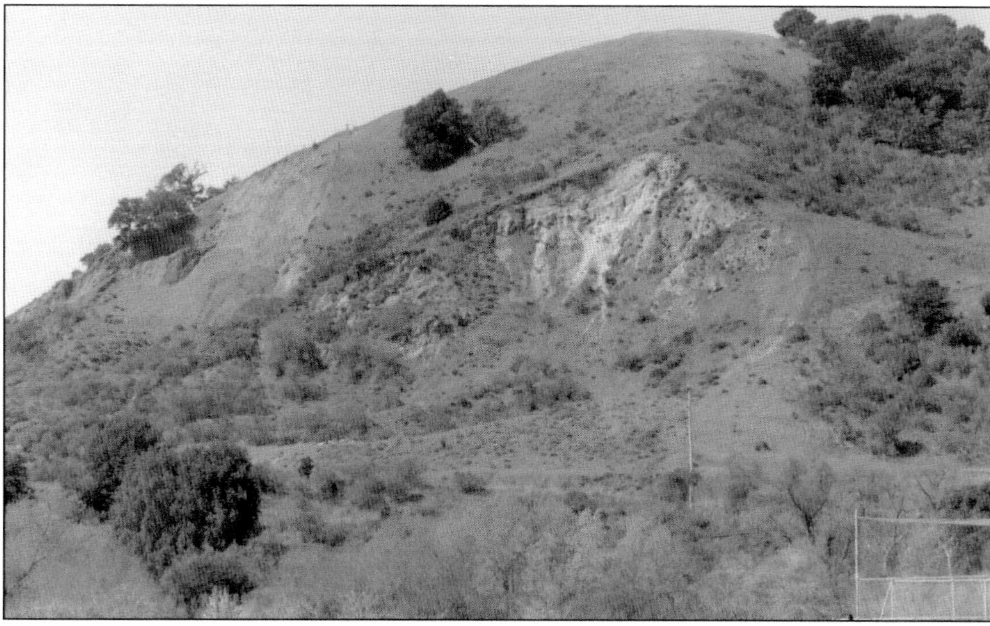

Remnants from a quarry that was operated at the Valle Vista railroad stop near the Upper San Leandro Reservoir can still be seen on the hillside as motorists drive around the bend from Moraga toward the Valle Vista hike staging area, on land now owned by the East Bay Municipal Utility District. Light volcanic rock from the quarry was once loaded onto railroad cars with a steam shovel. Crushed rock from this quarry was broken down by blasting and used to line rail beds. The crushed rock was also placed alongside the rail beds for ballast in order to keep the wooden cross ties in place. The quarry had its own rock crusher right alongside the railroad tracks.

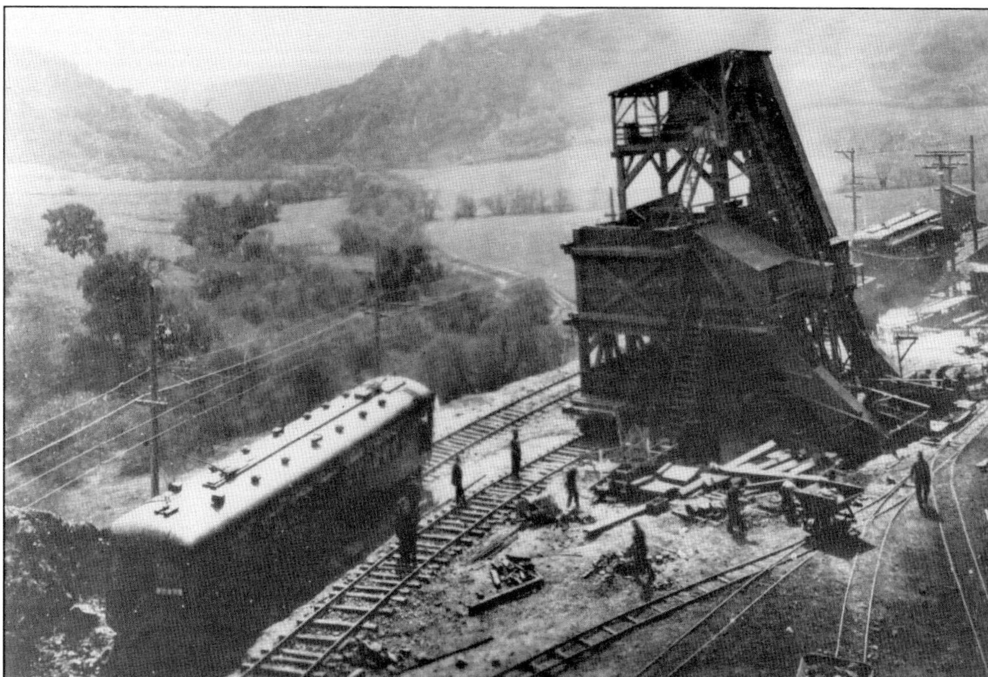

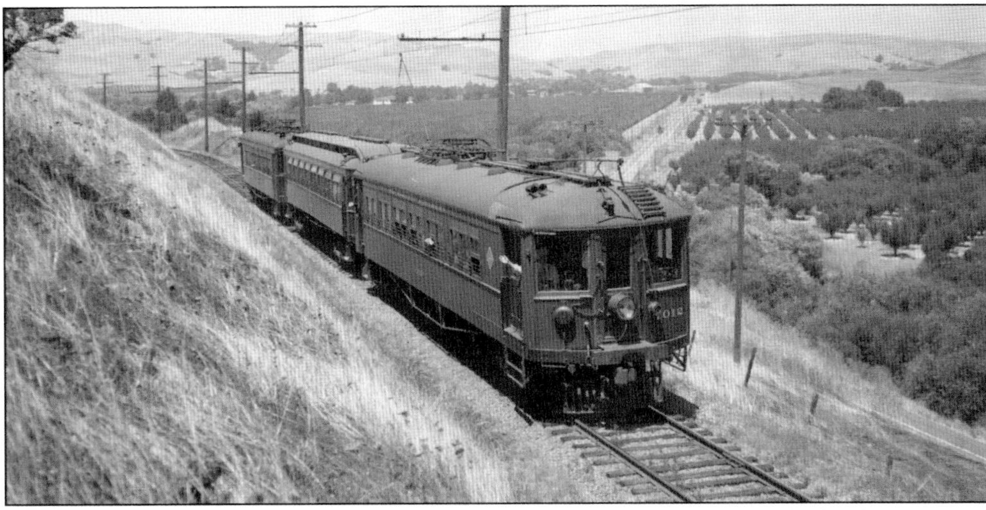

Before it was protected as watershed land by the water companies that took the land via eminent domain, Valle Vista was once a commuter community. Its water supply came from the springs at the Moraga adobe, whose water ran through a pipe to a reservoir in the original Moraga townsite at what is now Viader Drive. Valle Vista was situated on what are now the western outskirts of Moraga. It is currently a hiking and equestrian staging area, close to Redwood Park. The area previously occupied by houses is now mainly open space. It is hard to imagine that there was once a community there, but in 1928, there were about a dozen homes. Trains took commuters to work in Oakland and San Francisco. In this photograph, a train can be seen coming around the bend at Valle Vista. The orchards of the Moraga Valley serve as a backdrop.

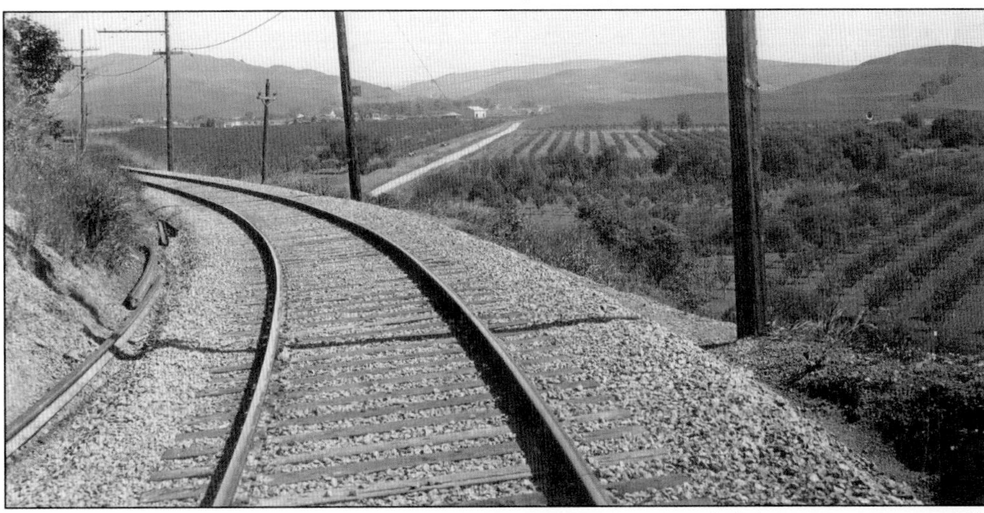

Rich agricultural surroundings were viewed by passengers as they rounded the quarry curve at Valle Vista. The beautiful location was attractive to railway passengers, who—beginning in 1913—might travel from over the hills in Oakland to picnic at Pinehurst Playground or Madrone Park in the Redwood Canyon area or travel just a little farther to the Moraga Valley for a pleasant day trip. Weekend excursion trains were made possible by the construction of the 3,200-foot Shepherd Canyon tunnel, completed in January 1913. The tunnel, lined with local redwood and concrete, ran through the Oakland hills, which had previously been a daunting obstacle to train travel. Families often welcomed the opportunity to travel to the slightly balmier climes just a bit east of Oakland to the beautiful valleys of Canyon and Moraga, where the fog had not reached.

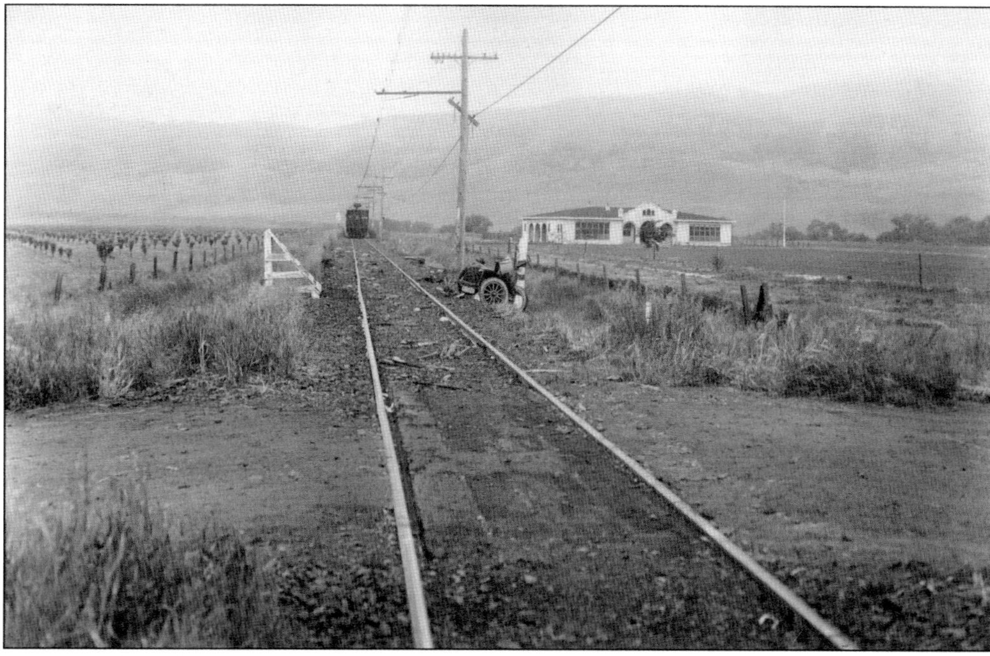

Train travel in the Moraga Valley was not without incident. A tragic accident occurred May 27, 1917, when the Comet, a train on the Oakland, Antioch & Eastern line, hit an automobile carrying sightseers from Oakland. The engineer claimed to have sounded his horn to no avail. The car was struck and demolished, resulting in the deaths of four people. The building in the background is Willow Springs School. (Photograph by Smith Brothers.)

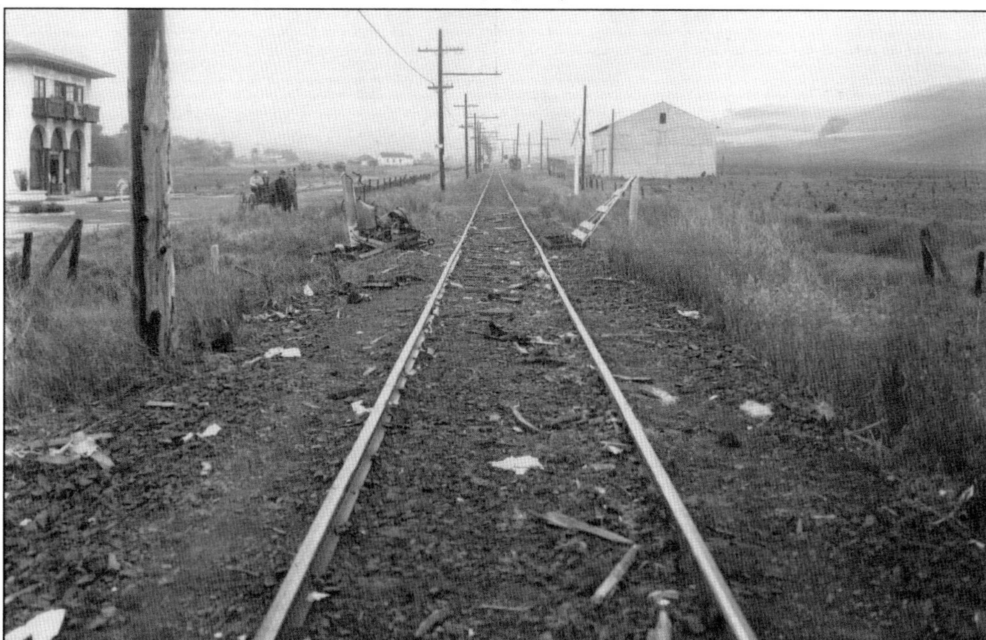

Another view of the destruction shows the Moraga Tavern (now known as the Moraga Barn) in the background. The accident occurred very close to the main train station in Moraga. (Photograph by Smith Brothers.)

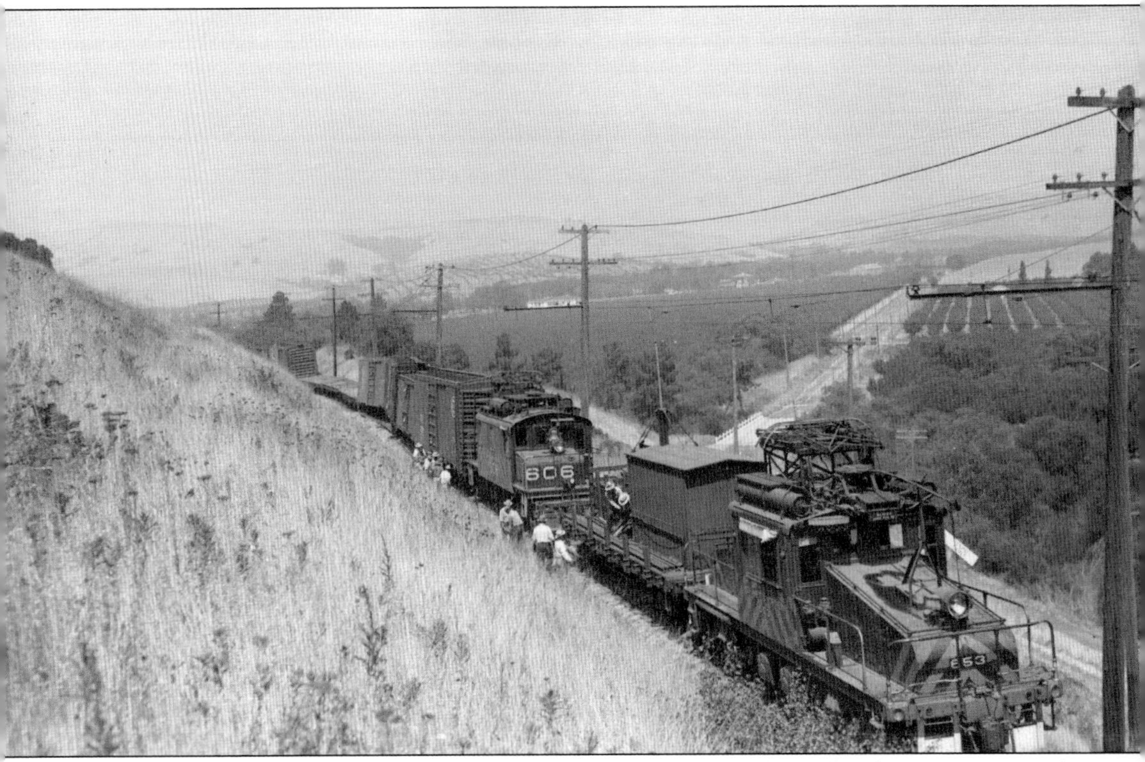

This photograph, taken in 1952, shows that Sacramento Northern freight train No. 606 has derailed at Valle Vista on the Moraga grade. Canyon Road can be seen below. Train No. 653 is backing in the wrecker car. Moraga was an important freight stop for the Sacramento Northern. Its main station location had cattle pens and a packing shed, and there was a good boardinghouse near the building now known as the Barn that also provided lodging, and at times served as a store and post office.

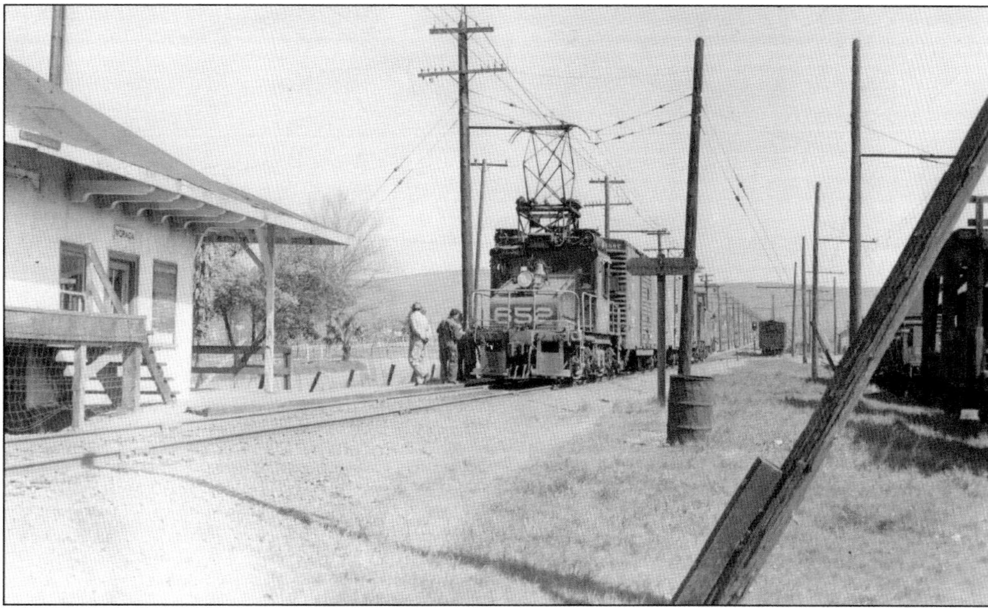

In the photograph above, a freight train comes into the Moraga station. Freight trains often carried livestock and produce from the Moraga Valley to destinations where they could be processed or sold. Below, an Oakland, Eastern & Antioch train stops at the packing shed near the main railroad station in the early 1900s in the Moraga Valley. The walnut and pear packing shed was perfectly situated for walnuts to be processed, packed, and shipped off. Although Moraga is known primarily for its Bartlett pears, walnuts were also harvested in many locations in the Moraga Valley, including the Carroll Ranch. Local settler Mary Ann Maddock Carroll, born in 1855 in Louisiana, remained on the Carroll Ranch, which had been purchased in 1865. She recalled that in about 1938, a huge walnut tree there had been flourishing on the property for over a century. Walnut trees can still be spotted here and there all over town

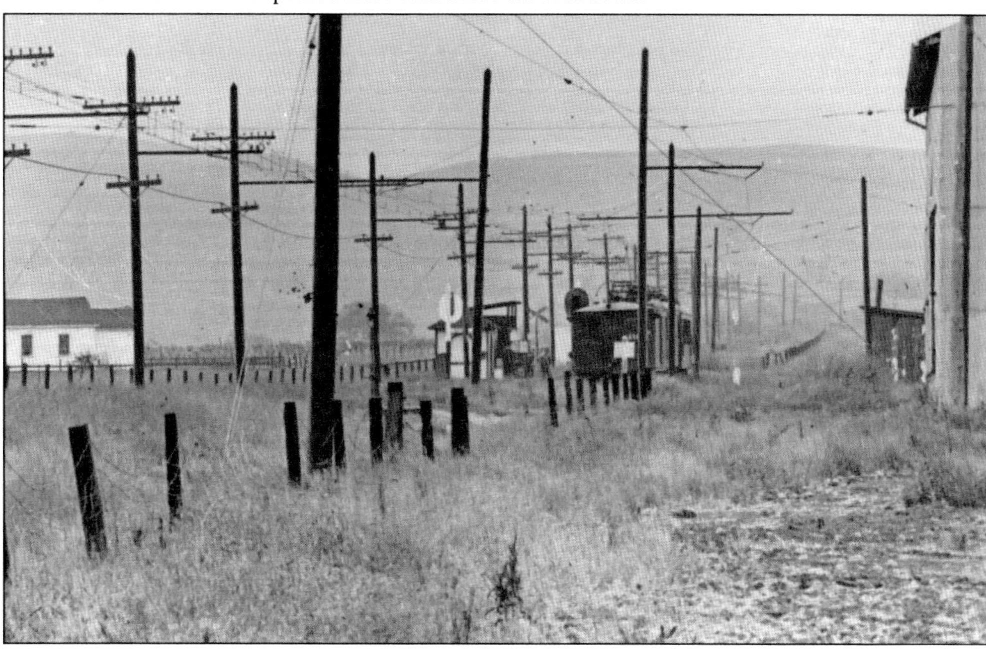

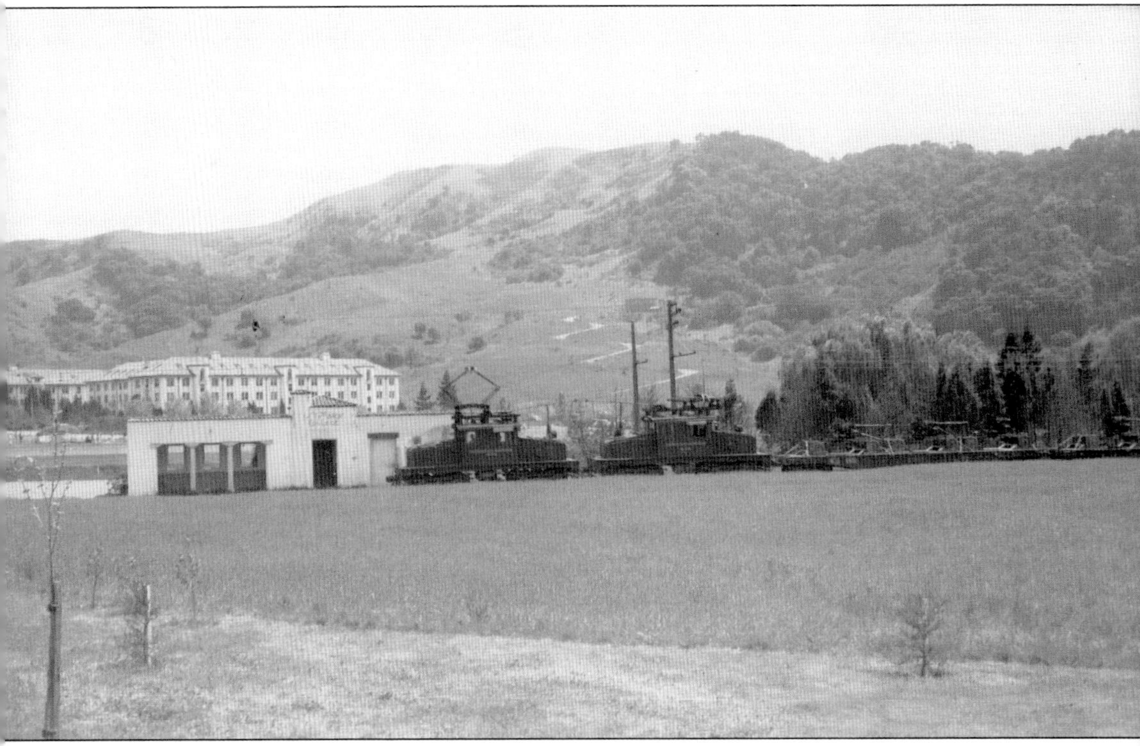

Sacramento Northern trains Nos. 604 and 603 are bringing military equipment to St. Mary's College post–World War II. After the stop at St. Mary's, the railway continued northeast on the Oakland to Sacramento railroad branch through Lafayette, Saranap, and Walnut Creek and on to Pittsburgh. After 1957, there was no longer any freight service. (Photograph by Tom Buckingham.)

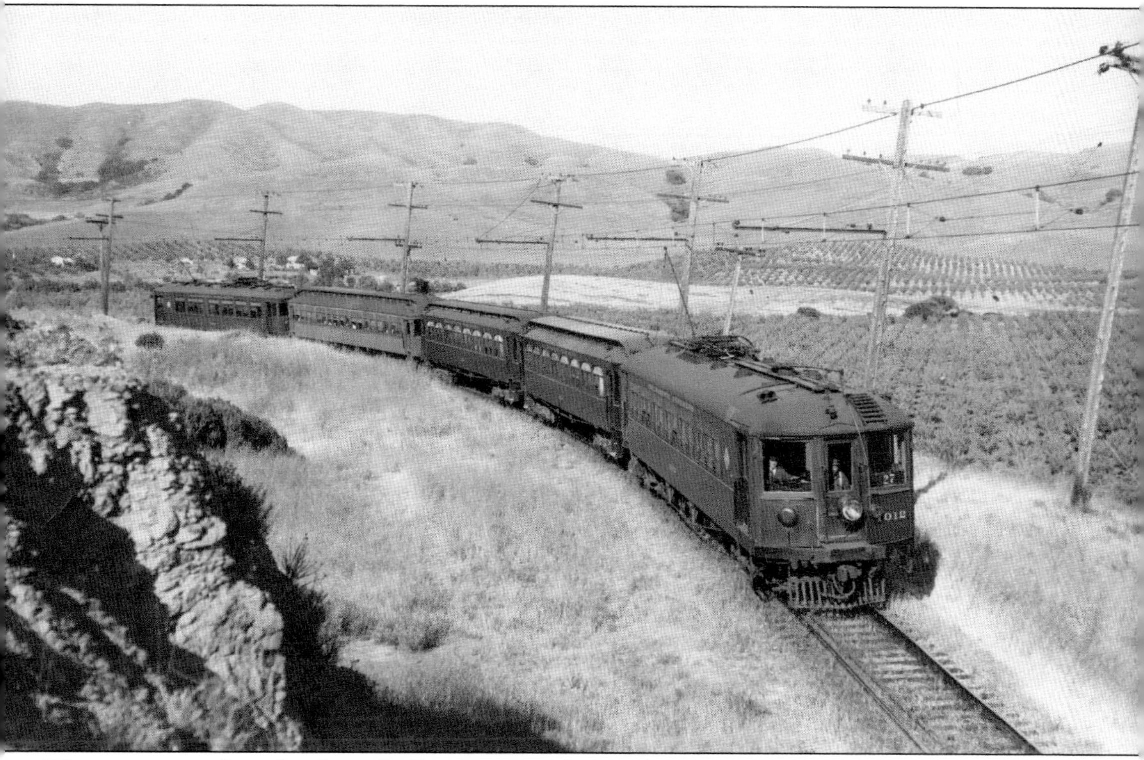

There were very few schools in the East Bay Area before the 1950s. Students often had to travel far, often by train, to get to their school. Here, school train No. 27 takes students to school in Canyon or Oakland around 1940. As it rounds the curve at Valle Vista, an outcropping of volcanic rock can be seen. This rock is called the Moraga formation, created when sedimentary rock was laid down between lava eruptions in the Miocene period. The Moraga formation is noted for its lava vesiculation. Boys and girls rode in separate cars of the train. School trains also took Moraga Valley students to high school in Concord. (Photograph by Art Alter.)

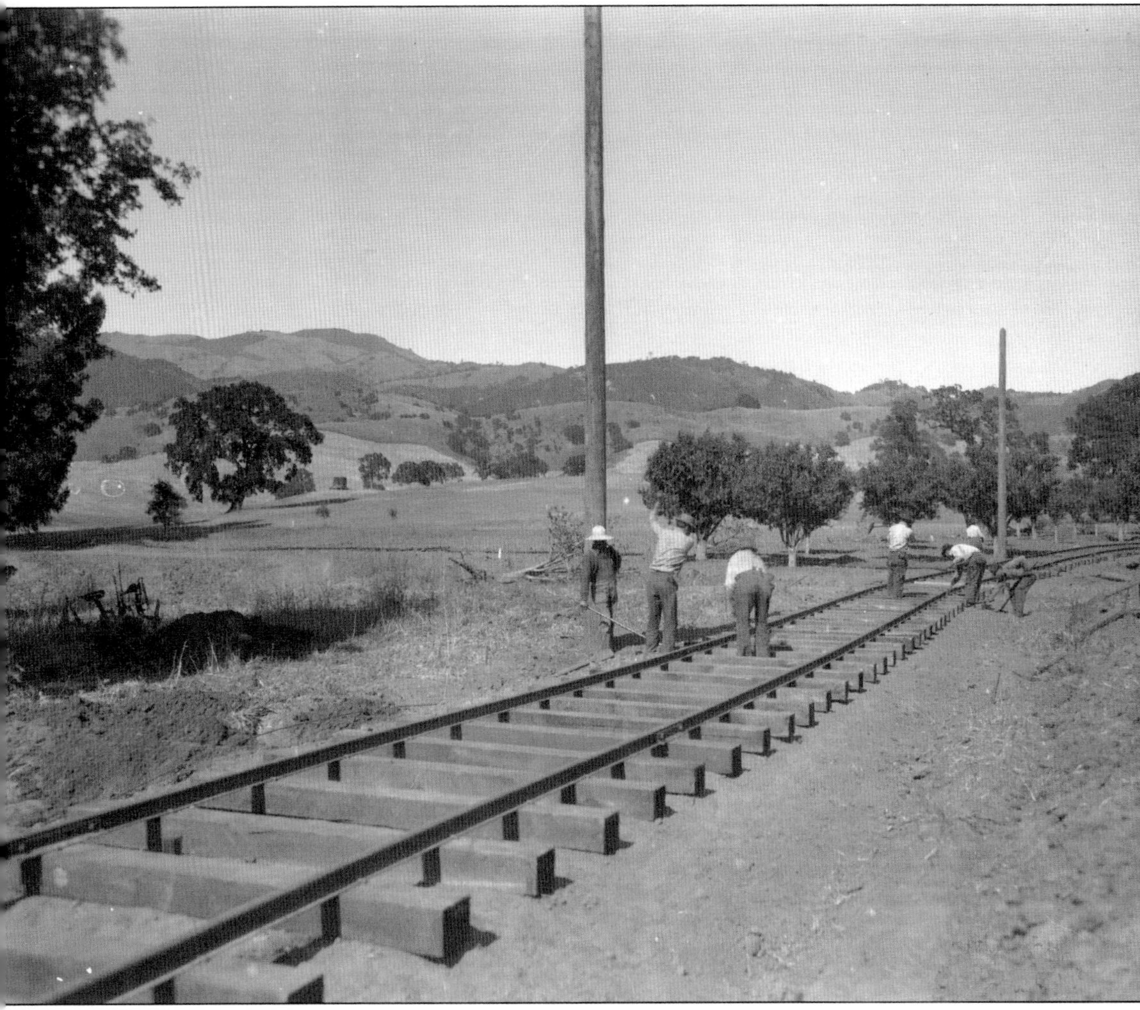

Workers are setting track in the East Bay in 1914, creating the means for transporting passengers and freight and uniting the local communities. This photograph shows construction on the Oakland, Eastern & Antioch Railway Danville branch, between Danville and Diablo Park. The railway was incorporated in 1911 to build a railroad from Bay Point to Sacramento. The railway also leased the San Ramon Railroad, which ran from Saranap to Danville on the main line. According to an early promotional brochure, the principal founders of the railway were A.W. Maltby of Concord, Walter Arnstein of Alamo, Samuel L. Napthaly of San Francisco, and Harry A. Mitchell of San Francisco. (Photograph by Eston Cheney.)

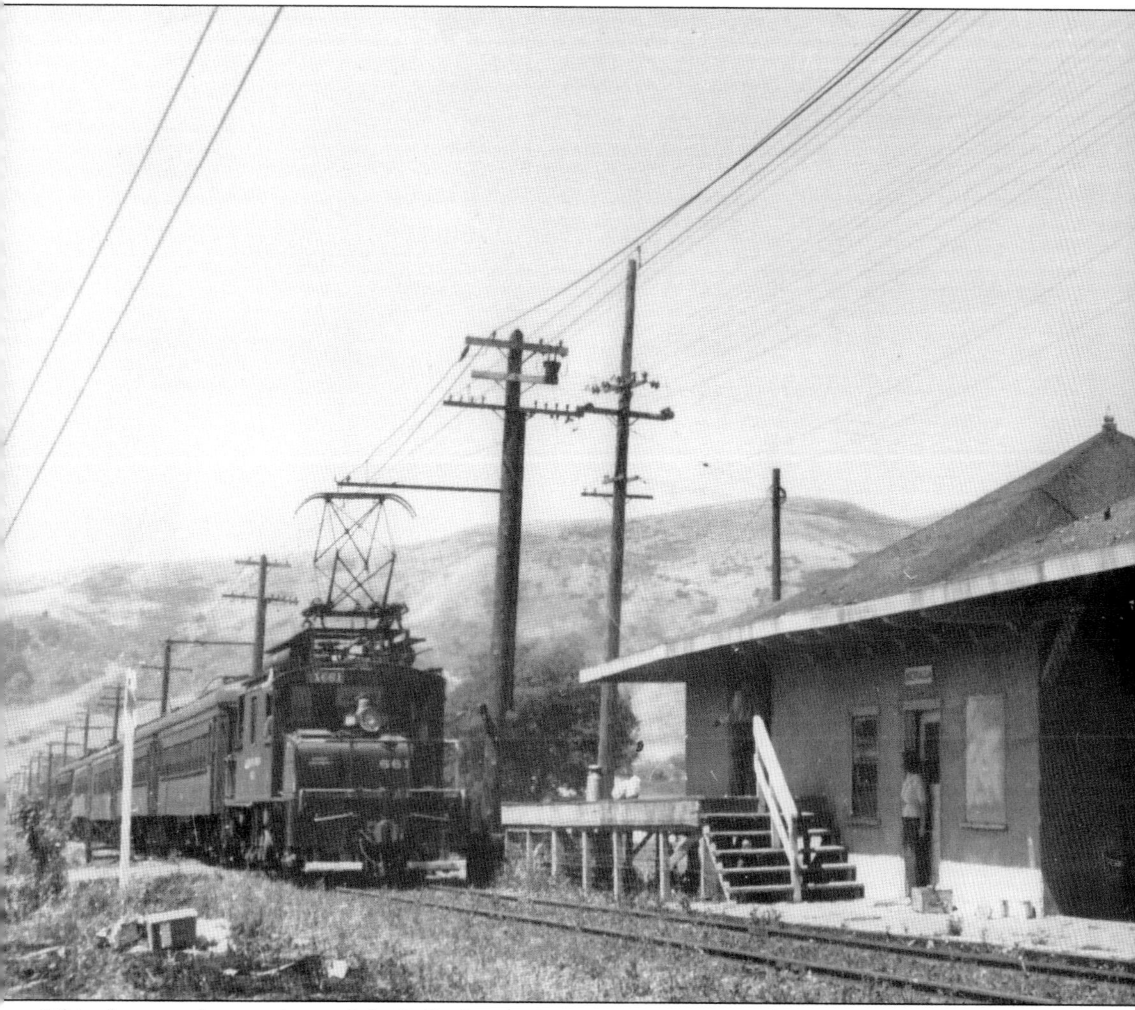

This photograph was taken in July 1941 after the last passenger cars ran through the Moraga Valley from Oakland to Chico. The empty trailers are being brought to Chico. The end of passenger travel was a financial decision made by the railway company, at that time the Sacramento Northern Railway, based on lower fares from competing lines for holiday destinations, increased automobile traffic, and high operating costs. Freight traffic did continue, however, until 1957. Subsequent to the last passenger trip, trains continued to carry travelers on excursion trains managed by the Bay Area Electric Railway Association. (Photograph by Richard Jenevein.)

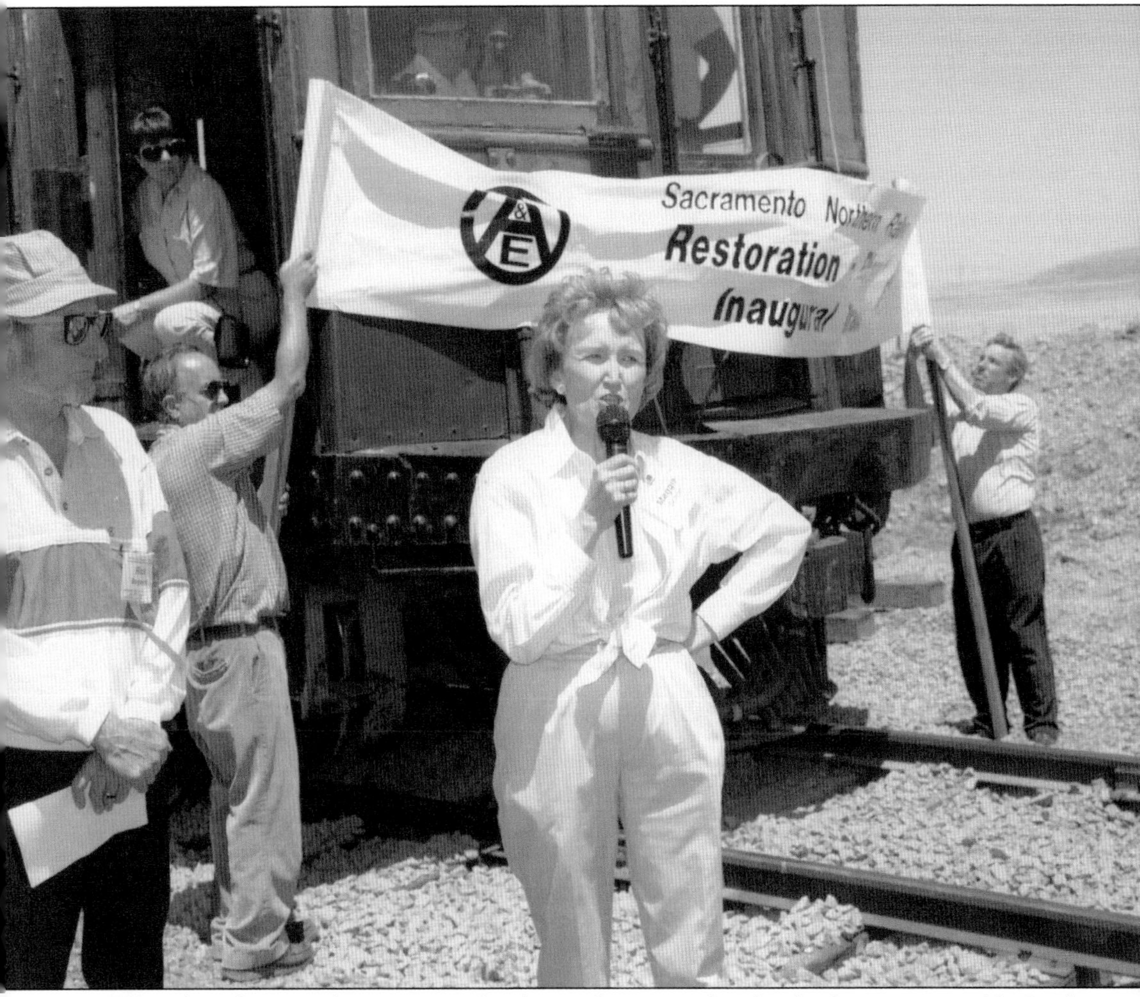

Efforts have been made to preserve local train history and make this history accessible. In this photograph, Maggie Skinner of the Moraga Historical Society and Rick Borgwardt, board member of the Bay Area Electric Railroad Association, are present at the Western Railway Museum in Rio Vista as the newly re-set electric wires are tested on July 7, 1994, on passenger motor No. 1005. Visitors to this museum can ride restored interurban trains to get a sense of train travel in the past. (Courtesy of the Moraga Historical Society.)

Three

Orchards, Farms, and Ranches

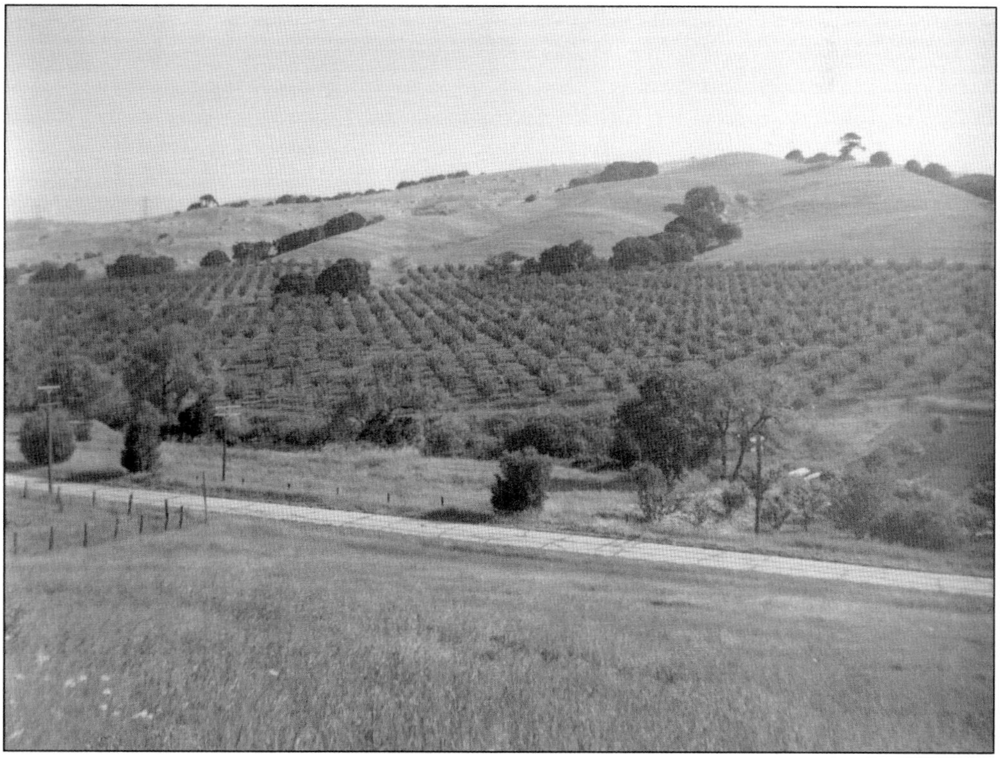

The town of Moraga is almost synonymous with the pear orchards that have long existed here. Ask any resident to name the main identifying feature of the past in this area, and the answer will almost universally be "pear orchards." Not only did the Moraga Valley boast plentiful harvests of large delicious Bartlett pears, it also provided fertile land for many other crops, including peaches, apricots, plums, walnuts, and apples. Ranching was established early in the days of the Mexican land grant. Farming followed shortly after. Although much of the former ranch and farmland has given way to subdivisions, livestock can still be seen grazing on hillsides, and pear and walnut orchards still grace the valley.

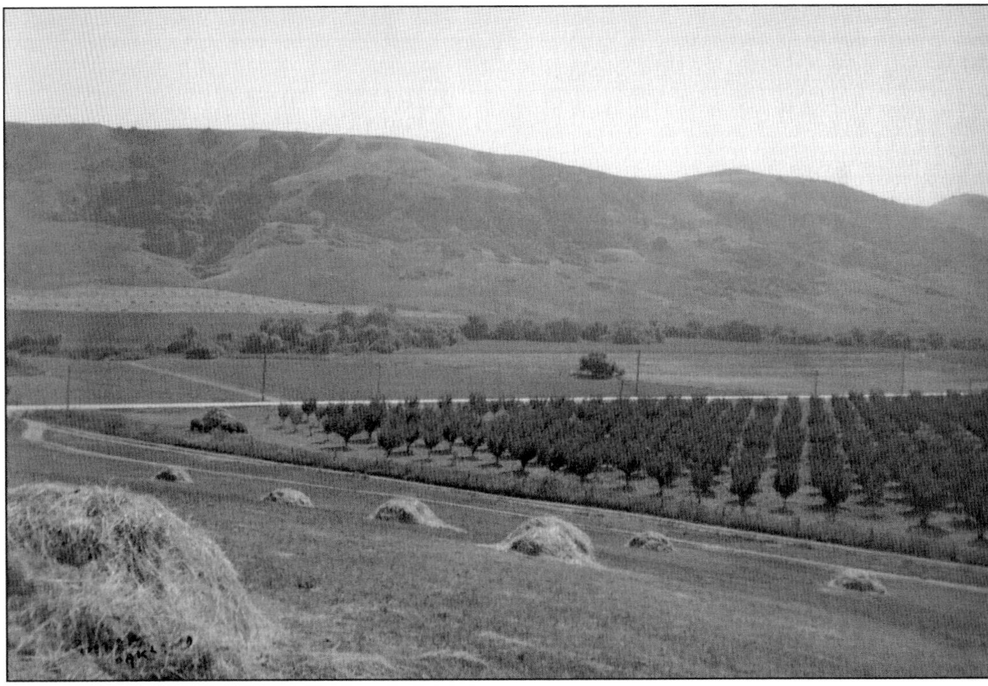

Rows of fruit trees grow in the Moraga Valley. In the picture above, taken in 1935, hay has been gathered into piles. The Carroll Ranch shown below was situated at the intersection of streets now known as Rheem Boulevard and Moraga Road and dates back to 1865, when land there was purchased by Michael Carroll. The land continued to be owned by the Carroll family until 1983. This view looks west over Jonas Hill Road (now Moraga Road) toward Rheem Valley.

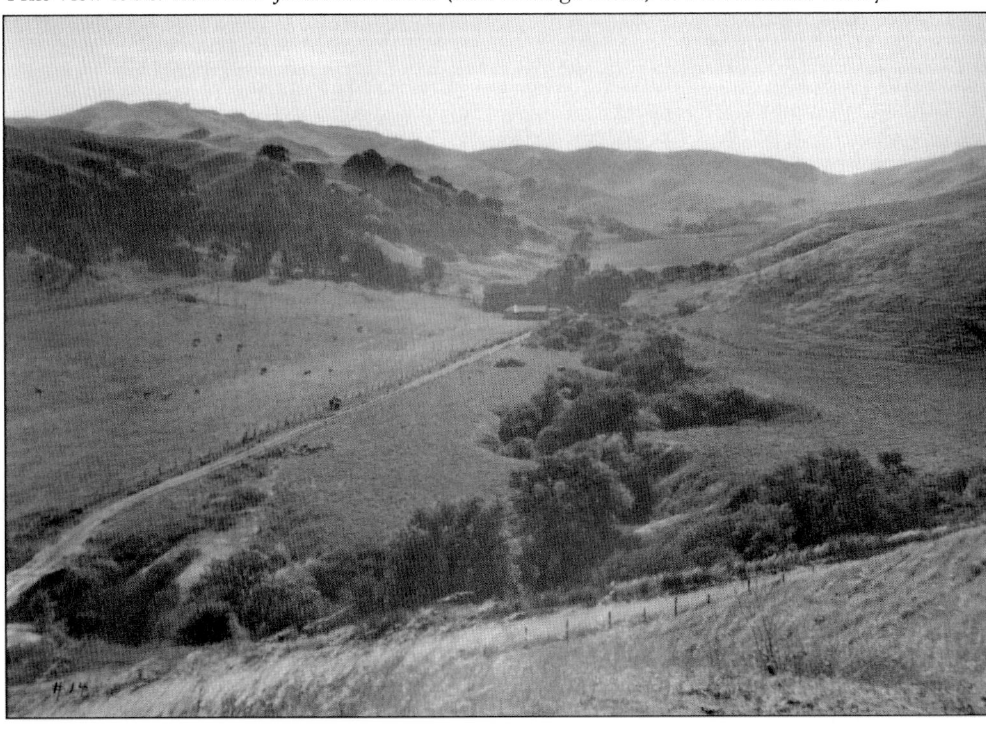

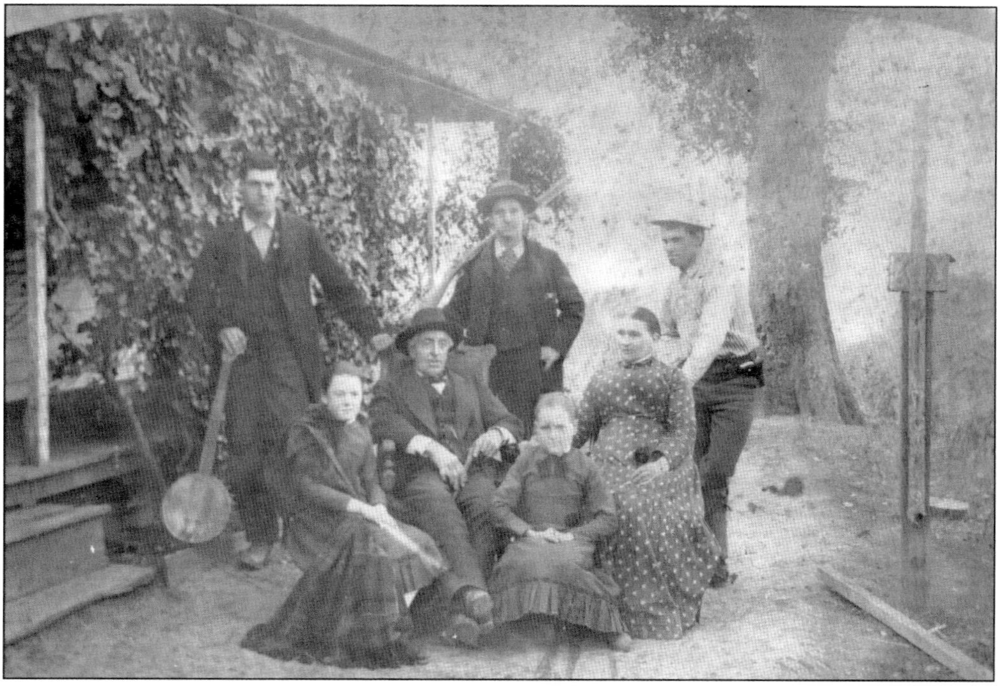

The Kendall family ranched at "the Bluffs," the rocky hills above Bollinger Canyon Road. The patriarch, Samuel Kendall, sailed from Boston on the ship *Edward Everett*, arriving in San Francisco in July 1849. Born in New Hampshire in 1812, he married Frances Mary Armstrong, who was born in New York in 1837. She was of Irish ancestry. The couple is shown above with their five children Charles, Samuel, Tim, Mary Fannie, and Jennie Morrow. They settled in the Moraga Valley in 1857, farming and raising livestock. The land above Bollinger Canyon Road is still partly semi-rural and has working ranches where cattle are raised and brought to market. Pictured at right are Gordon Frazell and his wife, Ynez, who bought a ranch here in 1944. Their daughter Susan and her husband, Sam Sperry, still ranch on the same land. (Right, courtesy of Susan Sperry.)

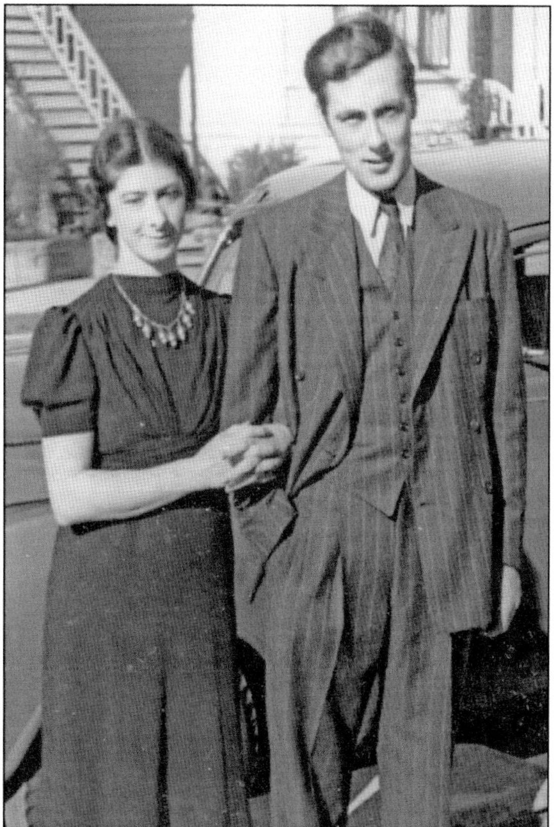

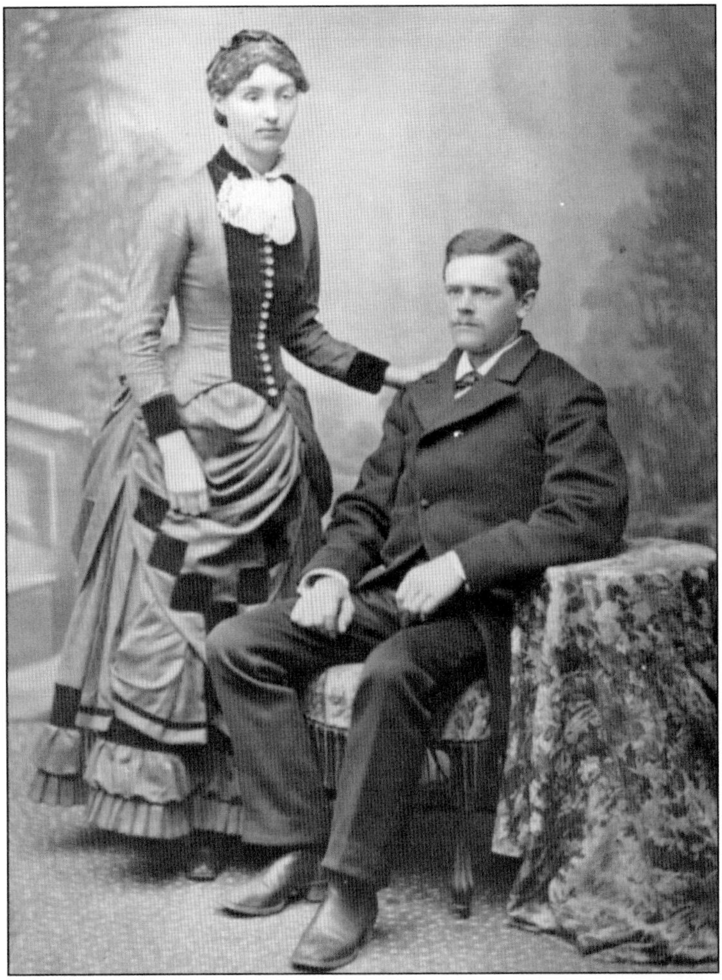

Native Californians Henry Harwood and Catherine Maloney married in 1884 and settled as tenant farmers on the pig ranch owned by Isaac Gann on Camino Pablo Road. Gann, born in 1813 in Tennessee, was an original purchaser of property from Joaquin Moraga in 1855. The pig ranch raised hogs for the Moraga Company. Henry and Catherine Harwood later moved to Oakland. They are pictured at left in 1915. The photograph below shows the home of the Harwood family in 1968. (Left, photograph by Schmidt.)

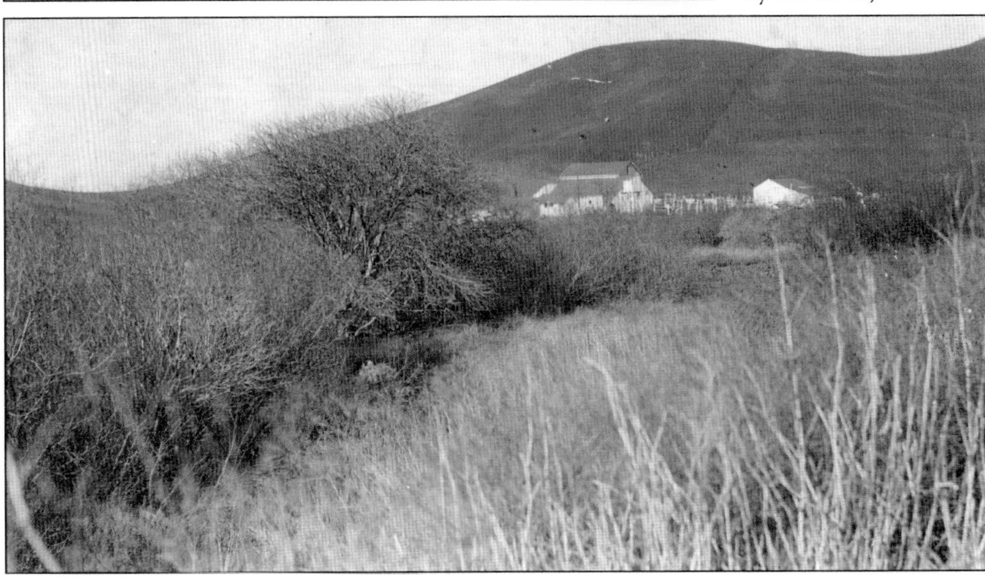

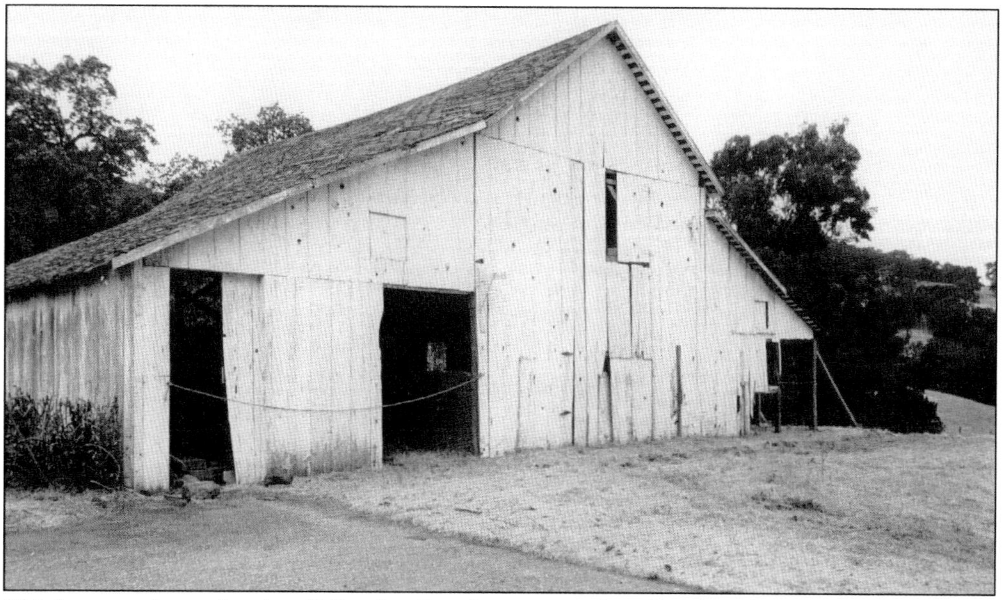

This barn was located at the old Sanders Ranch property where Frank and Lottie Sanders ranched in the early 1900s. Frank G. Sanders, a native Californian born in the early 1890s, was the son-in-law of John Metzler Carr, who was an early dairy farmer in the Fruitvale district of Oakland. Carr acquired land in the Moraga Valley, which he then turned over to his son Alfred J. Carr and Frank G. Sanders.

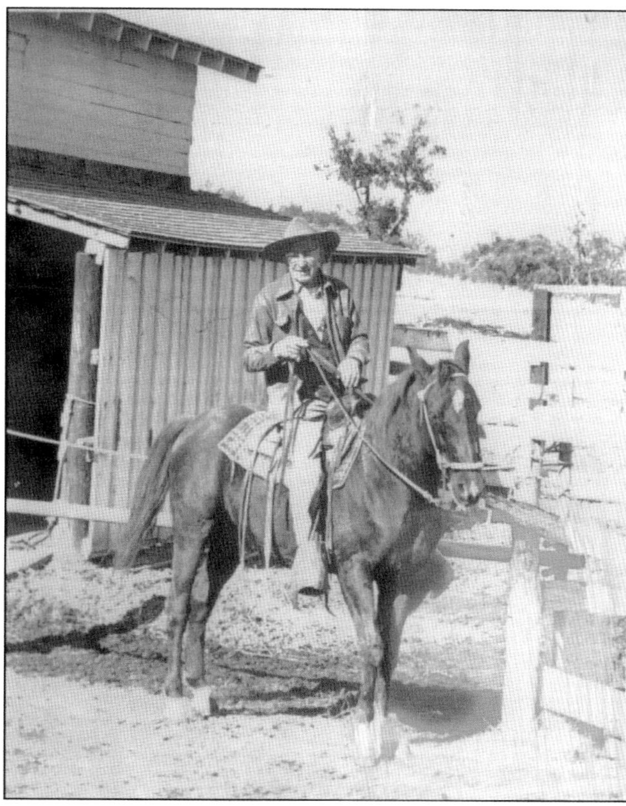

In the 1950s, ranching continued at the Sanders Ranch. Situated close to the area at the end of Camino Pablo, which has been developed into the park Rancho Laguna, the former Sanders Ranch was transformed into a subdivision and an upscale gated community in the 1990s. Nearby, however, the Carr Ranch will remain relatively undeveloped. It has recently been sold to the John Muir Land Trust, and the 600 acres will be preserved as open space accessible to the public by trails. The ranch area boasts grasslands, oak and bay trees, and wildlife including golden eagles, American badgers, and mountain lions.

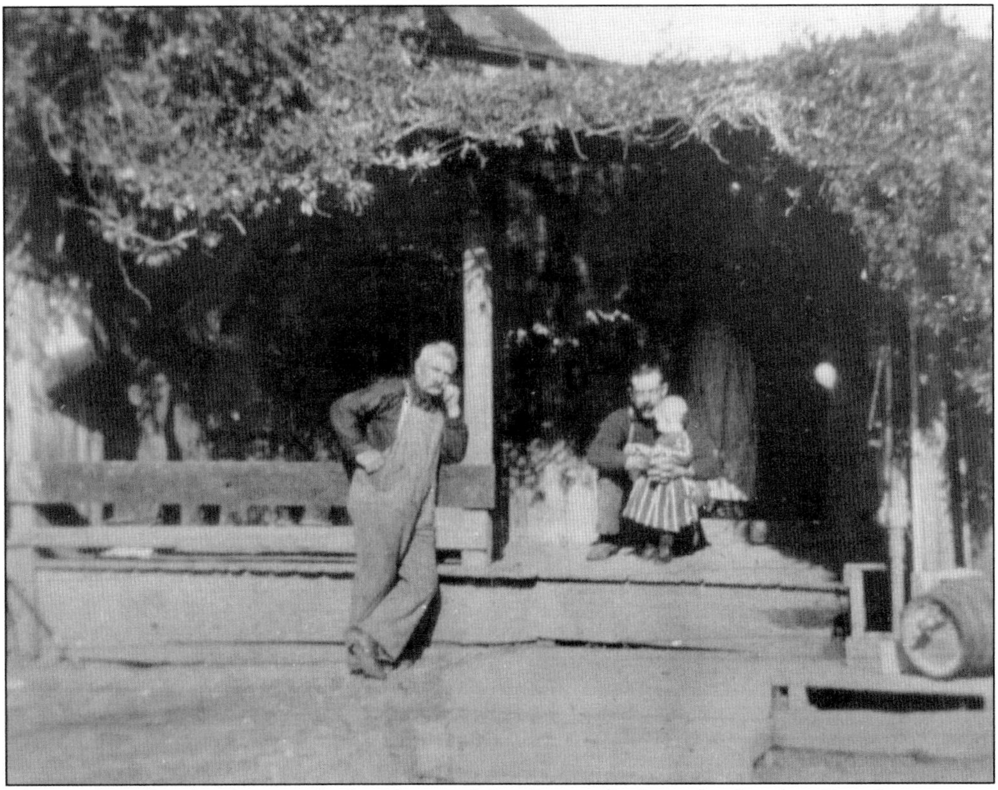

The Madsen family, along with the Harwood family, ranched on the Sanders Ranch as tenant farmers. Erich Madsen and his wife, Annie Hansen, both hailed from Denmark and married in 1870. Before moving to the Moraga Valley, they resided in Petaluma. Their five children were all born in California. Below, haying is in process on the Madsen Ranch with equipment, ranchers, and horses. Erich Madsen used a hay press to compress hay into bales. (Above, courtesy of Louis L. Stein Jr. collection.)

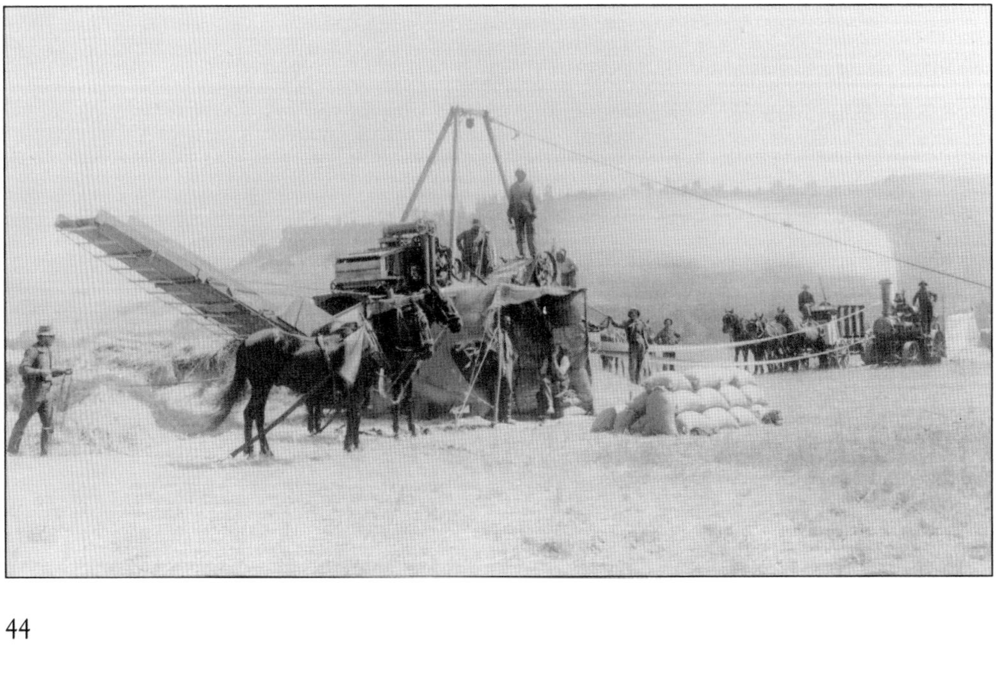

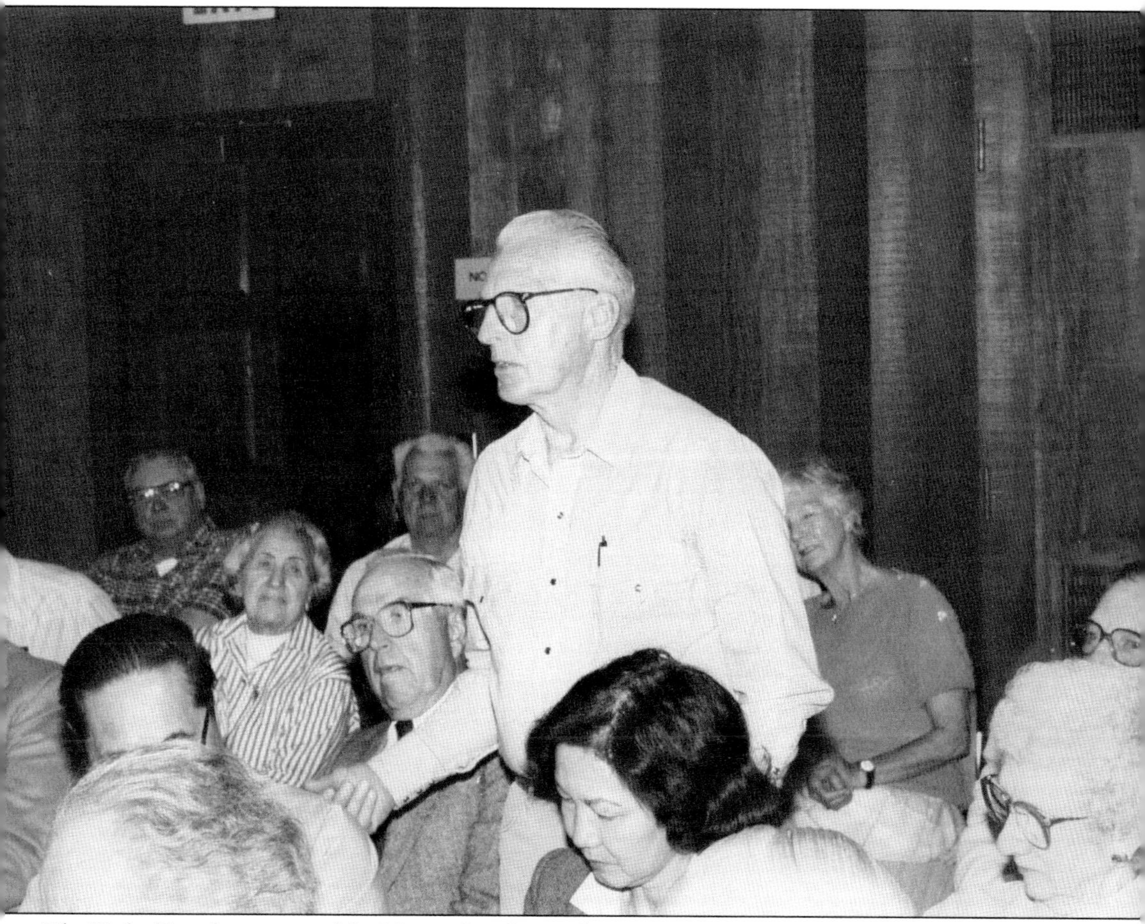

The Trelut Ranch was east of the Moraga Land grant between Las Trampas Ridge and Rocky Ridge on the outskirts of the current town of Moraga, at the end of Bollinger Canyon Road. Brothers Ernest, Etienne, and Leon emigrated from France and ranched here after they arrived in 1873. Ernest Trelut, born in 1858, was issued homestead land in Contra Costa County by the Bureau of Land Management in 1894. The ranch was well known for its vineyards and wine production, an endeavor that has recently become popular again in this area. Frank Trelut was a descendant of the family who remained in Moraga. Pictured here standing, Frank spoke at a gathering of the Moraga Historical Society that featured "old-timers."

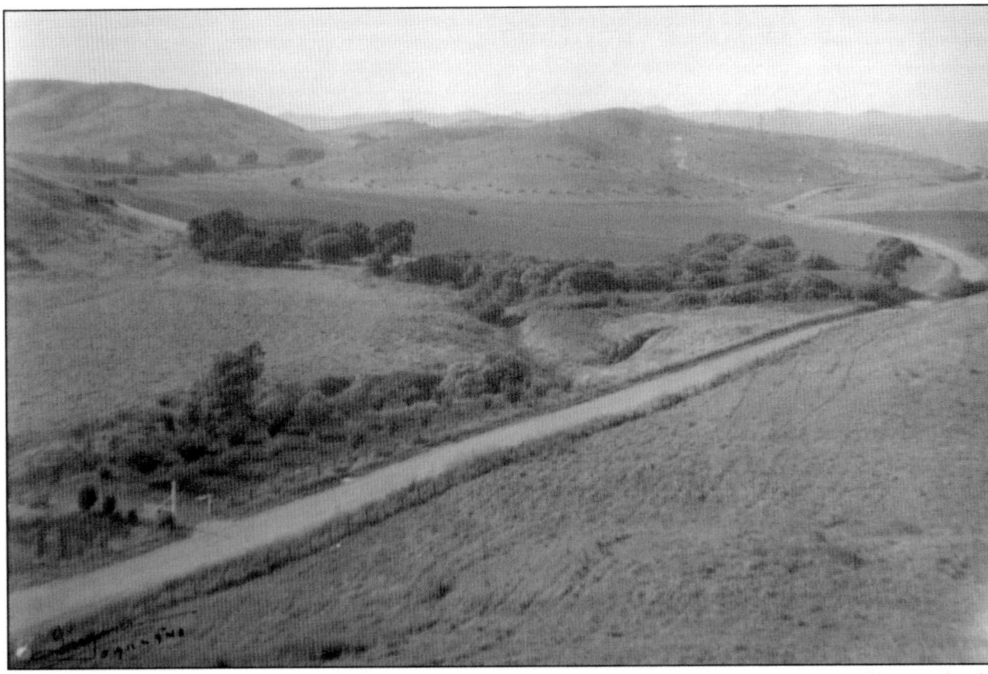

The photograph above shows the Bosqui Ranch on Moraga Road (near the current site of Campolindo High School) as it appeared in 1935. Edward Bosqui, a well-known printer, only lived in the Moraga Valley for a few years in the mid-1800s. He sold his ranch in 1864. The photograph below shows walnut trees in 1956 in the area that was later developed for the construction of Campolindo High School. Walnut trees were planted by the Moraga Company, and walnuts were shipped for many years from the Moraga Valley. Walnuts were processed by the Walnut Growers Association. Walnut orchards can still be found in Moraga today. (Photograph by Louis L. Stein Jr.).

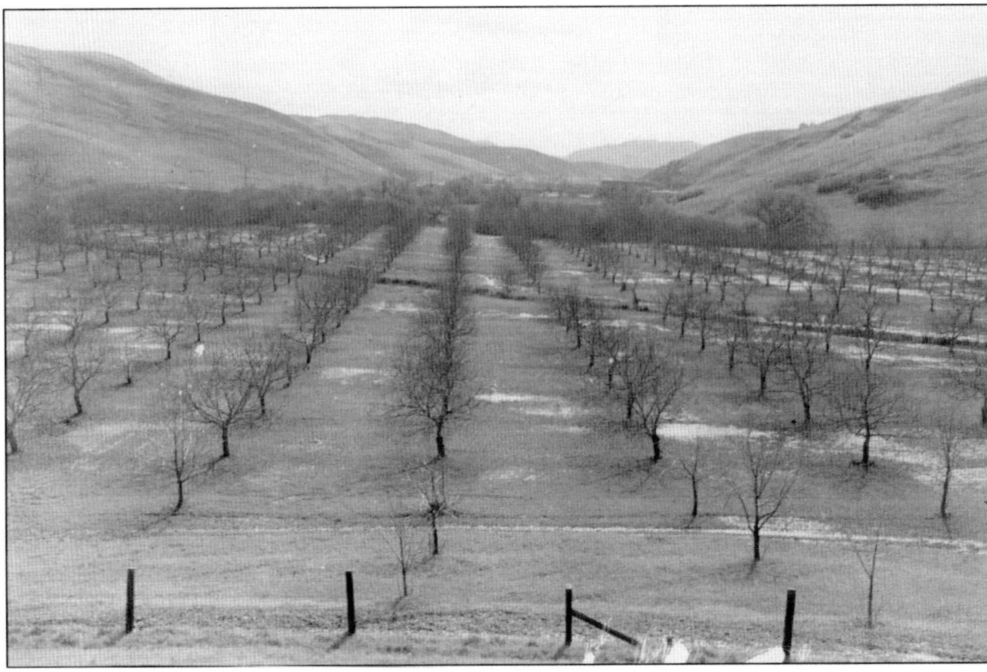

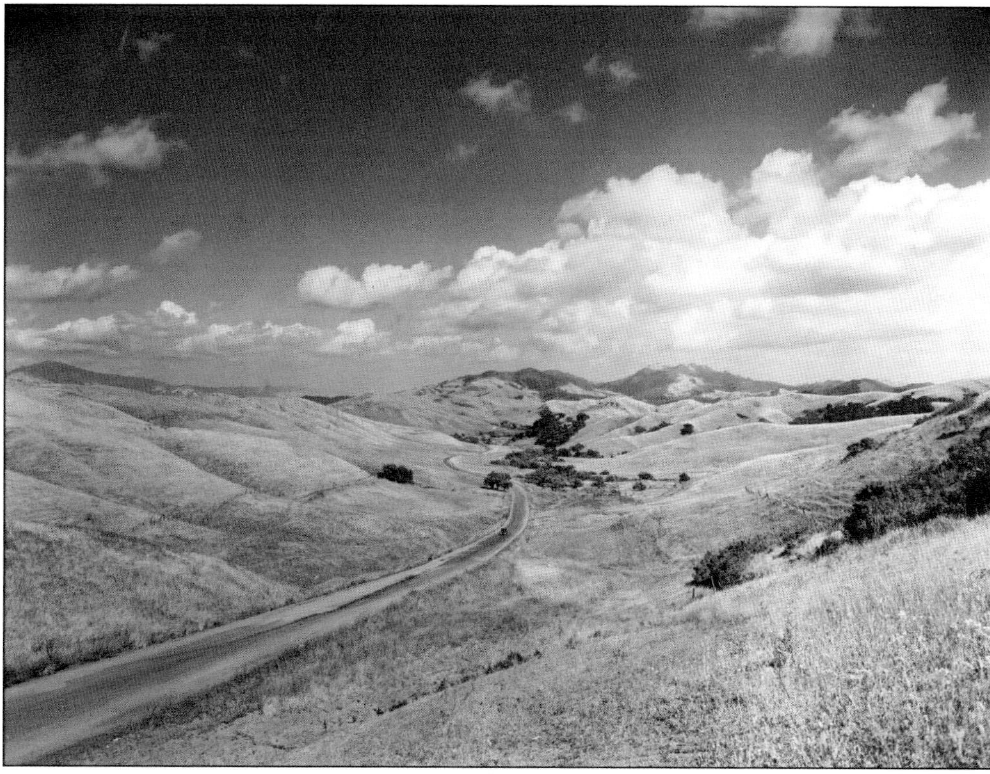

Joseph Nunes was a dairy farmer in this area, residing in the Moraga family adobe from 1903 until his death in 1918. In 1905, he took over the dairy and farming business run from the adobe property from Frank Neves, raising grain, beans, and corn. Born on San Jorge Island in the Azores, Nunes married Isabel Martin in 1902, and the couple had nine children. His first dairy product was butter, which he sold to stores in Oakland and Berkeley. The rolling hills of his farm, seen above in 1935, are still a typical sight in Moraga. From this viewpoint, Mount Diablo can be seen in the distance to the left. The photograph of the adobe at right was taken in 1935, when it was in decay. Five years later, Katherine Irvine, whose husband had bought the property including the adobe, began the renovation of the building. One of the eucalyptus trees seen in the photograph remained standing until recent years. (Right, photograph by Louis L. Stein Jr.)

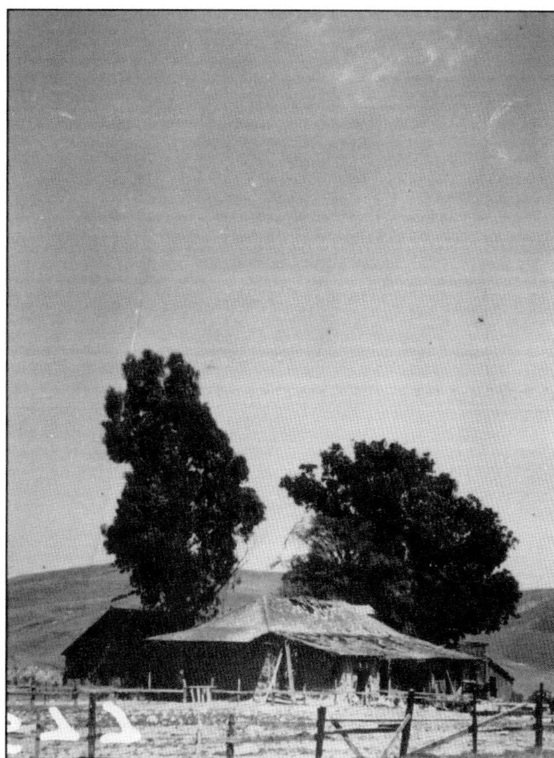

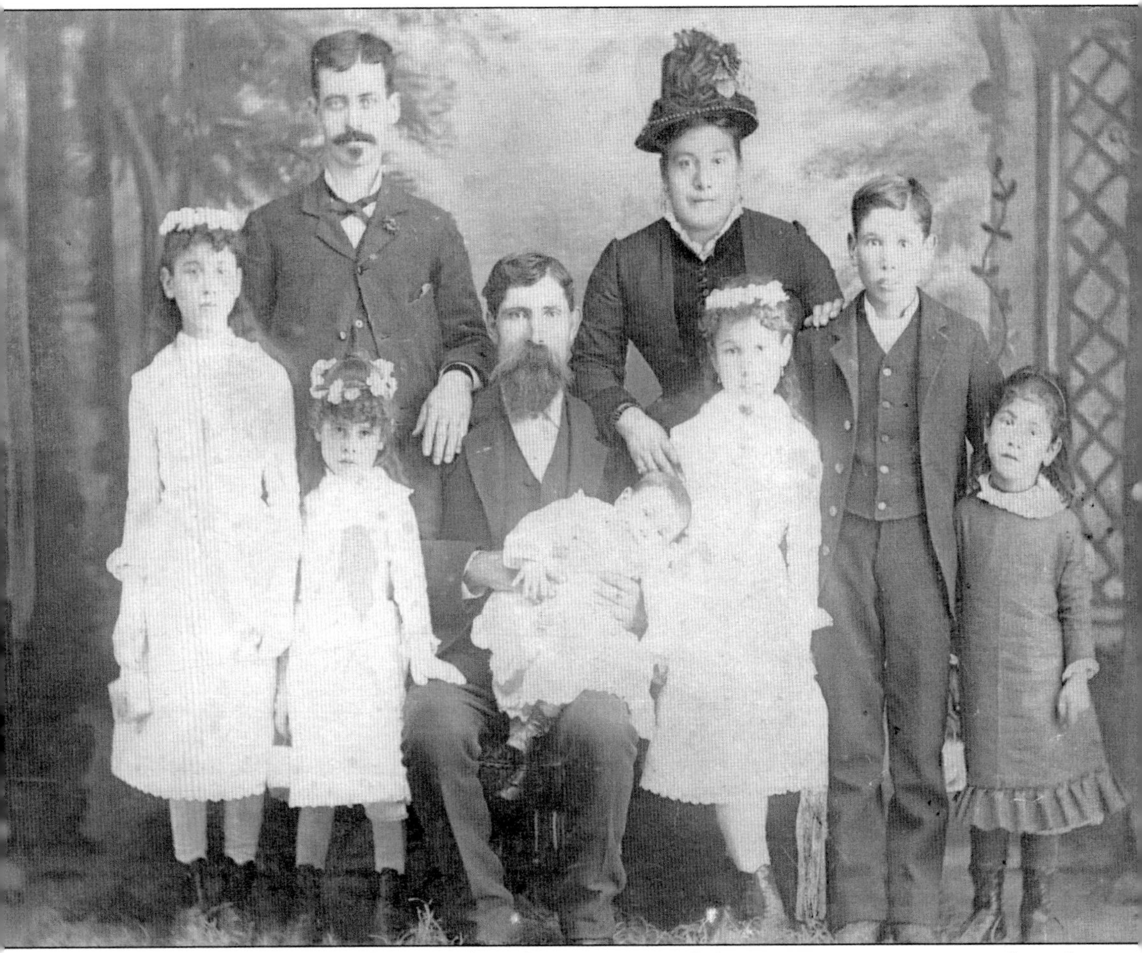

Joao Silveira Avila—or John S. Avila, as he was commonly known—was an immigrant from the Azores who married Gomacinda Moraga in the parish of St. Catherine of Siena in Martinez in 1873. The family resided briefly in the adobe as renters after Moraga family ownership had been lost. Gabriel Moraga, brother of Gomacinda, was the last to reside there as an owner, and he was physically evicted with his family from the premises after losing the property. Gomacinda, who died in 1892, was born in 1854 to Joseph de Jesus Moraga, son of land grant recipient Joaquin Moraga, and Maria de la Cruz Sibrian. The family of John and Gomacinda is shown here on August 5, 1886.

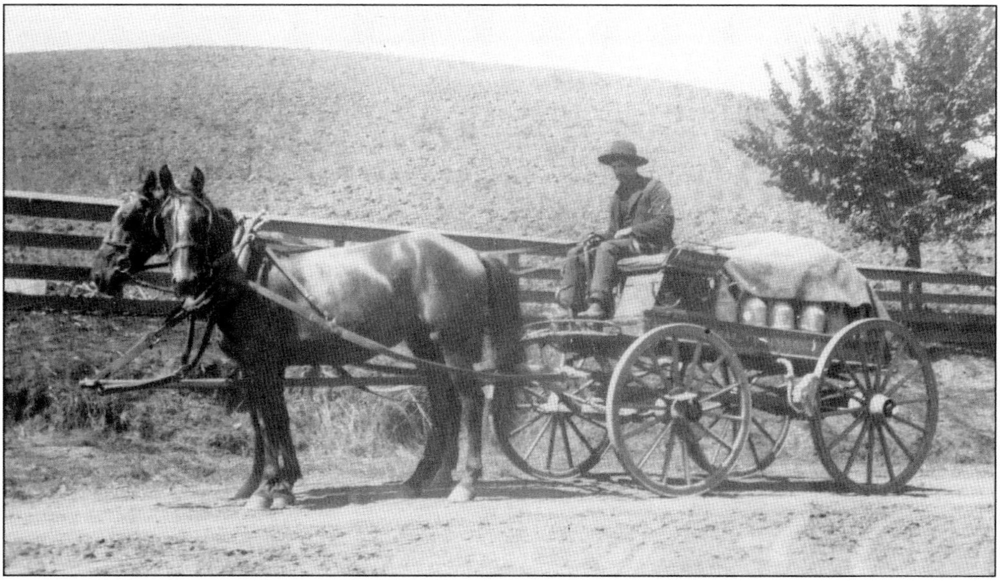

The photograph above from the Louis L. Stein Jr. collection shows Joe Azevedo driving a cart for the Central Creamery. Families like the Azevedos from Portugal were instrumental in starting up dairies in the Moraga Valley, replacing some of the ranching economy. The small industries of the valley demanded that roads be created and improved for the hauling and distribution of goods. Below, work is being done on Moraga Way. The route as it is known today was originally graded in 1922. In later years, it was connected to St. Mary's Road. Once called the Moraga Boulevard and then the Moraga Highway, it is now known as Moraga Way. Possibly confusing to visitors, it intersects with Moraga Road, which leads to and from the nearby city of Lafayette, while Moraga Way leads to and from the nearby city of Orinda.

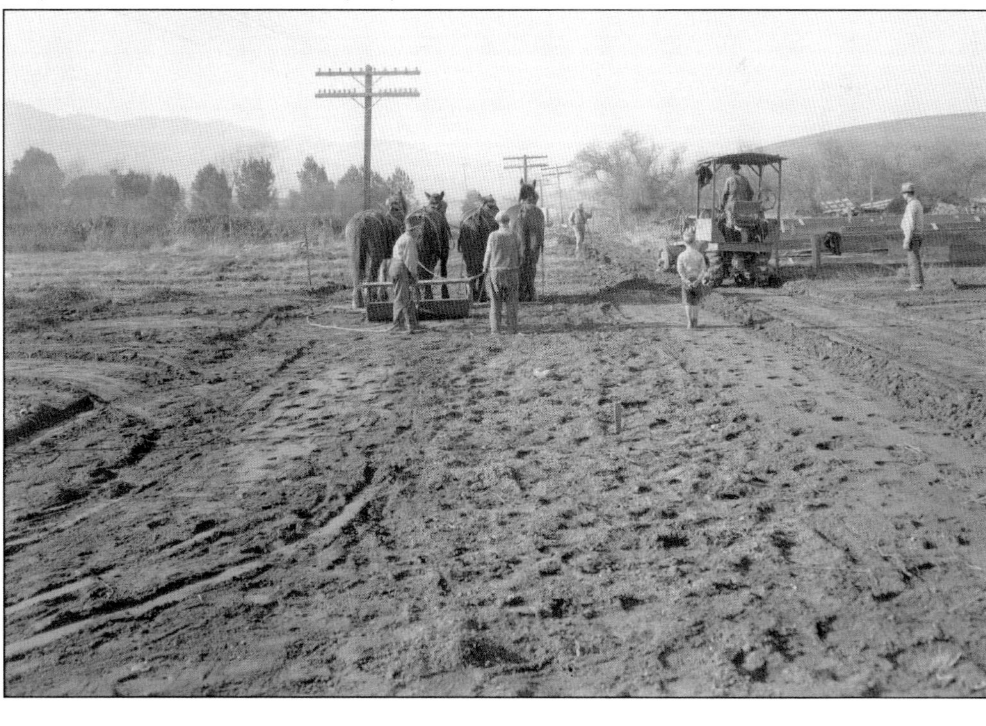

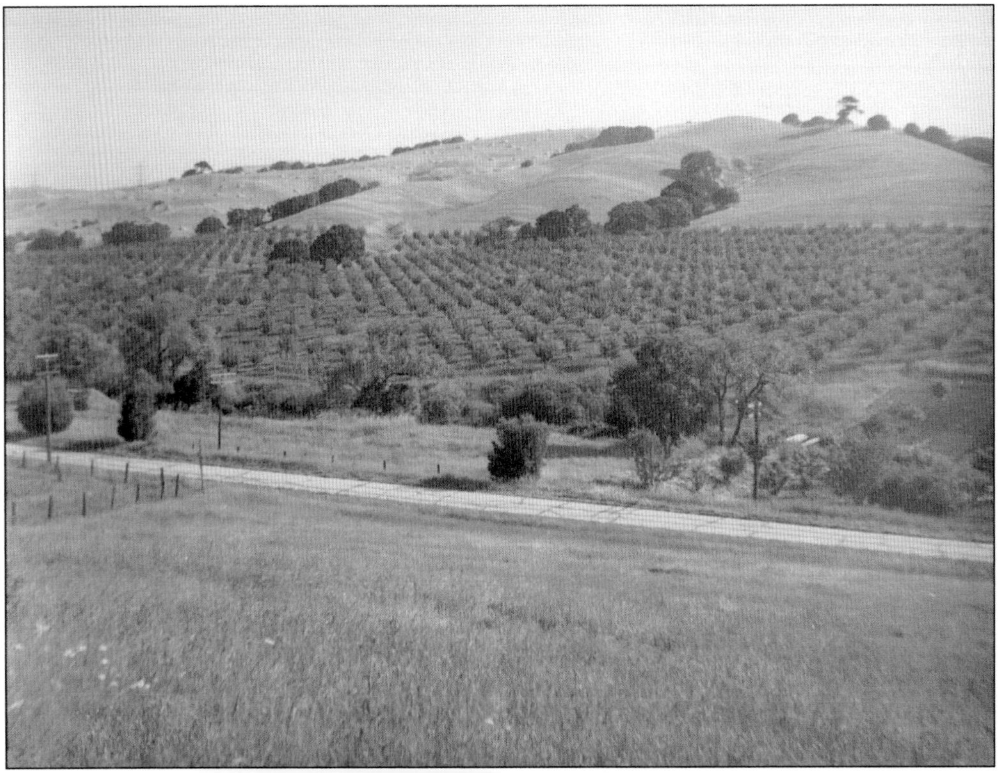

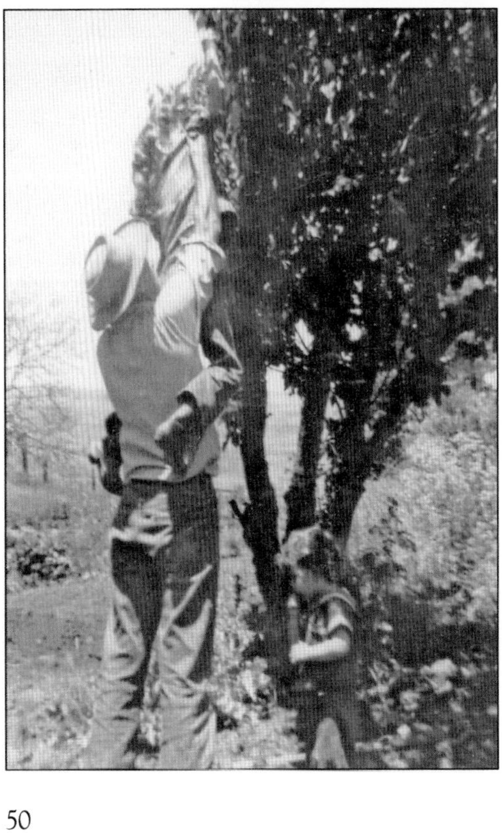

Moraga Company land was once home to pear orchards. The trees flourished, and some planted in the early 1900s by the Moraga Company founded by James Irwin still produce pears to this day. Pear picking by Moraga Company workers began in July and continued for about four weeks. Many other fruit trees were grown on local ranches. At left, Joan Frazell is hoisted by her father, Gordon, to pick cherries on the family ranch near Bollinger Canyon. Joan's younger sister Susan samples the fruit. (Left, courtesy of Susan Sperry.)

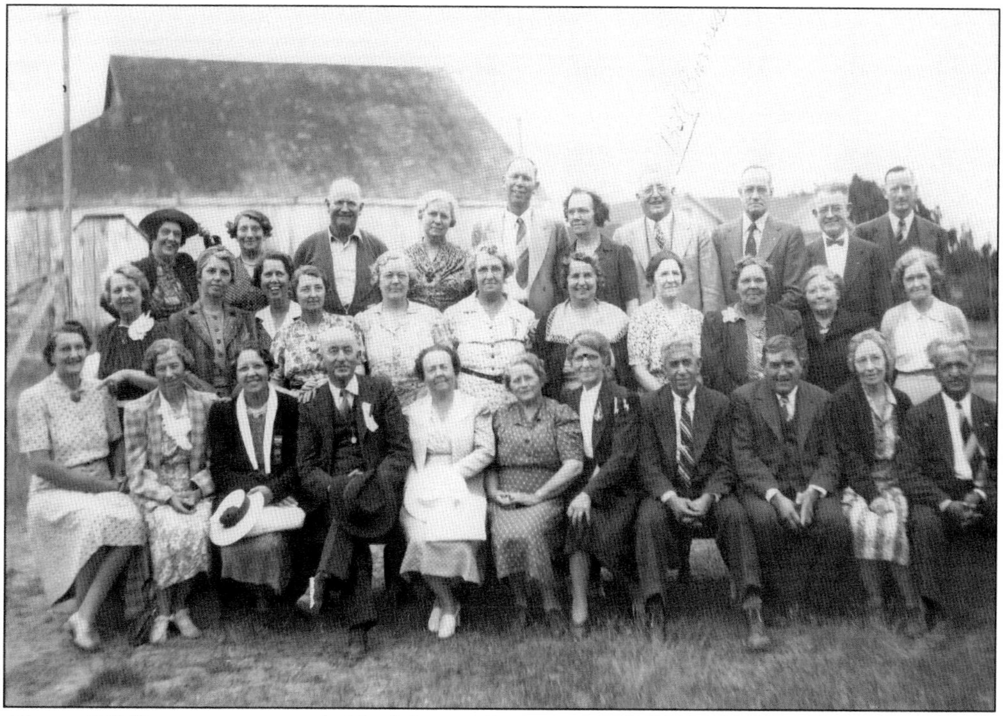

Above, Bill Barnes is surrounded by Moraga Company staff. Bearing a large grin, he is fourth from right in the back. Barnes was the longtime manager of the Moraga Company. In 1919, he became superintendent of the ranch property and was involved in all aspects of operations and property development. Below, Barnes (center) was at the 1966 dedication of the new Moraga Post Office along with Thomas Carroll, to his left, and Contra Costa County supervisor James Moriarty, to his right.

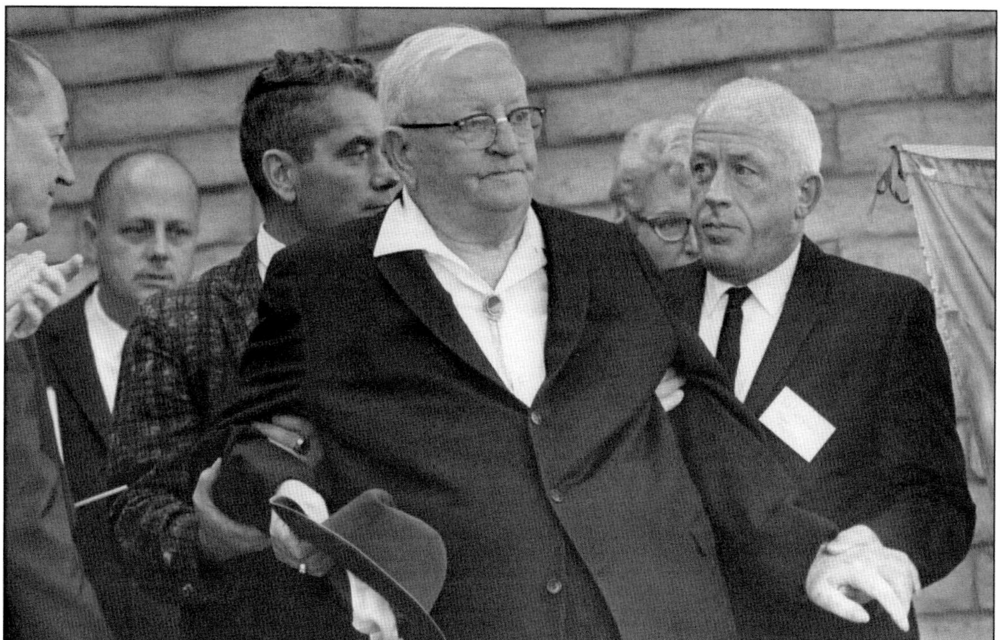

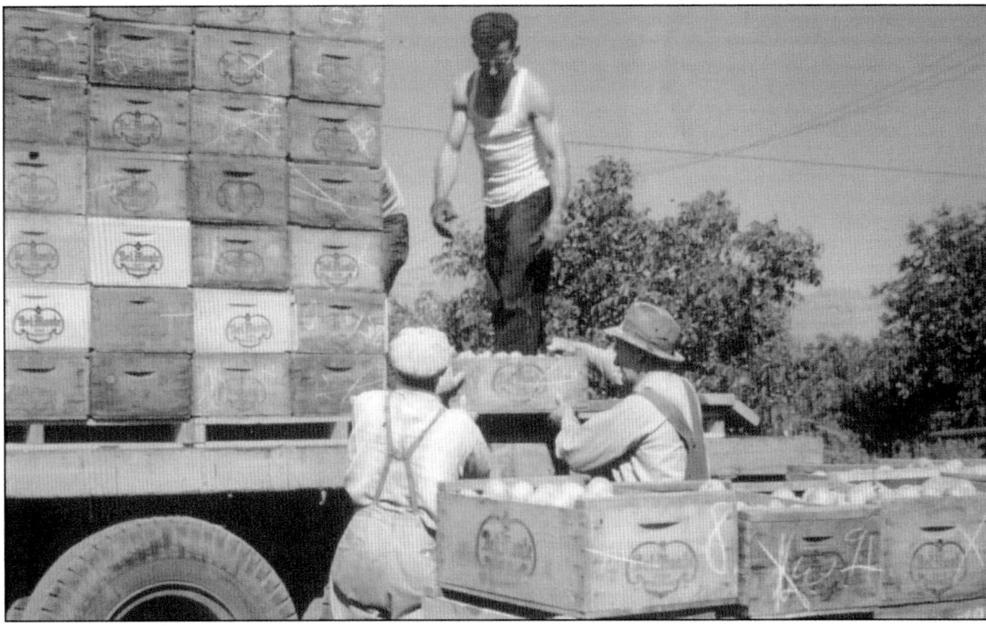

The above photograph, taken in 1940 by Moraga resident D. Reginald Tibbetts, shows workers loading crates of Bartlett pears onto trucks for transport to the Del Monte Cannery in San Leandro for processing. The photograph below also shows pears ready to be shipped off to the cannery. The work done in 1940 followed what had already been a long tradition of pear production. In 1921, Moraga Valley pears were first shown at the state fair, where they made a favorable impression. The same year, pears were shipped for the first time via the San Francisco–Sacramento Railroad to eastern markets and local canneries in the Oakland area.

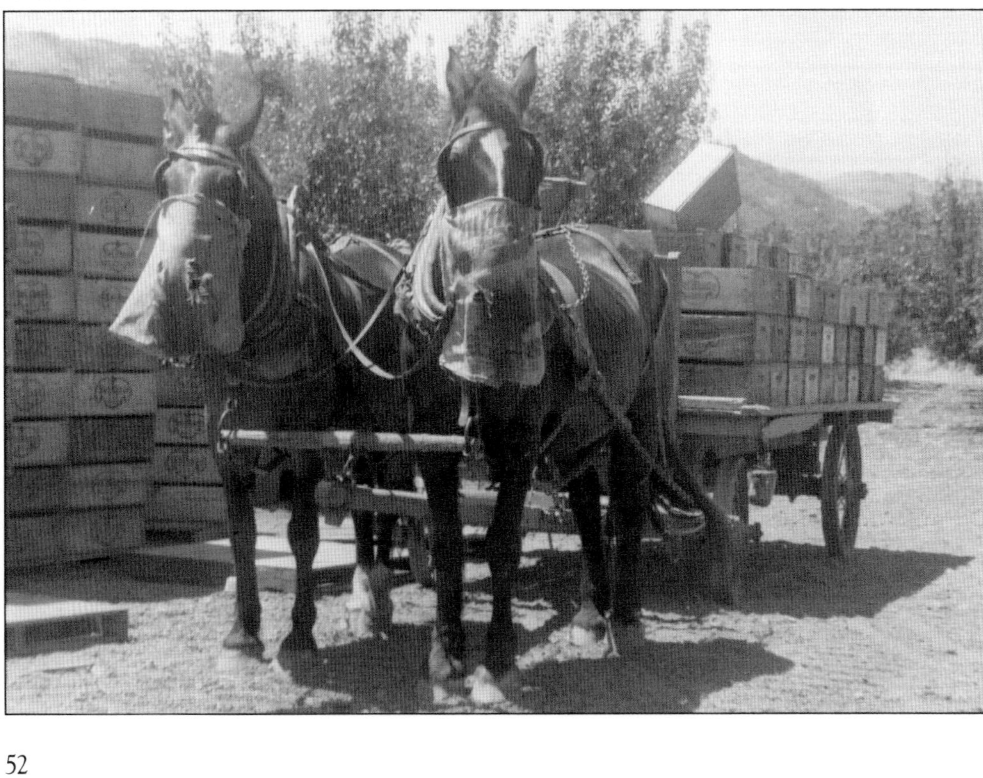

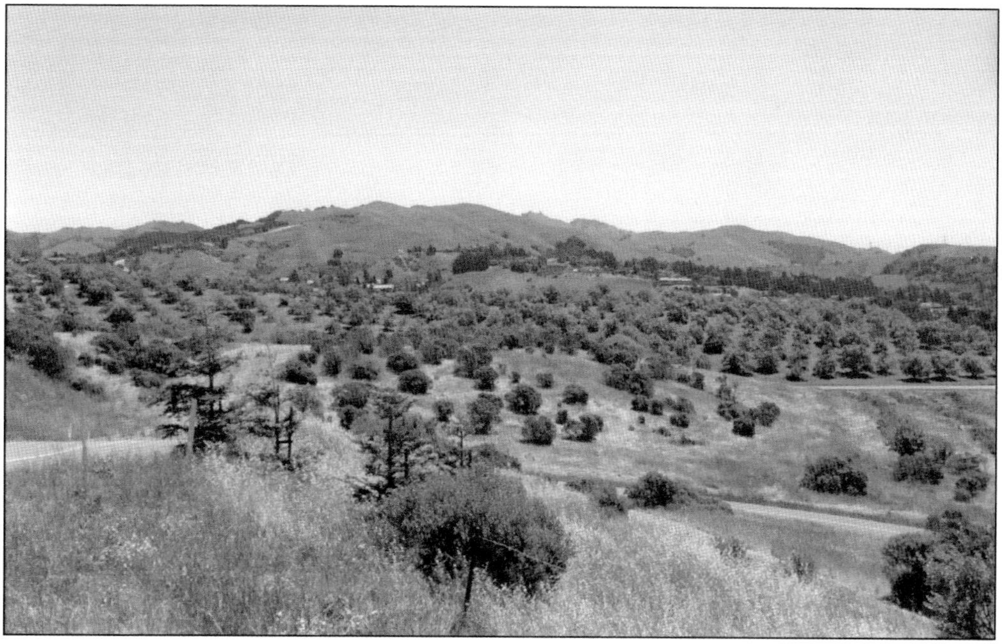

Remnants of pear and walnut orchards can still be found in Moraga years after they were first planted by the Moraga Company. Some of the trees are between 100 and 200 years old and still produce fruit. The above photograph is from 1994. There are still 100 pear trees on Camino Pablo near the Joaquin Moraga Middle School, although the recent fire blight is a serious threat to their survival. Community members pitch in on designated volunteer work days to harvest pears and control the blight.

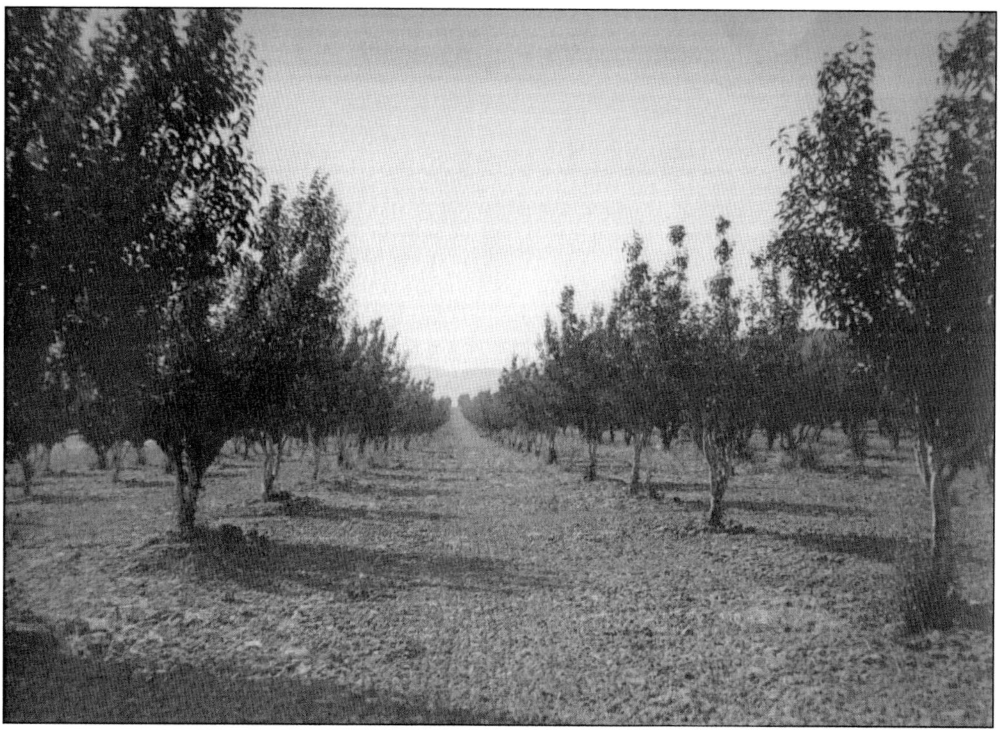

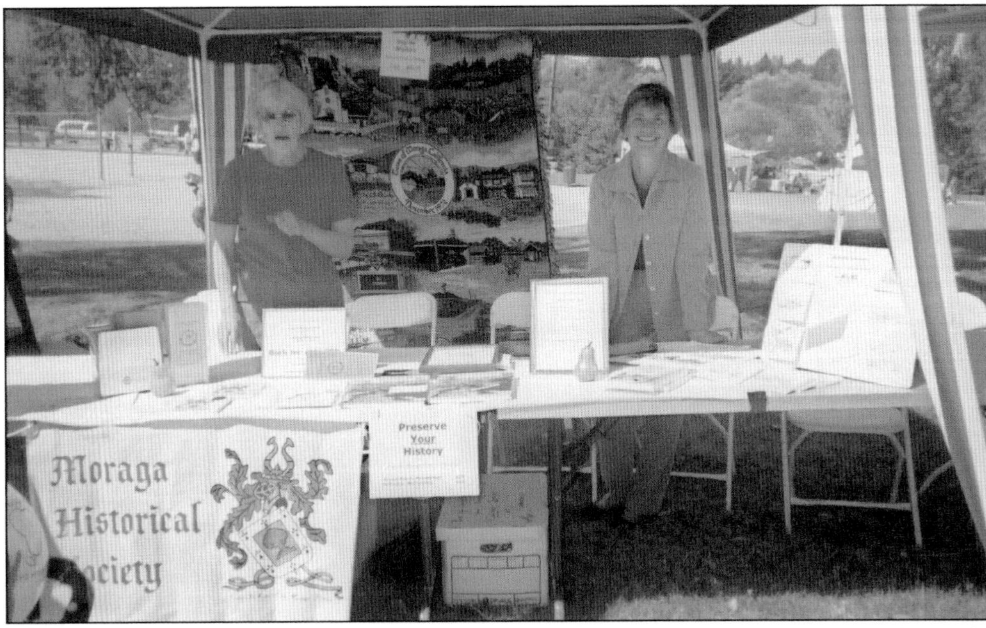

The Moraga Pear Festival is an annual fall tradition held on what is usually a sunny day at the Moraga Commons. Community groups man booths to offer information about their activities. Food (including locally made pear pies) and drinks are sold, and children play on the play structures and on rented inflatables. A pear recipe contest is held, and the winning recipes are published in a booklet. In recent years, with the addition of local wine tastings and grape stomping, the title of the festival was changed to the Moraga Pear and Wine Festival. This change reflects the renewed interest in the Moraga community in producing wine, a type of farming done in this community at the time of the very first Spanish settlers. Above, Donna Giorgi and Sue Holmes provide visitors with information on the Moraga Historical Society. The photograph below shows a band from the nearby Rossmoor retirement community playing for the festival audience at the Moraga Commons bandstand.

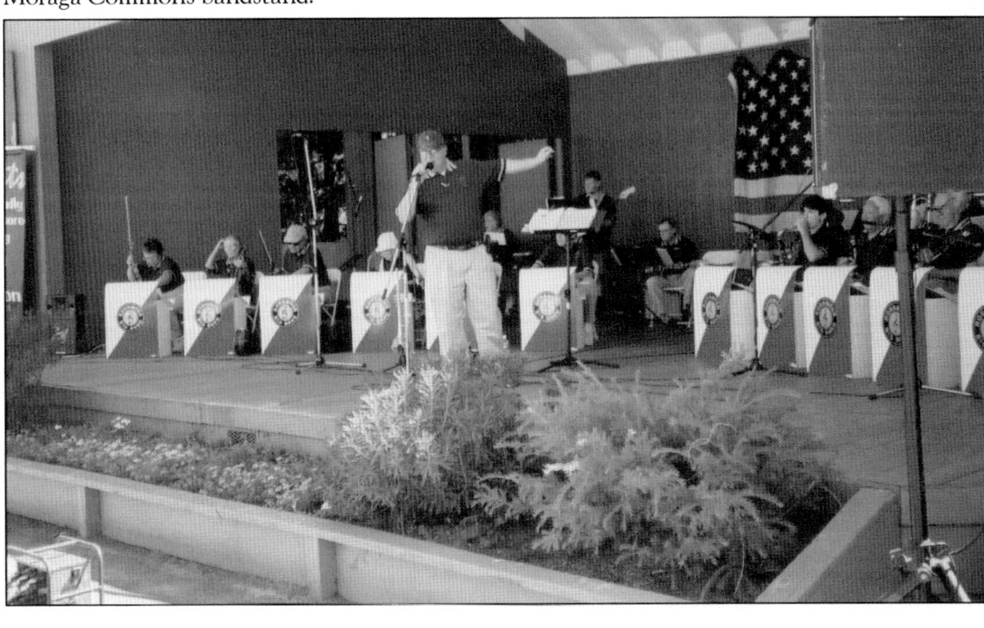

Four

A Bay Area Suburb

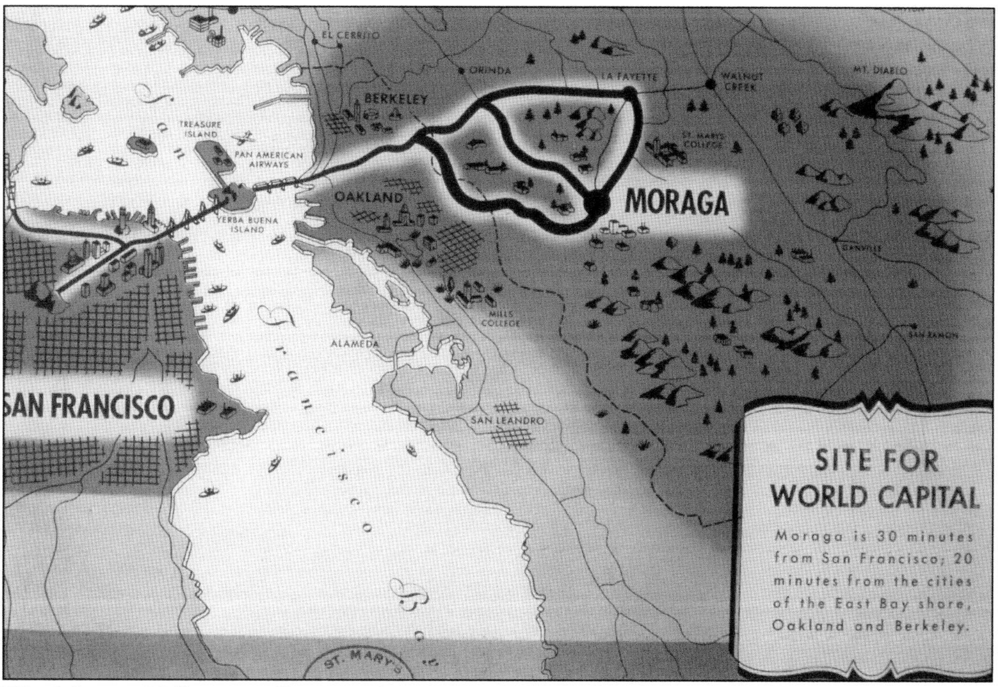

The Moraga Valley is well situated as an attractive environment near urban centers. Early developers saw a great opportunity to build a commuter community. Inspired to learn that San Francisco had been selected as the site for drawing up the United Nations charter in 1945, the Contra Costa County Board of Supervisors pitched the idea of locating the UN headquarters in the Moraga Valley to the Preparatory Commission of the UN.

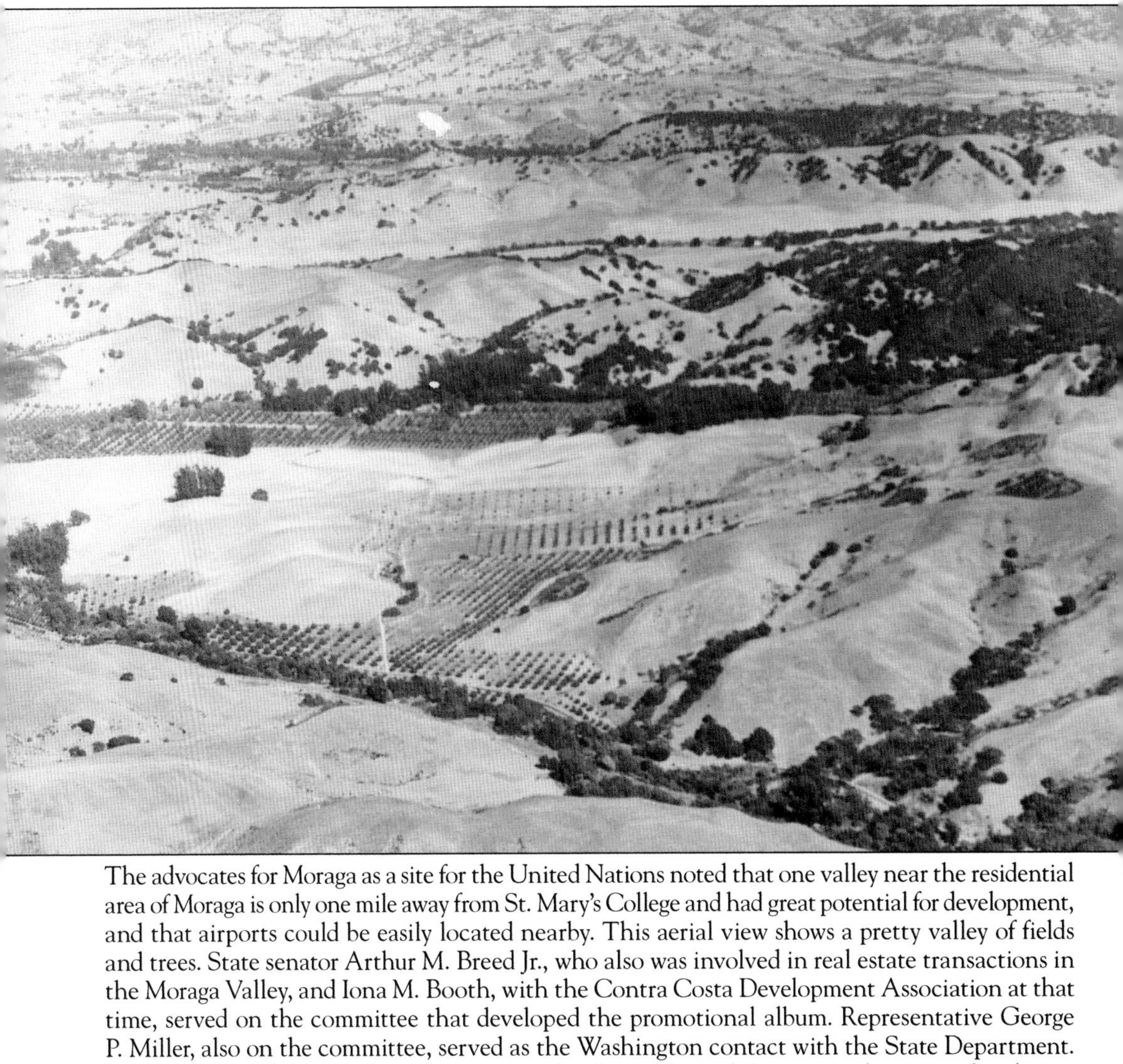

The advocates for Moraga as a site for the United Nations noted that one valley near the residential area of Moraga is only one mile away from St. Mary's College and had great potential for development, and that airports could be easily located nearby. This aerial view shows a pretty valley of fields and trees. State senator Arthur M. Breed Jr., who also was involved in real estate transactions in the Moraga Valley, and Iona M. Booth, with the Contra Costa Development Association at that time, served on the committee that developed the promotional album. Representative George P. Miller, also on the committee, served as the Washington contact with the State Department. Photographs and descriptions in custom-made albums showed the many advantages for placing the UN in this area, including the valley's proximity to San Francisco ("reached in 30 minutes of driving time"), the excellent climate, and the beautiful and relatively undeveloped location. The album also extolled the local redwoods and the beauty of nearby Mount Diablo.

An early suburban neighborhood, Valle Vista was developed by the Moraga Company in 1914. Commuters took the Oakland & Antioch Railway to Oakland and San Francisco. The water supply was piped from a spring at the Moraga family adobe. Herman E. Hespe and his wife, Martha Sonerud Hespe, were native Californians, he of German, and she of Norwegian descent. They were early residents of Valle Vista. Their son Wilbur, shown at right, was born in Alameda County in 1913. After the family bought a lot in Valle Vista, Wilbur attended Willow Springs (later Moraga) School, where he had Florence Fontes for his first-grade teacher. Hermann was a farmer, while Martha commuted on the Oakland & Antioch to her job at Pacific Gas and Electric Company in San Francisco. The family moved to southern California by 1930.

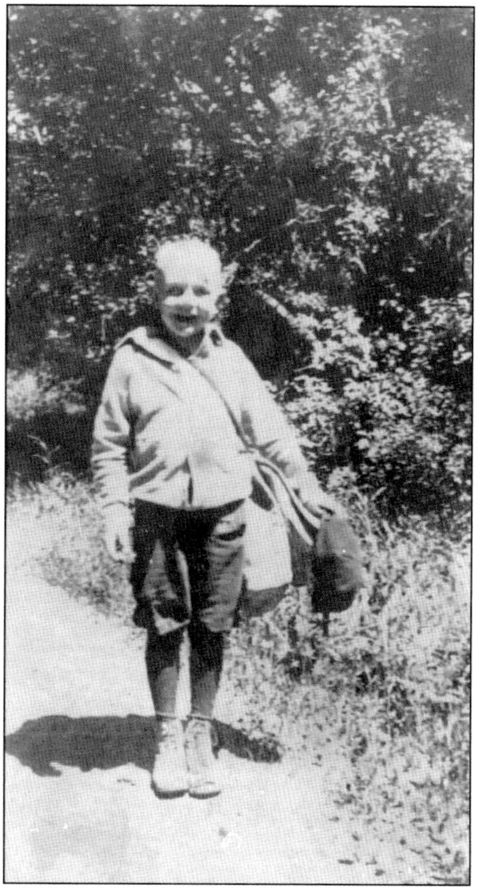

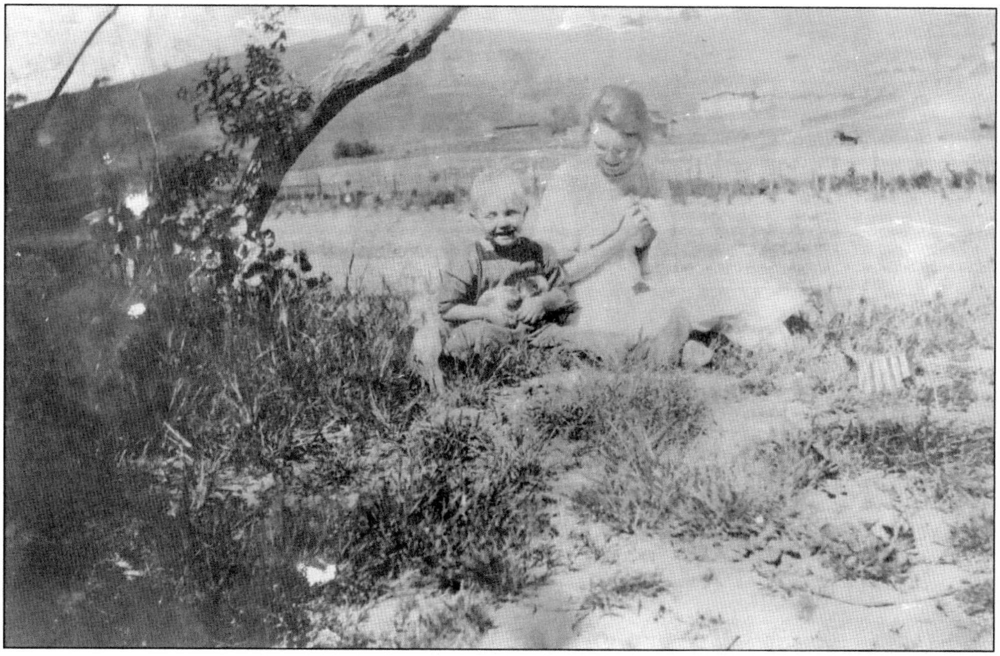

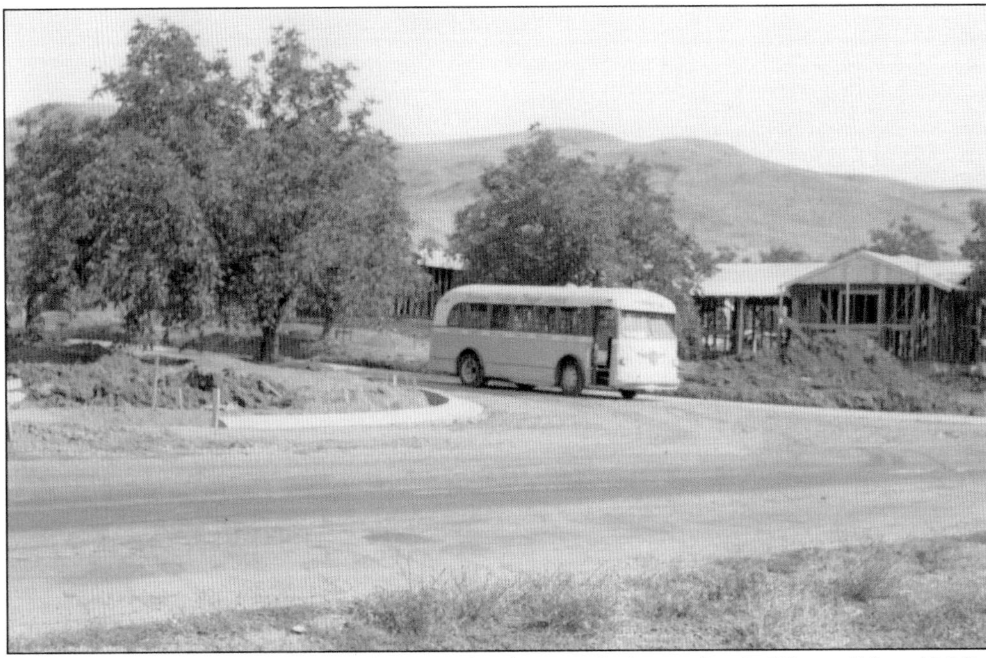

This Moraga Valley Stage Lines bus, shown in the photograph above taken by Warren Edward Miller, ran from Oakland to the Moraga Valley in the early 1950s. A converted US Navy bus, it served commuters in the developing community. The line ran over Skyline Boulevard through Canyon and Moraga communities to a terminus at Glenside Drive in Lafayette. Bus lines have continued to operate through the Moraga Valley. The commuter bus pictured below was operational in 1992. Since 1980, a bus service known as the County Connection has provided service throughout Contra Costa County from neighborhood stops to Bay Area Rapid Transit stations.

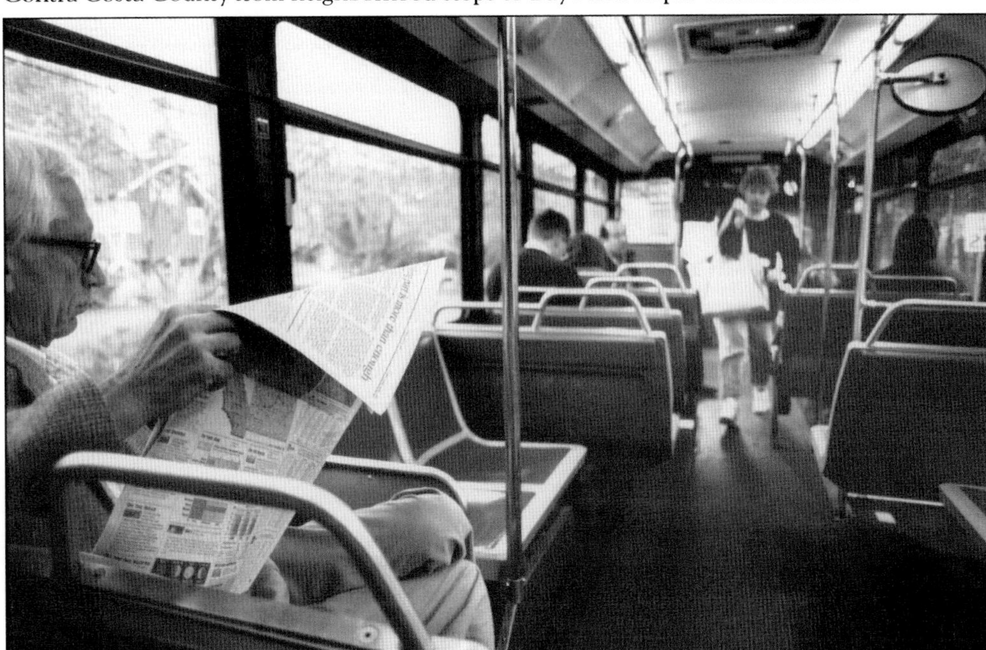

Five

MORAGA BECAME A TOWN

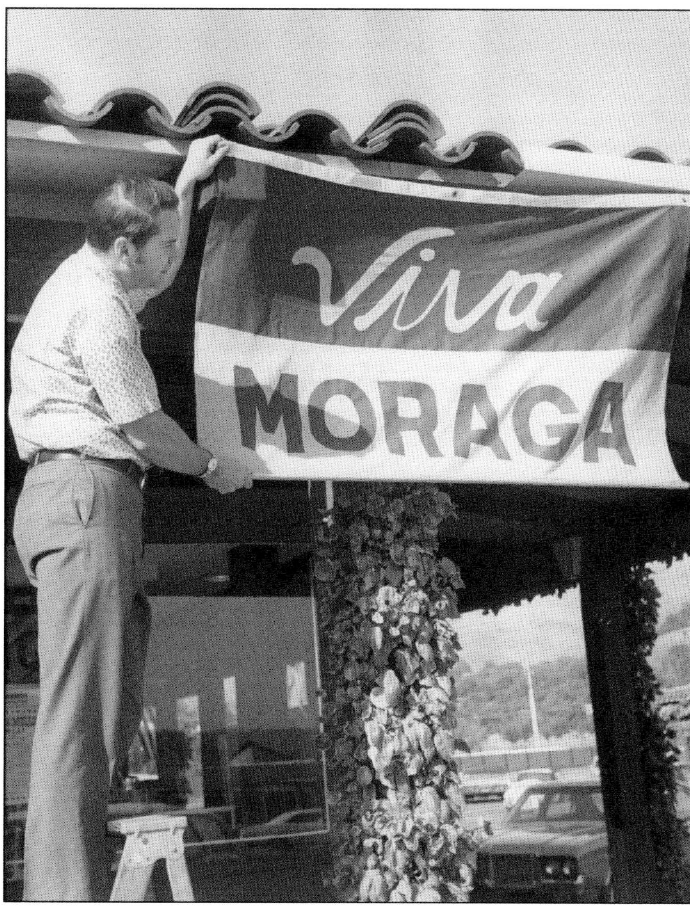

Moraga became an incorporated town in 1974, but before town boundaries were established, people had been living in the residential community for over a century. The families and their homes had been documented in the US and state census. Like residents of any town, they had established businesses, roads, water resources, schools, a college, a postal service, a fire department, and places for worship and for recreation. The small town was ready to thrive and to build on its strong community foundation when the incorporation papers were signed. (Photograph by *Midweek Sun*.)

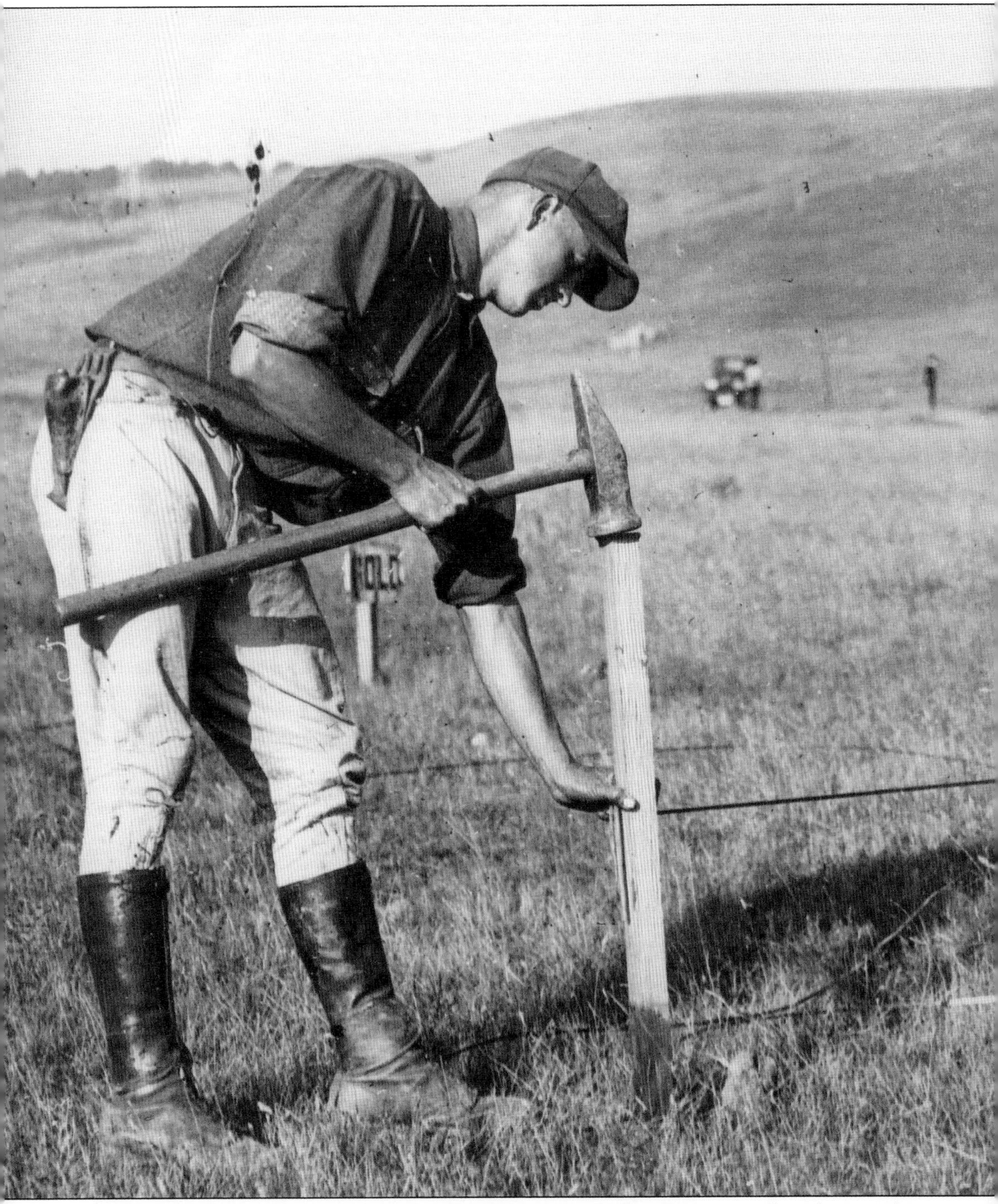

From left to right, instrument man Lee Simmons, engineer Frank Draeger (kneeling, working as rear chainman), and chairman Shirley M. Whitehead survey property in the Moraga Valley in 1922. Draeger worked from 1922 to 1977 as a civil engineer for the various companies that surveyed and developed land in the Moraga area and beyond. Draeger himself bought what was known as the Don Trego Chicken Ranch at the corner of Woodland Road and Moraga Way. Working for Wilson & Company for 55 of the 65 years the firm was in business, Draeger was highly involved

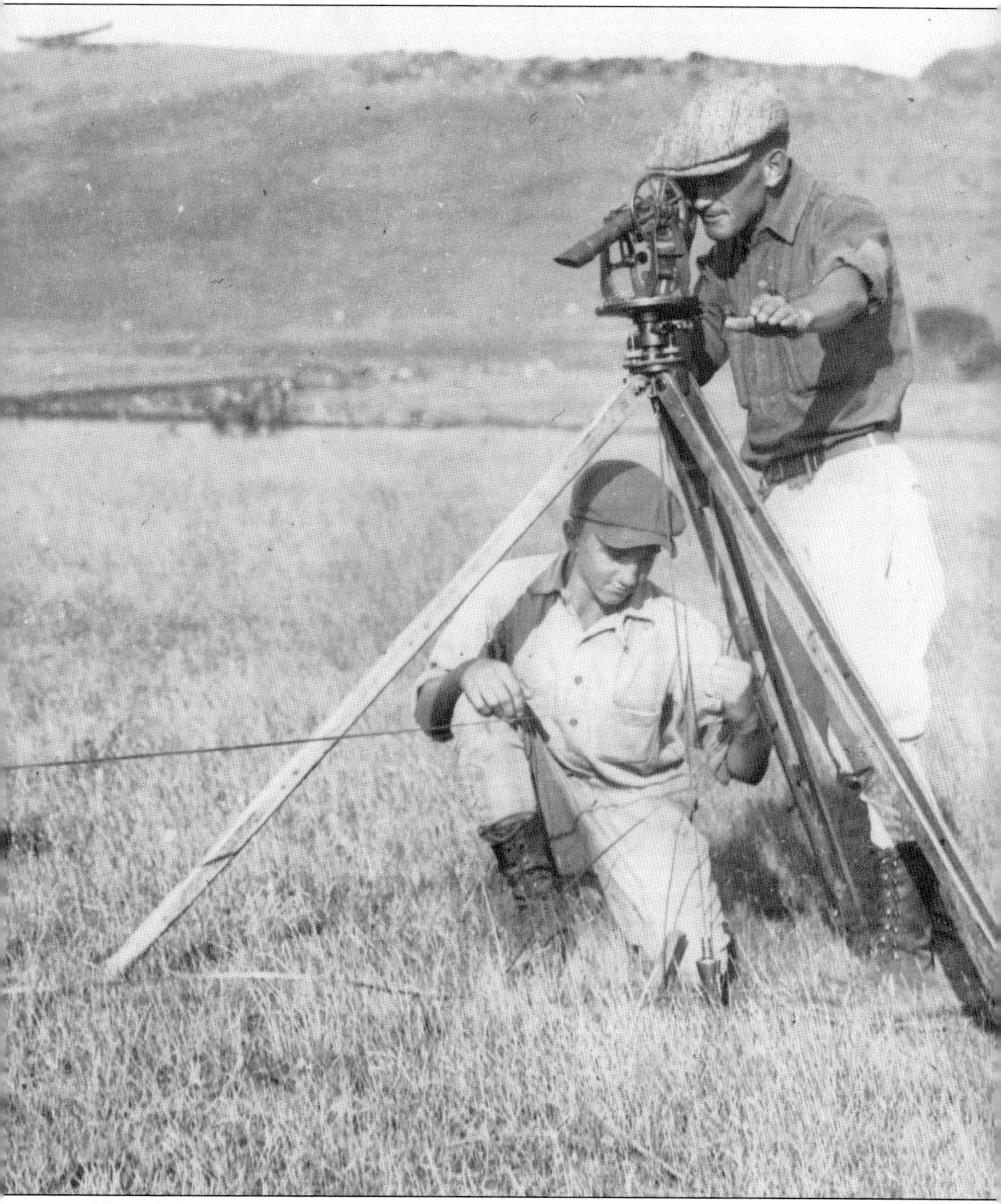

in and knowledgeable about the land and people of the Moraga Valley. He wrote a manuscript detailing his memories of development of the Moraga Ranch called "Developing the Moraga Company Ranch: 1922–1977." He concludes by noting that his work was pleasant and interesting, and that he was fortunate to have had the opportunity to take part in the development of the "beautiful Rancho Laguna de los Palos Colorados."

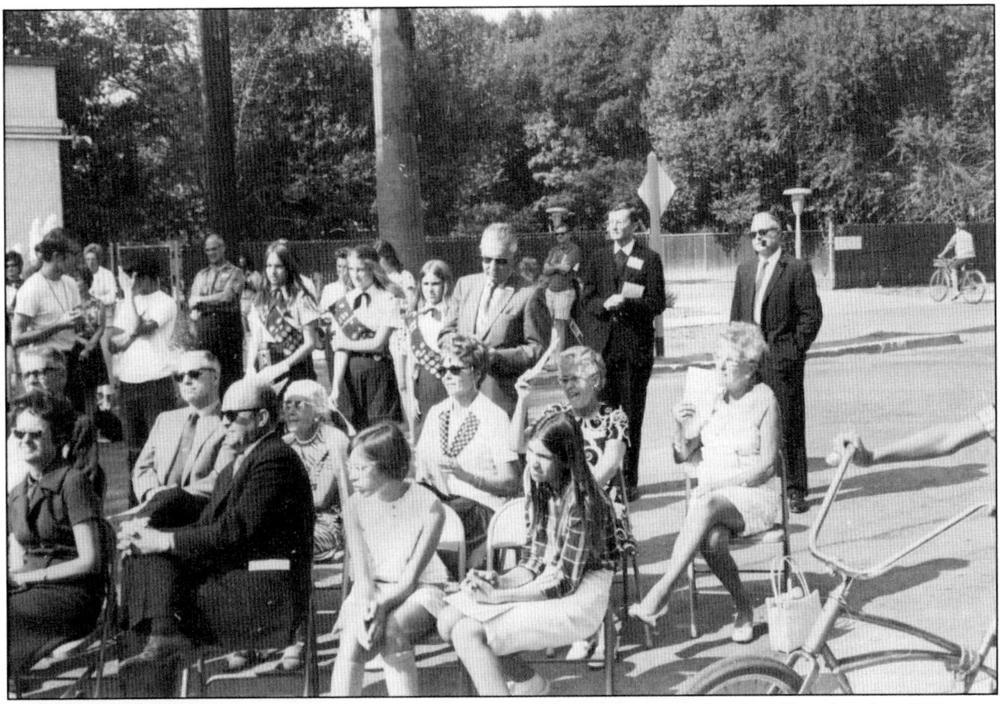

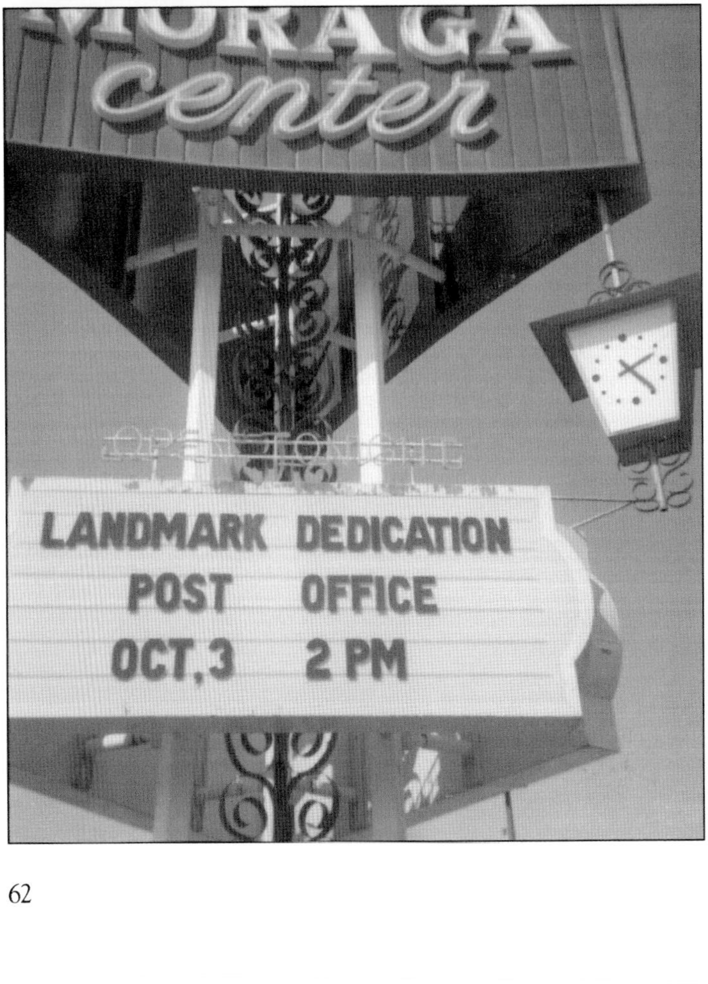

On October 3, 1970, a plaque was dedicated by the Moraga Historical Society on School Street to commemorate the creation in that locale of the old townsite, first conceived by A.A. Grant and J.A. Williamson in 1894, based on plans developed by R.N. Burgess. The townsite undertaking was furthered in turn by the Moraga Company and by the Utah Construction and Mining Company. Although this location eventually failed as a central townsite, it has always been an important historic part of town, and the old post office where the plaque was dedicated continued to serve the Moraga community until recent years.

Long before Moraga became a town, the valley had schools for the local children. The first school that can be documented in the Moraga Valley was established in 1855, a private one-room schoolhouse with Philip Sage as its teacher. The Willow Spring School District dates from 1857, when the one-room schoolhouse joined the public school district. This small school was located near what is now the Moraga Commons park. The building was moved to another location to serve as a recreation hall, and eventually, the structure burned down. Below, it can be seen that there were quite a few students at the school in 1911. As the population of the area grew, the Moraga Company provided land for a new school, which was also called Willow Spring School. This larger school opened its doors to students in 1917 and closed in 1958. The building still exists and has been the home for a preschool and a church.

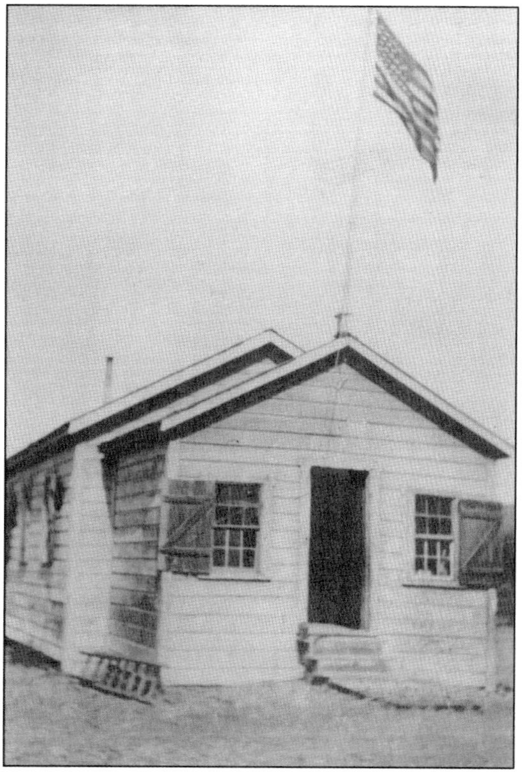

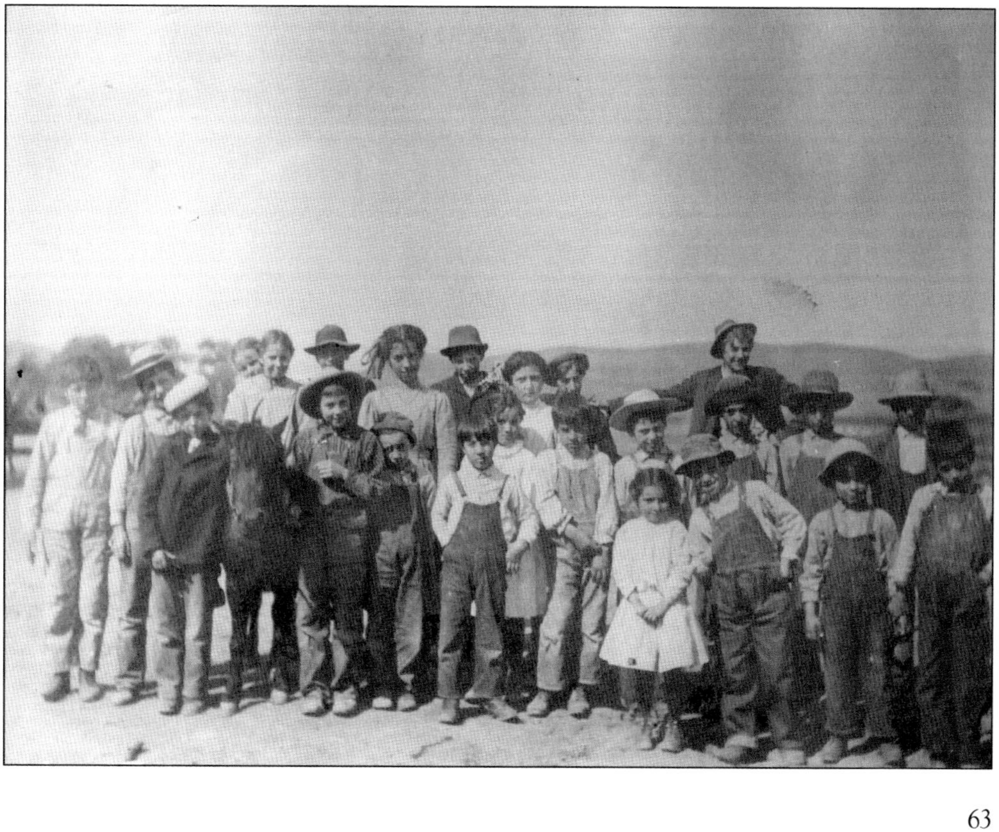

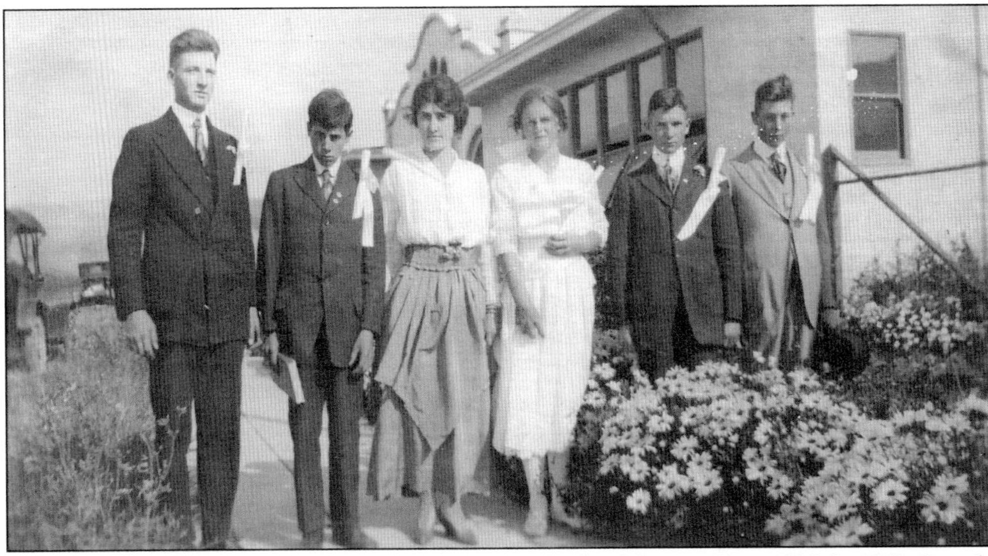

Florence Fontes, seen above, taught at Willow Spring School from 1909 to 1920. In 1958, Donald Rheem Elementary School was built. Camino Pablo Elementary (established in 1960) and Los Perales Elementary (1966) followed shortly. The middle school for children in Moraga, Joaquin Moraga Middle School, was opened in 1967. The local high school, Campolindo High School, opened in 1962 on land known as the former "tule pond" near the Carroll Ranch property. Campolindo is part of the Acalanes Union High School District, which has traditionally boasted excellent test scores and student achievement. The swampy land of the pond at the high school site, now filled in, gave its part to the original name in the land grant: Rancho Laguna de los Palos Colorados (ranch of the lake of the redwoods). Below, at the location of the tule pond, now a playing field for the high school, Otto Vasak, Moraga Historical Society president Mary Cowan, and Tom Carroll unveil a plaque dedicated by the Moraga Historical Society in 1984 to mark the location of the laguna.

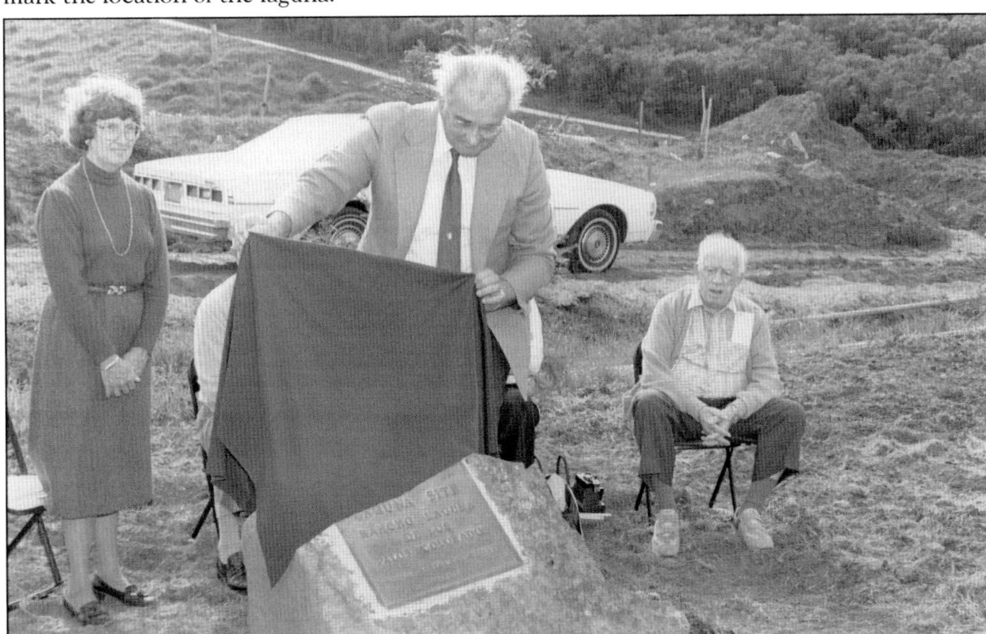

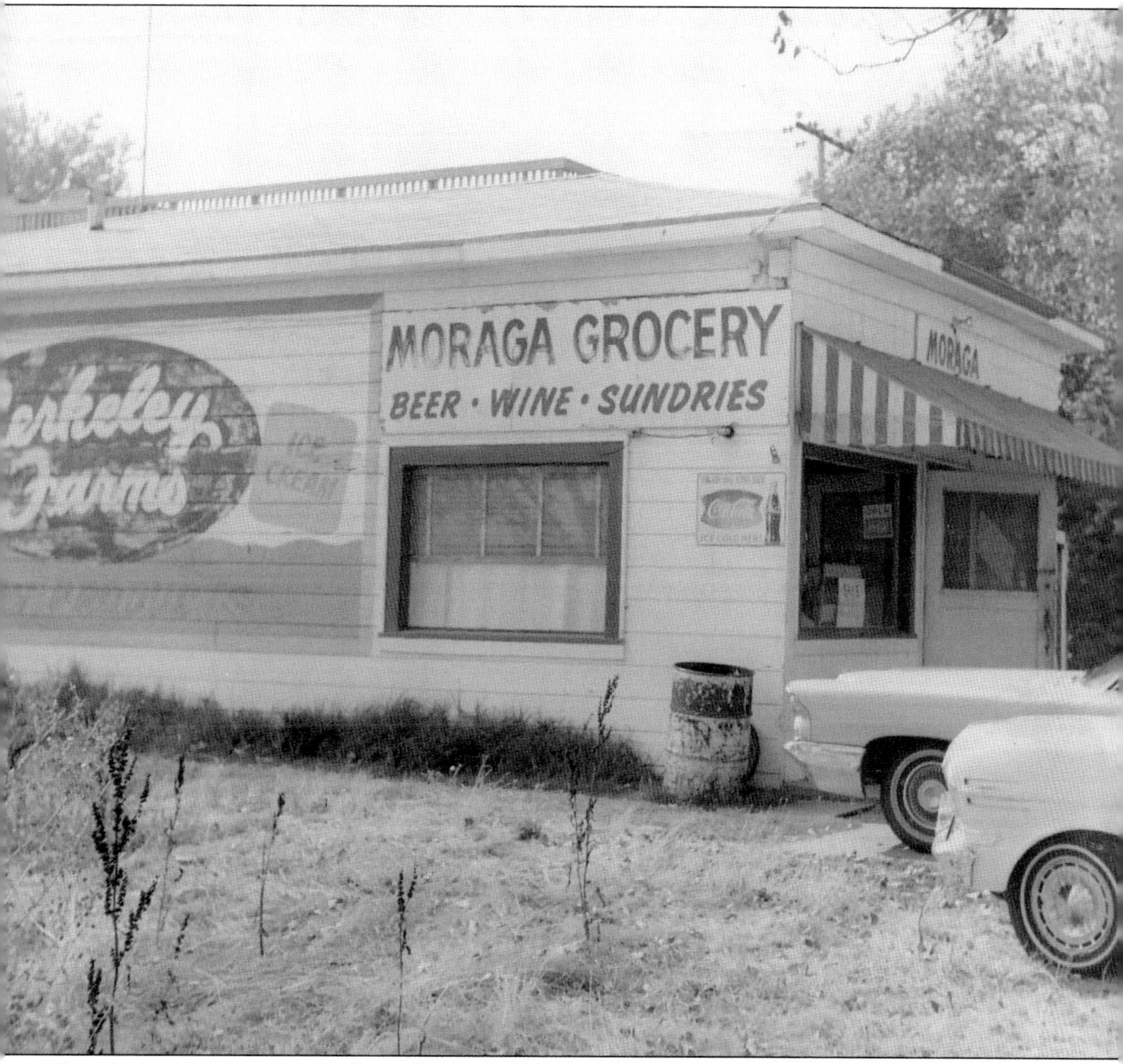

This store on Munster Street (now Country Club Drive) sold groceries to early residents in the Moraga Valley from 1920. The location where it stood remains quiet and charming, a part of the originally designated townsite in the early 1900s. Wide tree-lined streets preserve a sense of former times. The earliest store in the area was John Courter's, established in 1854 at the intersection of Larch Avenue and Canyon Road. It served teamsters, lumberjacks, tourists, and locals and had a saloon. Courter's store burned down in the 1920s.

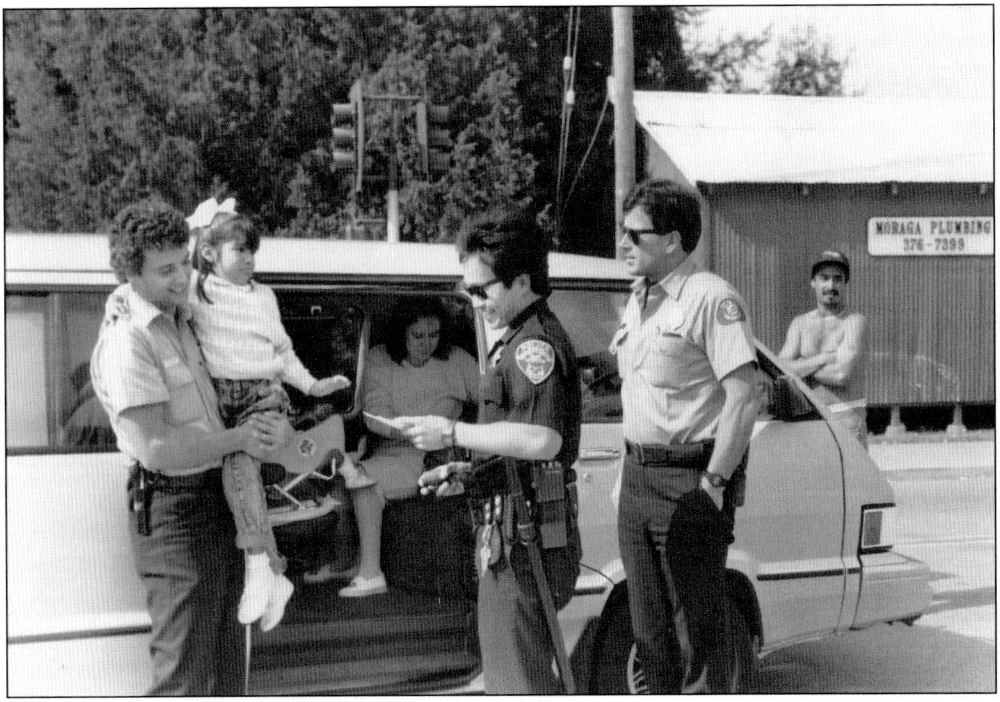

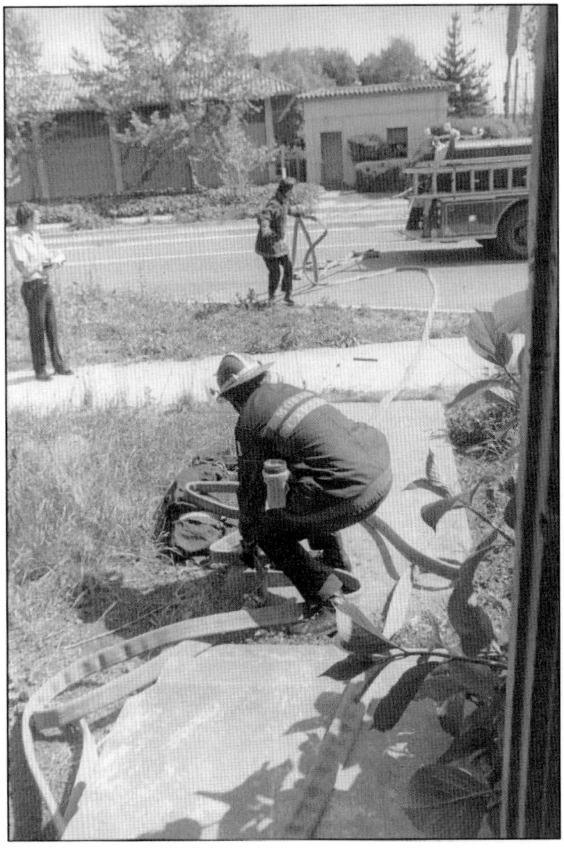

Moraga has had local firefighters since 1946, at which time all in the department were volunteers, with the station manned from the Moraga Ranch. By 1955, the volunteers were accompanied by three paid firemen. As the town grew, fire trucks and ambulances were acquired. In 1996, the Orinda and Moraga Fire Districts were consolidated. When Moraga was incorporated as a town, it collaborated with the local city of Lafayette to create a joint police force. In 1980, Moraga established its own independent police department. Police officers and firefighters provide a friendly presence at community events.

There are two shopping centers in Moraga, with one in Rheem Valley and one near the area originally designated to be the center of the Moraga townsite, at the intersection of Moraga Road and Moraga Way. Rheem Valley Shopping Center has been home to many small retail stores, supermarkets, and several restaurants. Until 1957, the area was known as Moraga Center, which is somewhat confusing, as that is the name currently used for the shopping center on Moraga Road and Moraga Way. The long strip in Rheem Valley has ample parking and easy access off Moraga Road. The photograph at right dates from the 1970s. In the 1980s, Center Street, which runs parallel to Rheem Boulevard, was developed. The Safeway store, which took over from the proprietors of Clark's supermarket, was the first completely air-conditioned market in Contra Costa County. The store was closed in 1985 when a new Safeway opened in the Moraga Shopping Center at the intersection of Moraga Way and Moraga Road.

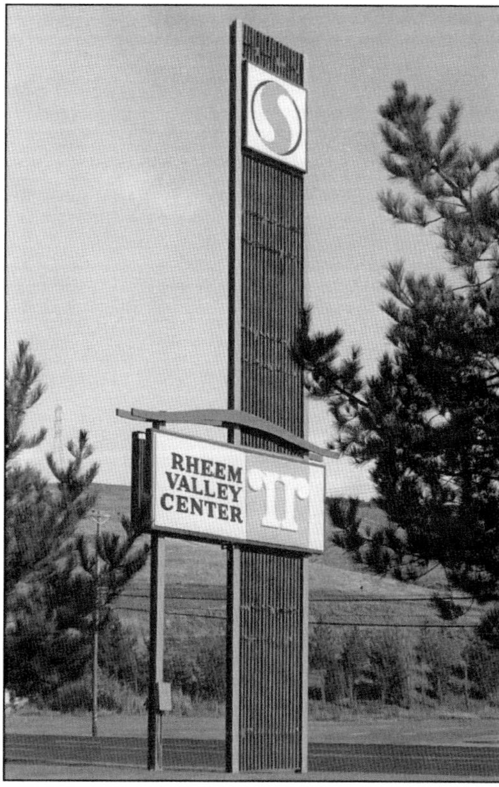

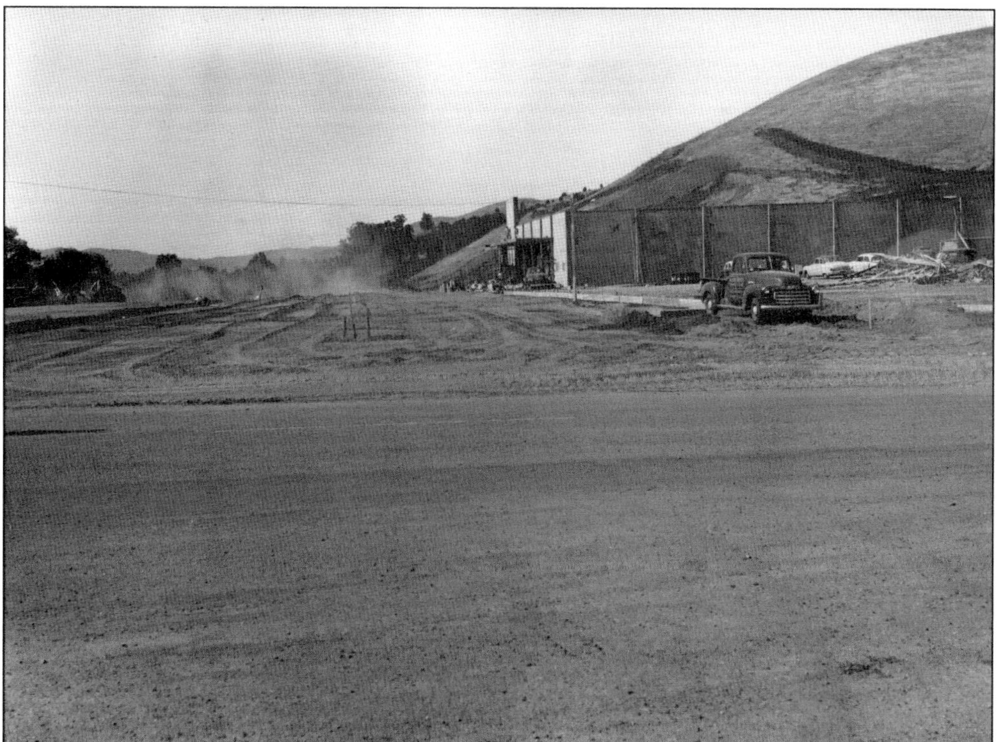

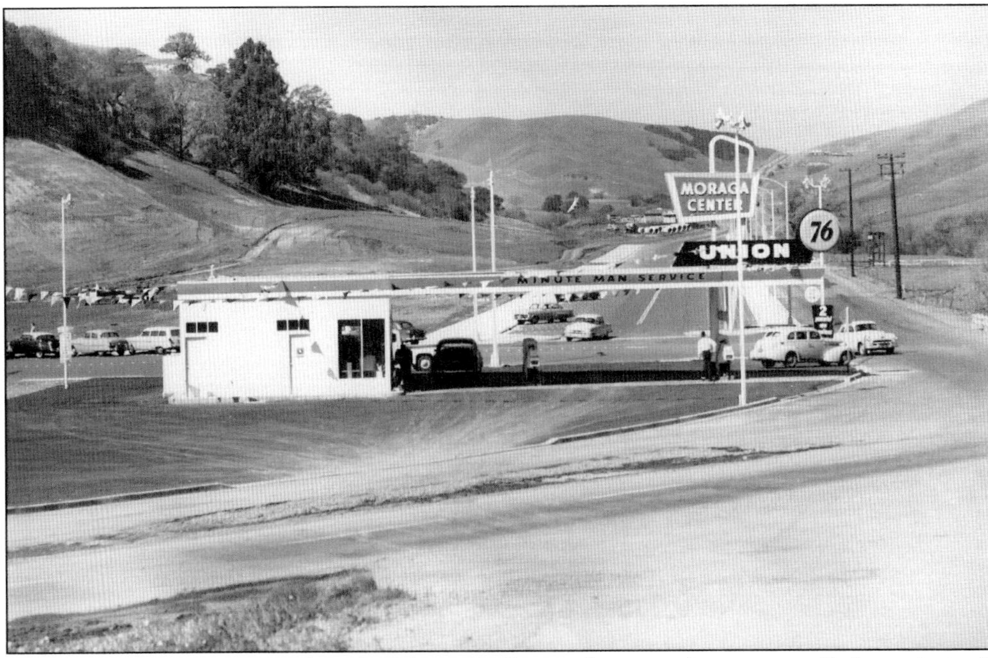

This service station operated in the Rheem Valley at the time that it was called, confusingly for today's residents, Moraga Center. Below, the intersection of Rheem Boulevard, which runs straight through the valley ahead, and Moraga Road, which runs toward Lafayette on the right and towards Moraga Way on the left, can be seen. Moraga Road was widened at that intersection, requiring deep cuts in the adjacent hill. Hillslide erosion management is an important matter for Moraga, a town of steep hills and valleys.

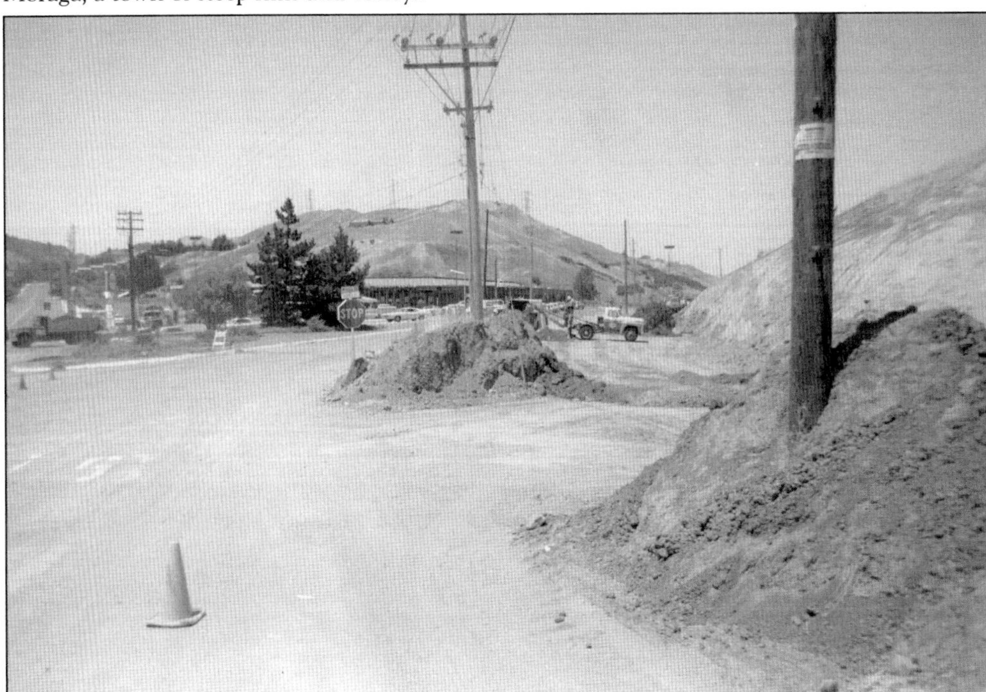

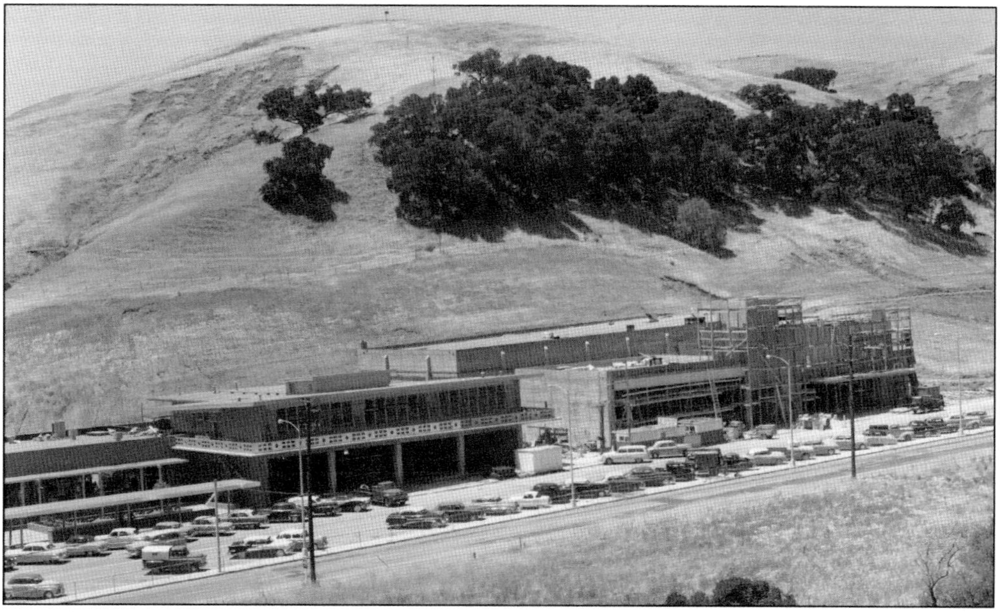

The photograph above shows the Rheem Valley Shopping Center in its early years. Seen from the hills across Moraga Road, the two buildings under construction to the right are in front of the Rheem Theater, a large square building with parking on Center Street, which runs parallel to Rheem Boulevard. The photograph below, taken from the shopping center parking lot, shows the hills across Moraga Road where it meets the section of Rheem Boulevard, which runs down to St. Mary's Road. The shopping center sits below the "Rock" seen on the hill where cows have, until very recently, roamed on pastureland. The Rock is itself an old icon, visible from a distance along Moraga Road to drivers heading north. The Rock almost always has intriguing words painted on it, usually by high school students, to champion their sports team, invite a fellow student to prom, celebrate class graduation, or provide entertaining comments. One memorable comment that ran for many years in the 1970s was "Betty Jane Please Shave Your Legs."

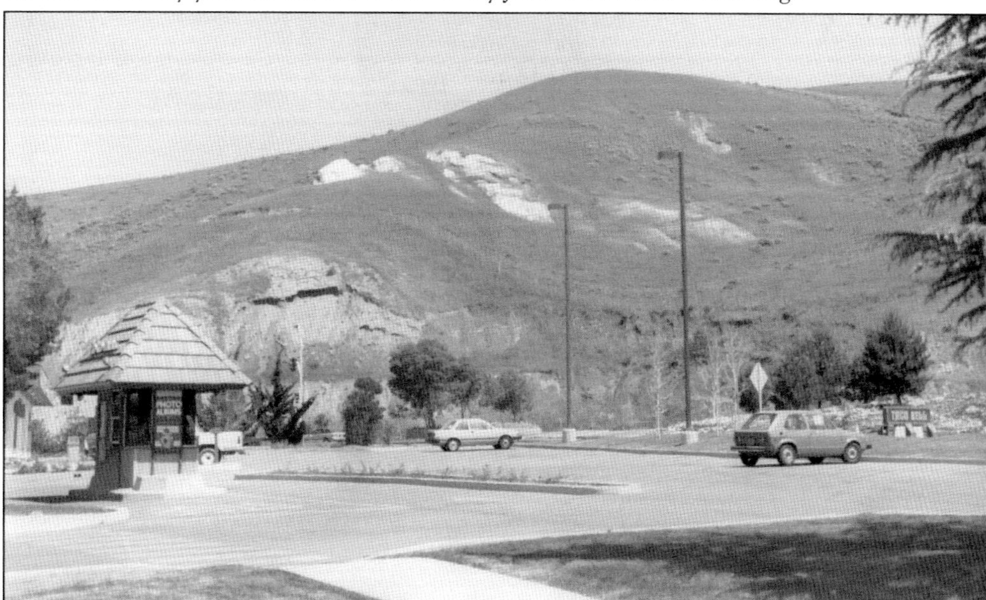

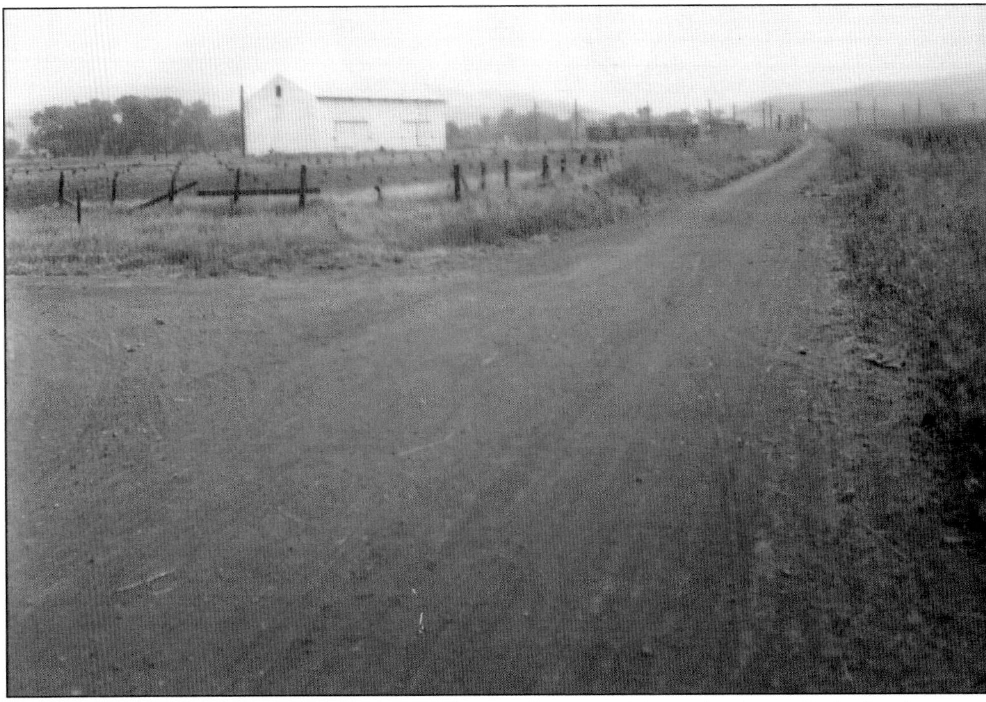

In the 1910s, the area that would become Moraga Shopping Center had very little development. What was once farmland, train tracks, dirt roads, and electricity poles became a busy shopping center in later decades. Below, construction for a supermarket is underway while undeveloped hills can still be seen in the distance. The flat location surrounded by hills is an ideal location for a commercial enterprise.

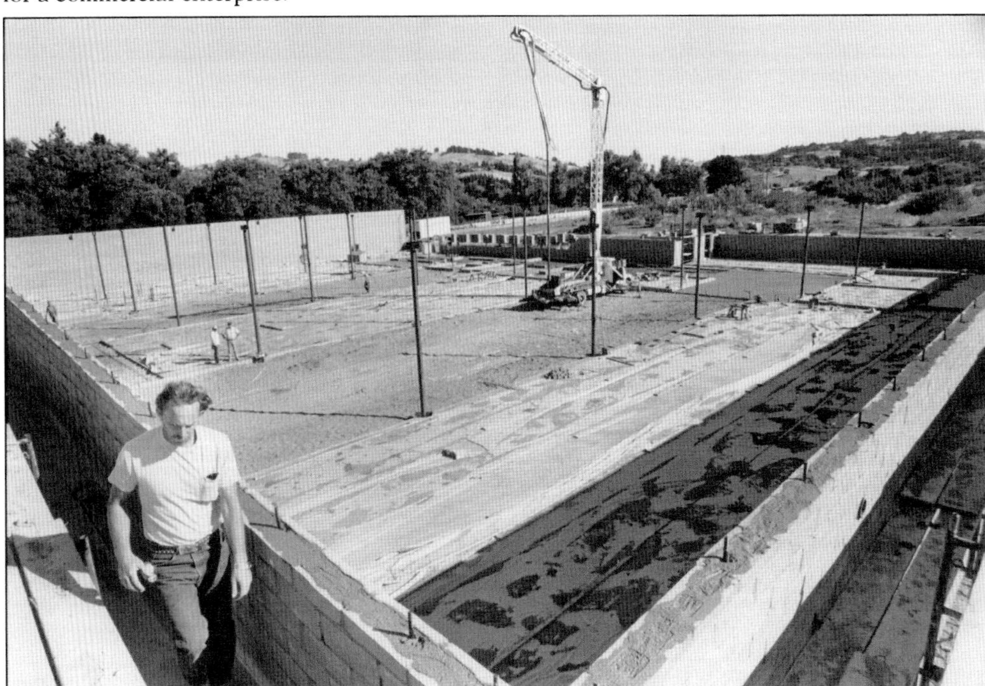

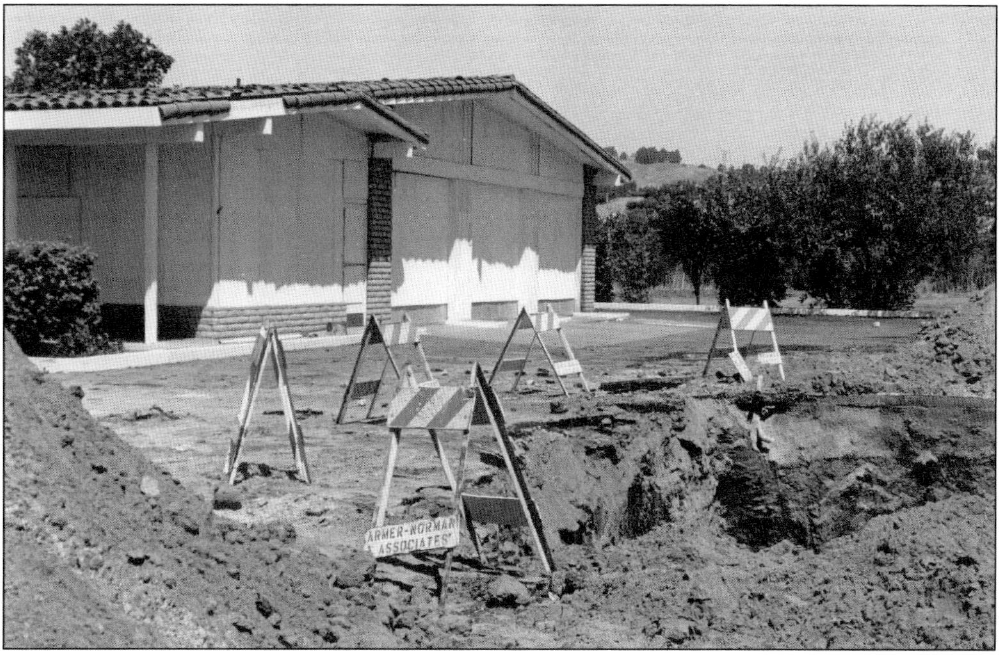

In 1984, ground was broken for a new service station near the shopping center on St. Mary's Road near where it meets Moraga Road. The same year, a surveyor worked to establish the location for the supermarket in Moraga Center at the intersection of Moraga Way and Moraga Road. First developed by Russell Bruzzone starting in 1964, the Moraga Shopping Center has long had an excellent location for shoppers coming from the Orinda direction down Moraga Way or, for those coming from within Moraga, from the Moraga Road direction. Although at one time destined to be easily accessible to traffic coming from the freeway, the area remains unconnected to any freeway and so remains a relatively uncongested place to park and shop.

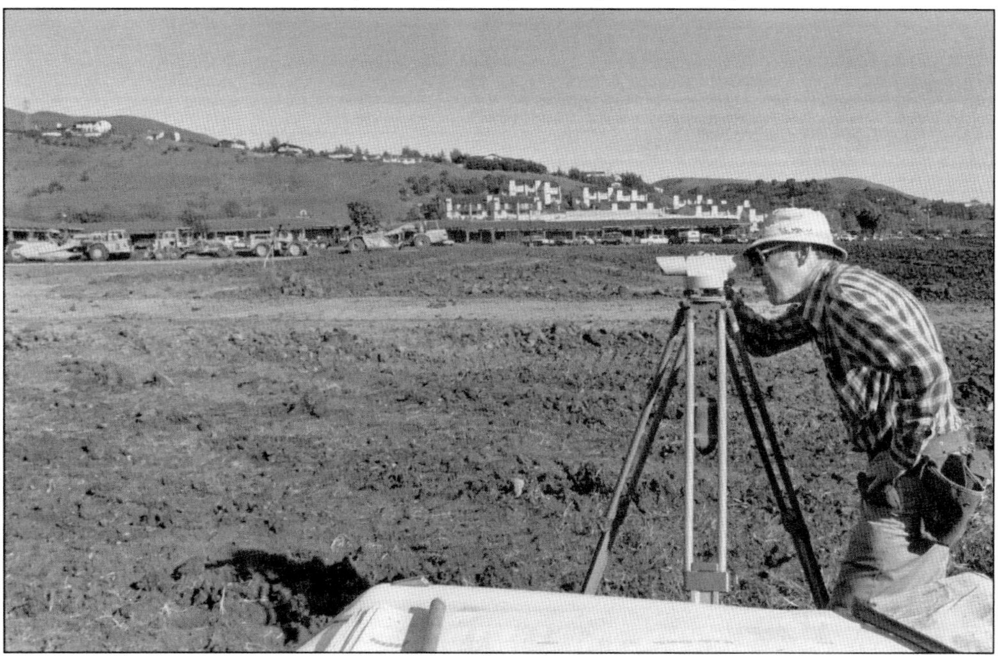

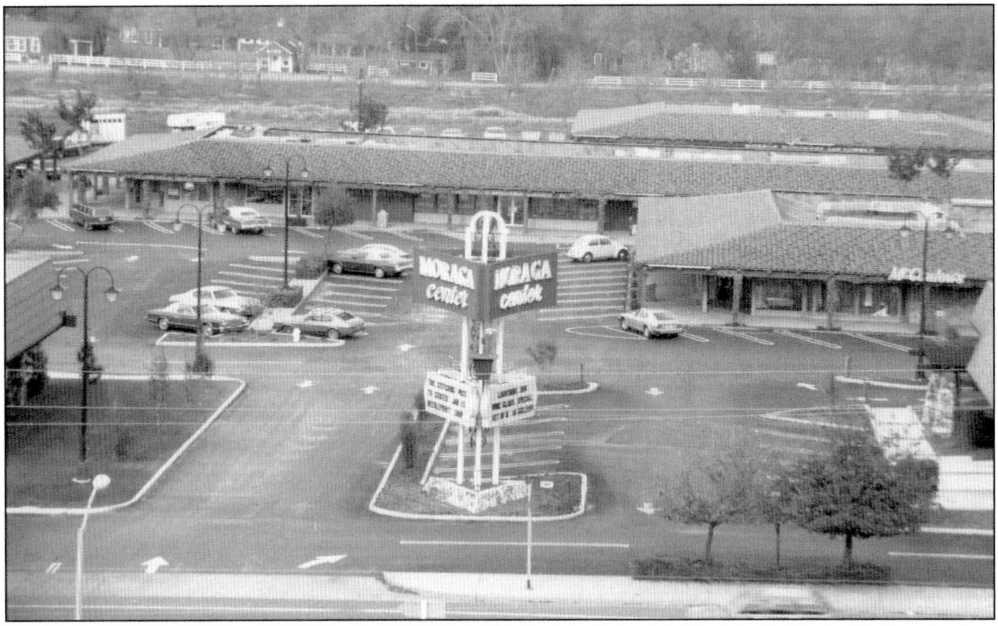

These photographs show the growing Moraga Shopping Center. Above, the Moraga Center sign appears at center, and the Ranch buildings are visible behind the parking lot. These buildings have housed stores, restaurants, and a horse barn and are still operational today. Below, the view from the hill across Moraga Road shows the Moraga Center sign to the right. Also in sight are the large supermarket, still in use today, a service station, and several bank buildings. In the distance, Moraga Ranch and the Barn (far left) can be seen. The Moraga Center has a clothing store, a hardware store, a gift shop, several restaurants, a preschool, and a delicatessen, and its parking lot on the Moraga Road side is the location for the weekly farmers' market. (Both photographs by Elaine H. Lind.)

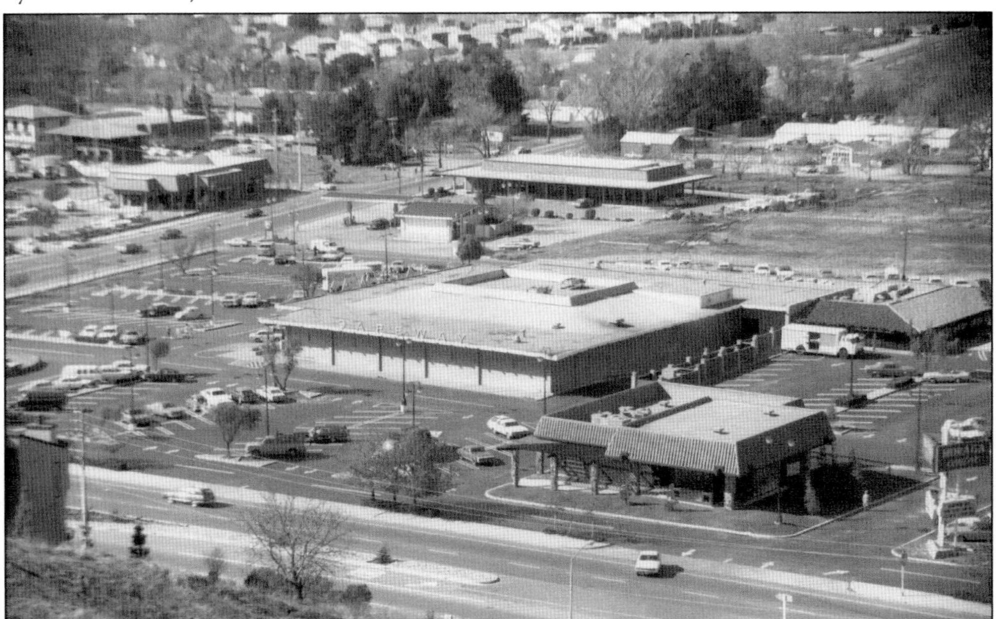

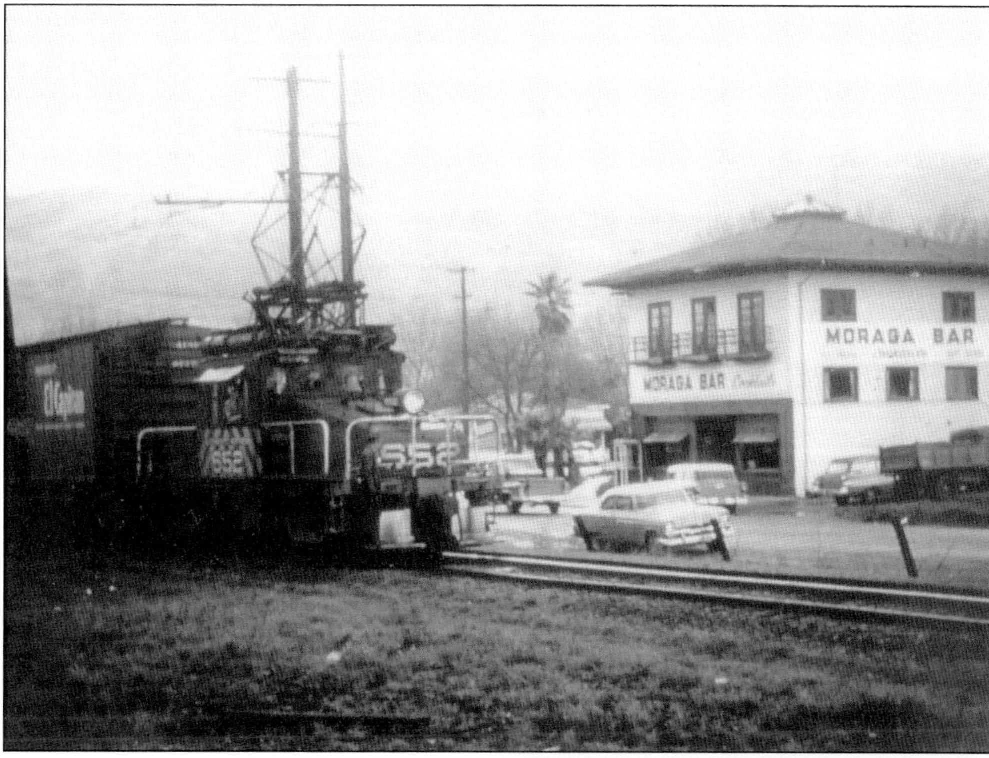

The square-shaped white building, known locally as the "Moraga Barn," was originally built in 1911 by Robert N. Burgess Sr. as a hotel and store to accommodate the needs of train passengers who stopped at the adjacent station. When John Fleuti bought the building about 1912, there were five rooms upstairs, each with a shower and basin. Fleuti conducted a general store in the building, later known as the Moraga Mercantile. A small post office also served the public from the store. Eventually a saloon was added, called the Moraga Bar. Legend has it that the word "Bar" became "Barn" due to Prohibition influence or concern about liquor laws. However, Helen Hetfield, Fleuti's daughter, stated in 1966 that her family added the "N" around 1960 just to make it more appropriate. A plaque to honor the history of the building was dedicated in 1994.

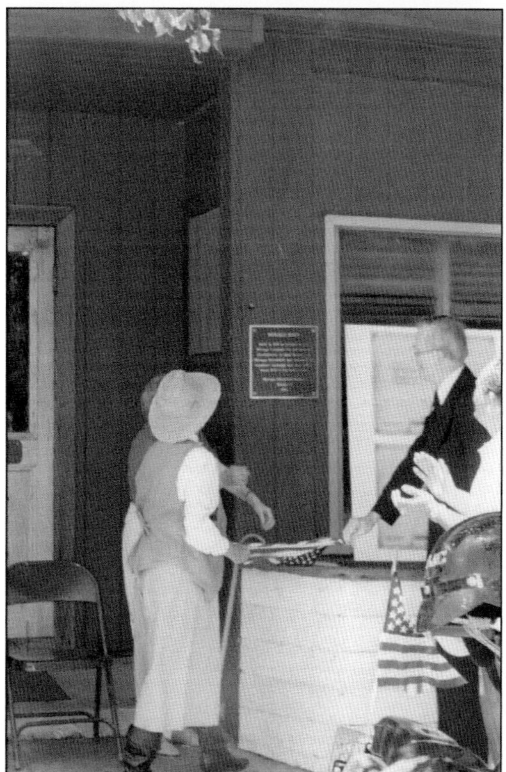

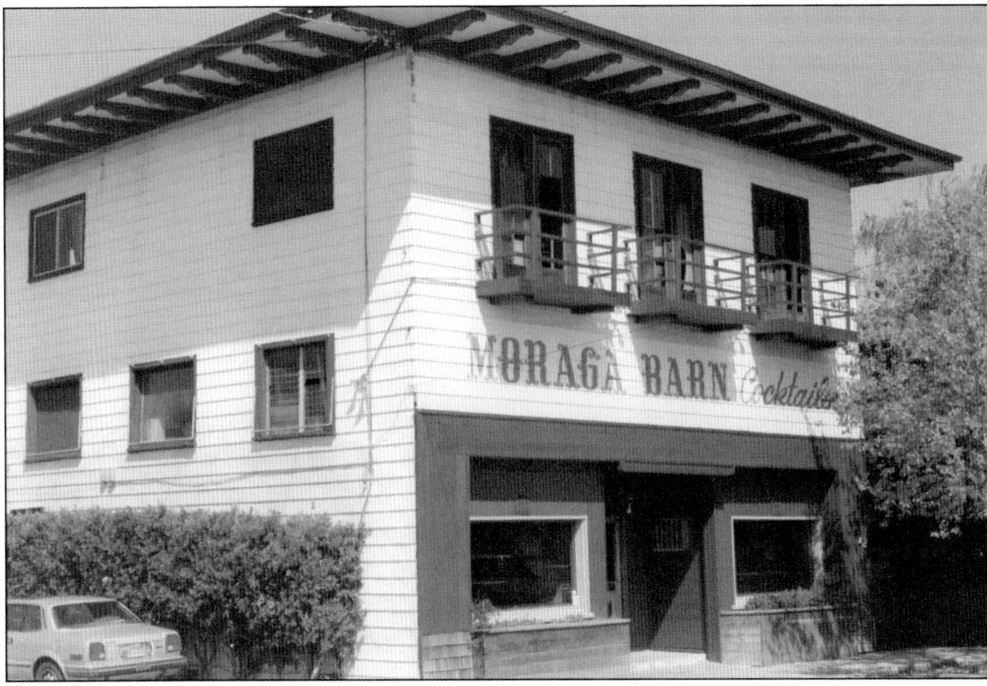

For years this building was known as the Moraga Barn. The name has stuck as it stands as an empty structure waiting for its next incarnation. Although the Barn building was until recent years open for business as a bar, it has changed ownership and has recently been partially renovated for office use. Due to financial roadblocks in continuing the renovation process, its future is uncertain.

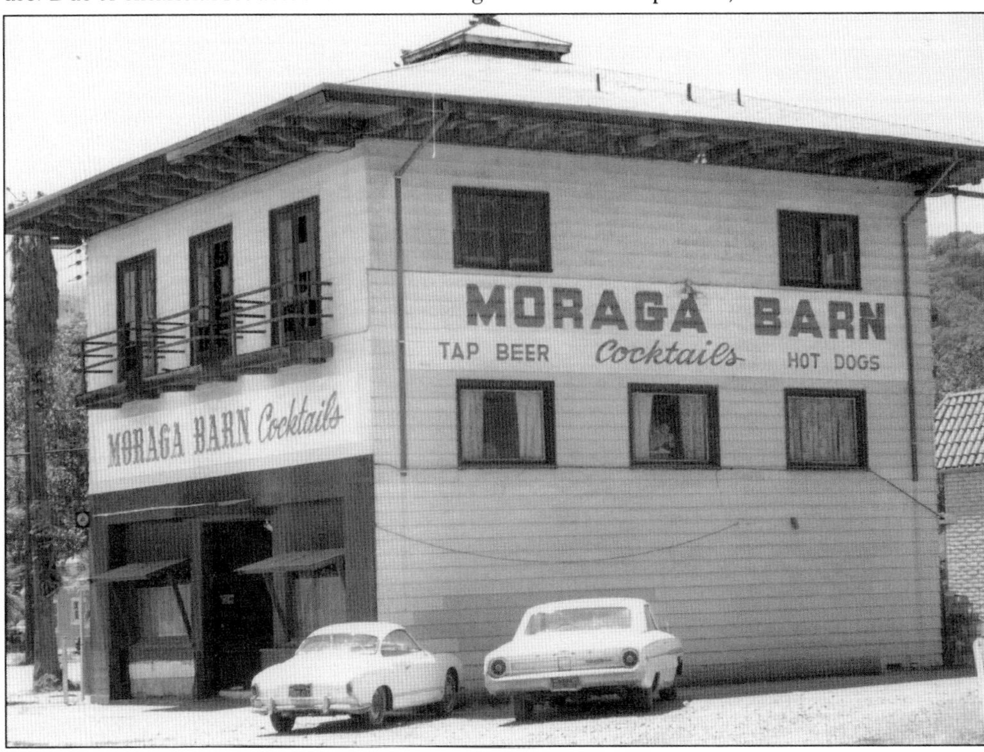

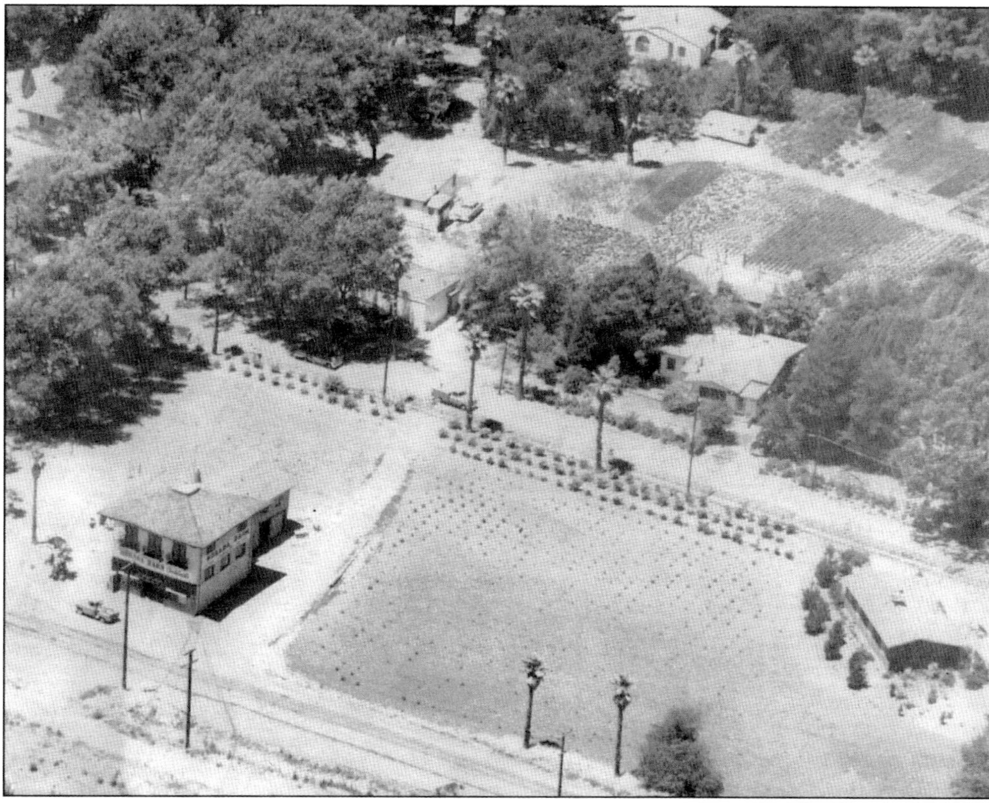

The aerial view of the Moraga Barn above shows its location in the area originally destined to be the center of town. In the photograph below, taken by Louis L. Stein Jr., the building, which was at that time a hotel and store, is set off from one of the streets intended by the initial developers to be in the center of town. The urns in the center were features of the planned townsite main streets. Although the subdivisions and commercial development plans did not come through, the urns and the Barn remain as vestiges of the past.

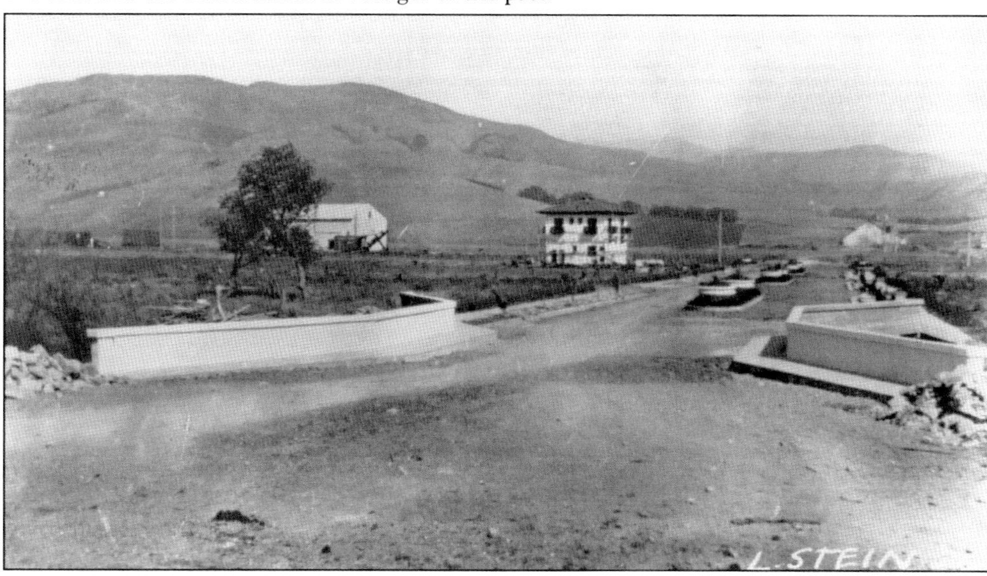

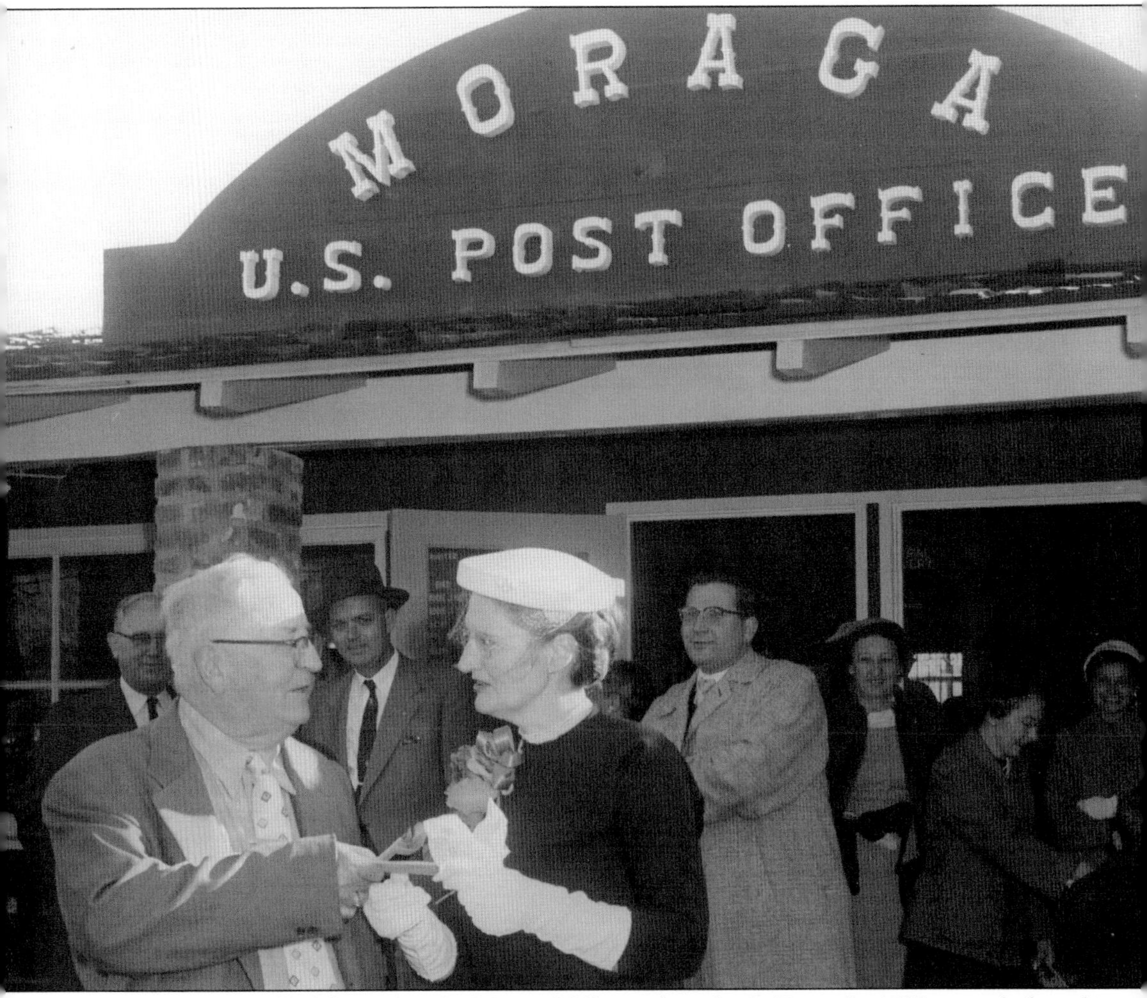

Mail was originally delivered in the Moraga Valley on horseback. From the 1850s, a rawhide sack called a *vaca* was nailed to a tree near John Courter's store. Locals put mail in the sack, where it would wait until a *vaquero* picked it up to take it on horseback to another rancho or settlement. Post office facilities were in later days established in saloons (the first in 1886), stores, and other permanent locations and were moved as needed based on increasing patronage. In this photograph, taken in 1955 at the dedication of the Moraga Post Office on School Street, Moraga Company supervisor Bill Barnes accepts the first general delivery letter to be received in the Moraga Valley from postmistress Elinor Dickenson. This post office was the first permanent building dedicated solely to postal service for Moraga residents.

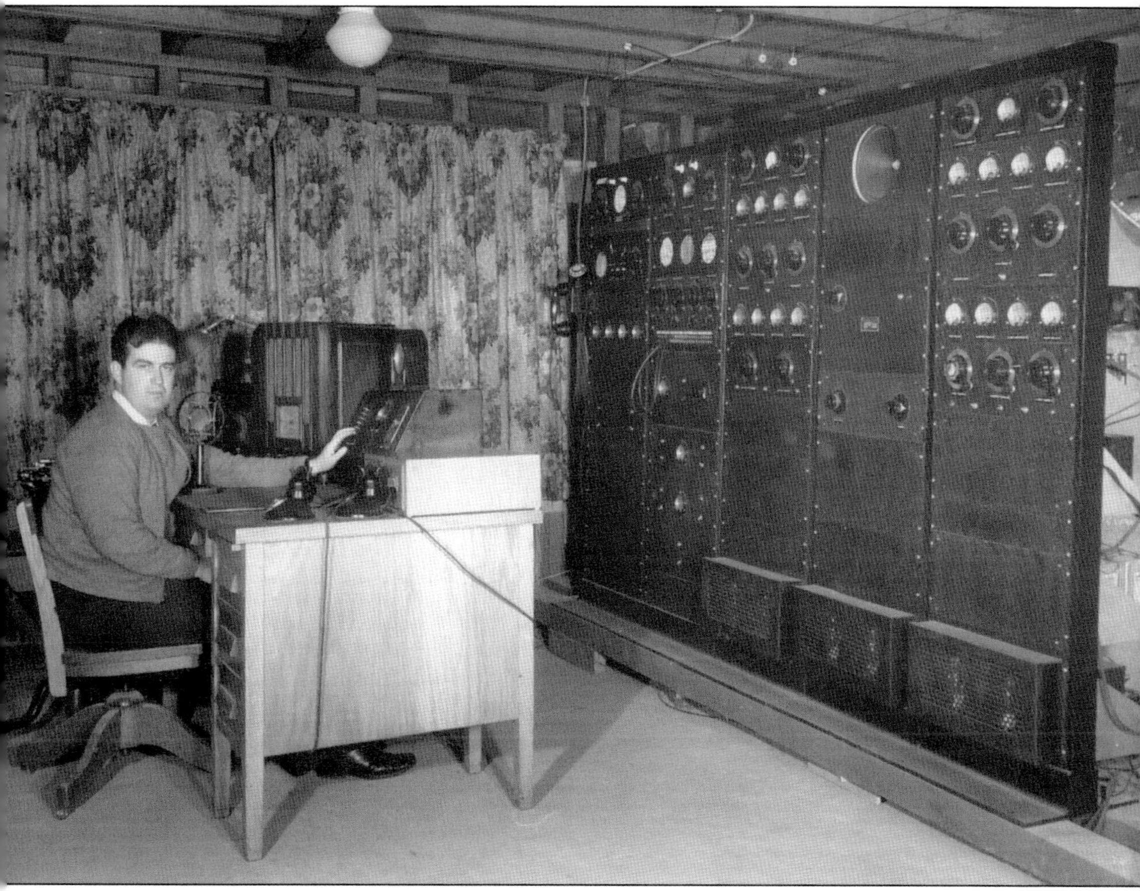

D. Reginald Tibbetts, a scientist and communications engineer, established a listening post in his home for news from Tokyo during World War II. He monitored Japanese broadcasts for the United Press, the Office of War and Information, and the US Navy, translating messages and breaking codes. At the same time, he worked covertly on assembling and shipping Geiger counters and atomic bomb equipment to be used in the war effort. He was made postmaster so that he could ship these items easily. Tibbetts was postmaster of the post office that was situated at the railroad station on Viader Drive (at that time called St. Mary's Road). He shipped the items to Los Alamos in laundry cases from St. Mary's, which he had relabeled to indicate they were carrying tractor parts to foil counterintelligence.

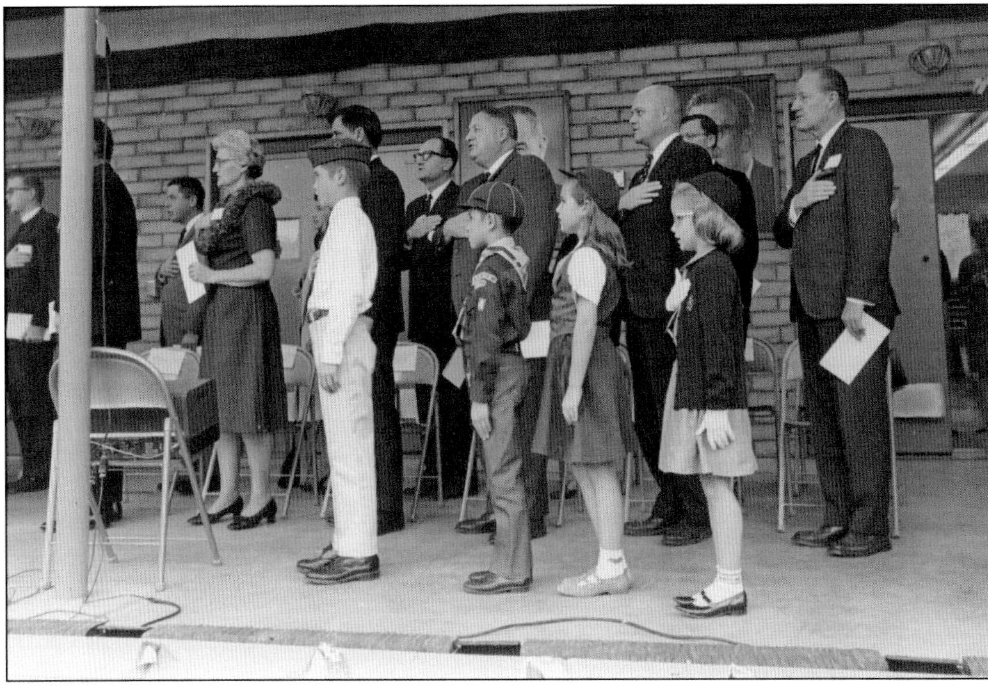

In 1966, a main post office was dedicated at the corner of School Street and Munster Drive (now Country Club Drive). In 1985, mail volume exceeded the capacity of the small post office, with letters and parcels overflowing onto the deck, and after some deliberations as to what would make the best spot, a new location was selected. In 1988, the main post office moved to a large building in the Rheem Valley Shopping Center, and the post office on School Street became a secondary location.

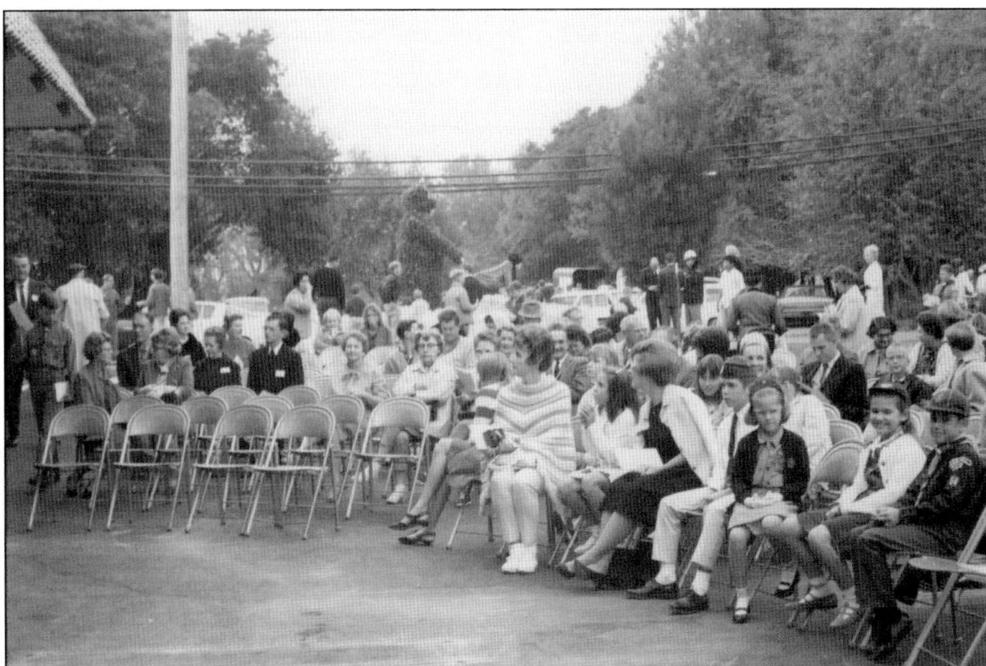

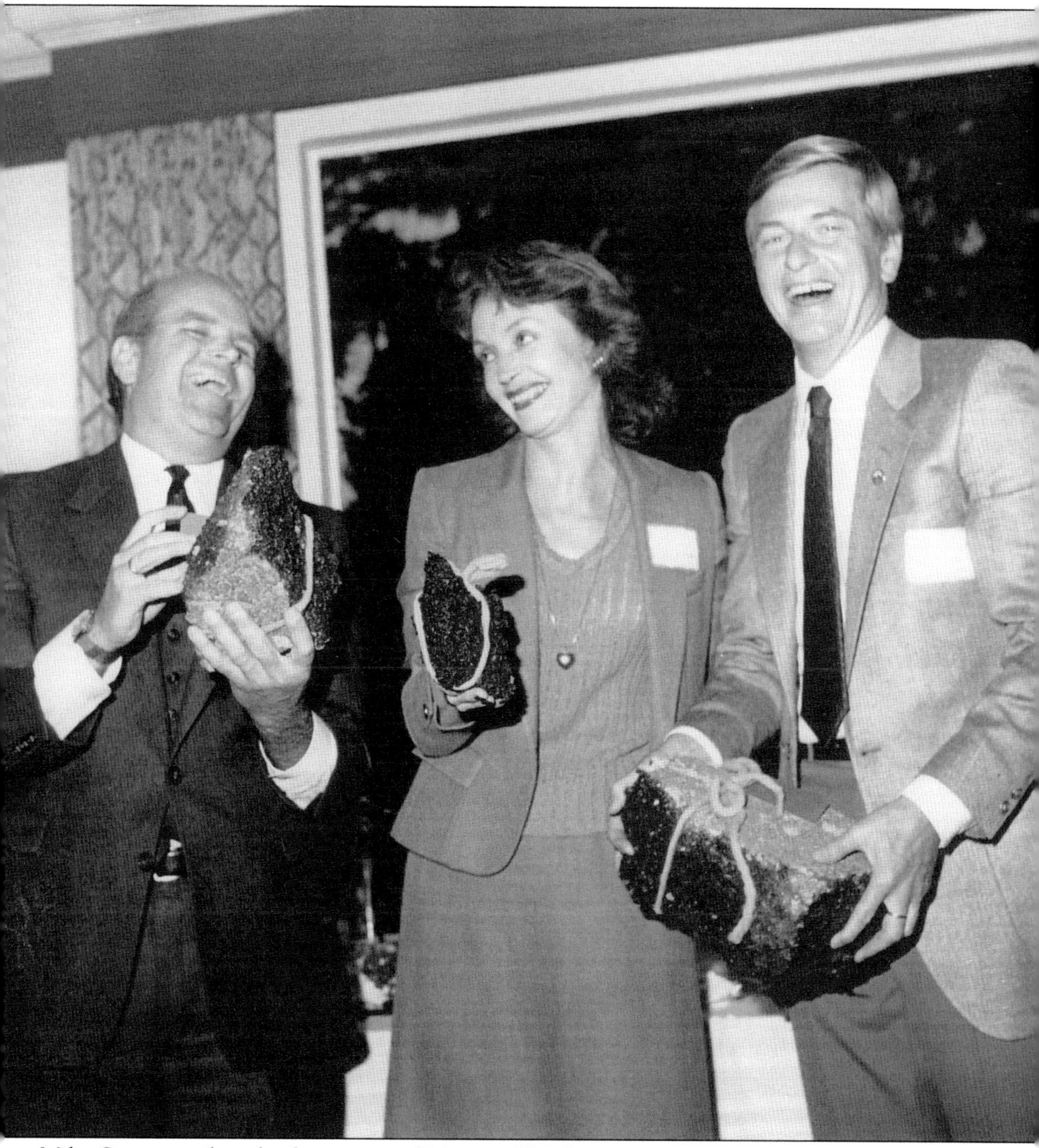

Mike Cory served as the first mayor of Moraga. The first town council, elected in 1974, was comprised of Mayor Cory and council members Merle Gilliland, Barry Gross, Bill Combs, and Sue McNulty, who received a certification plaque from California governor Ronald Reagan on the occasion of town incorporation. Cory is shown here with town council member Jay Fowler in 1988, receiving a tongue-in-cheek gift from the mayor of Lafayette, Gayle Uilkema. The deterioration in the chunks of asphalt cut from Lafayette streets was blamed (with a smile) partly on rainfall and partly on the traffic from Moraga residents, who must pass through either Lafayette or Orinda to get to a freeway entrance. Ironically, the important discussion of whether Moraga would have a freeway entrance or not played a role in the formation of the Moraga Community Association. This organization was instrumental in the work that led to the incorporation of the town.

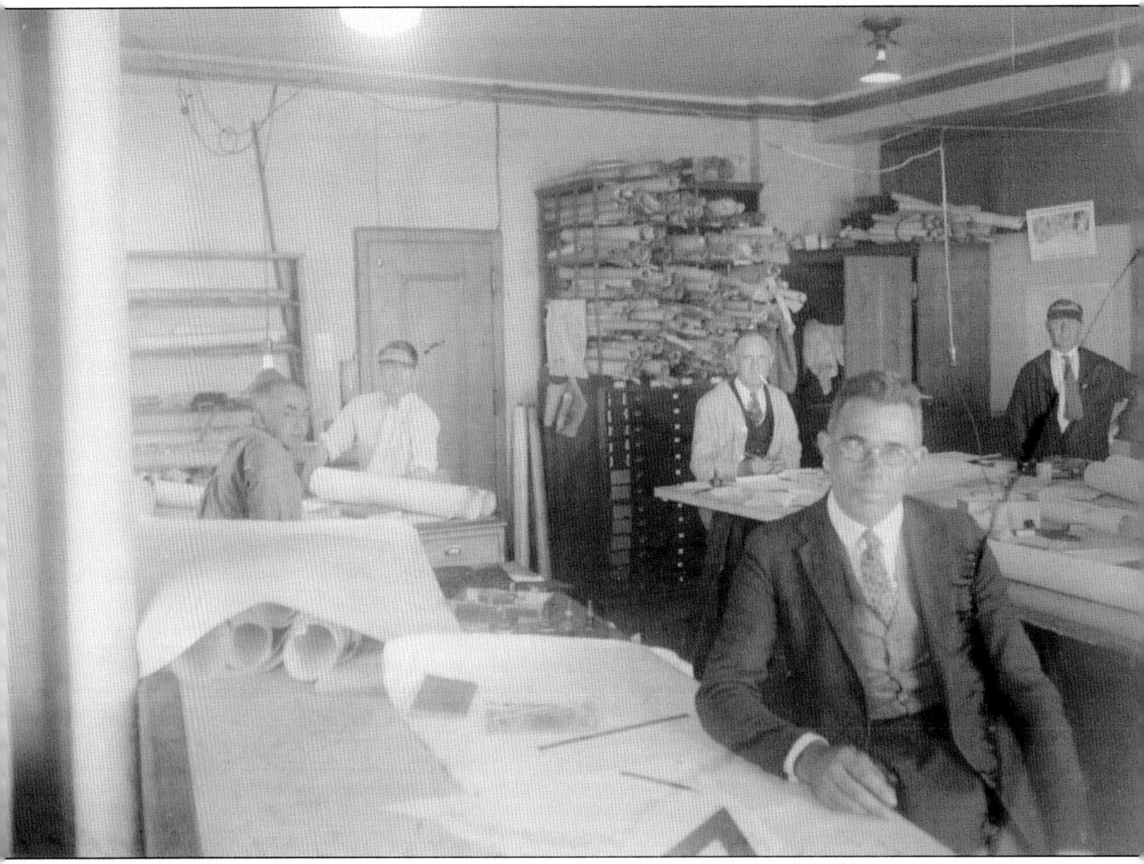

A Moraga townsite plan was drawn up after completion of the railroad line in 1913. This plan, drawn up by James M. Punnett, included 21 city blocks, a main street, two parks, and a playground. The plan was greatly modified by the Moraga Company and the engineering company it hired, James H. L'Hommedieu & Co., in 1925. The Utah Construction and Mining Company and the Preston Management Company bought 5,000 acres of the Moraga Ranch in 1954 from the Moraga Company, which acted as the principal holding company for the main stockholders Mayford Irvine, Eric Taussig, and the heirs of the late state senator A.H. Breed. The new owners proposed construction of a city with 8,000 attractive homes. The Utah Company did not build homes, but rather developed subdivisions and a shopping center. Frank Draeger, engineer for both of the real estate development companies, is pictured here.

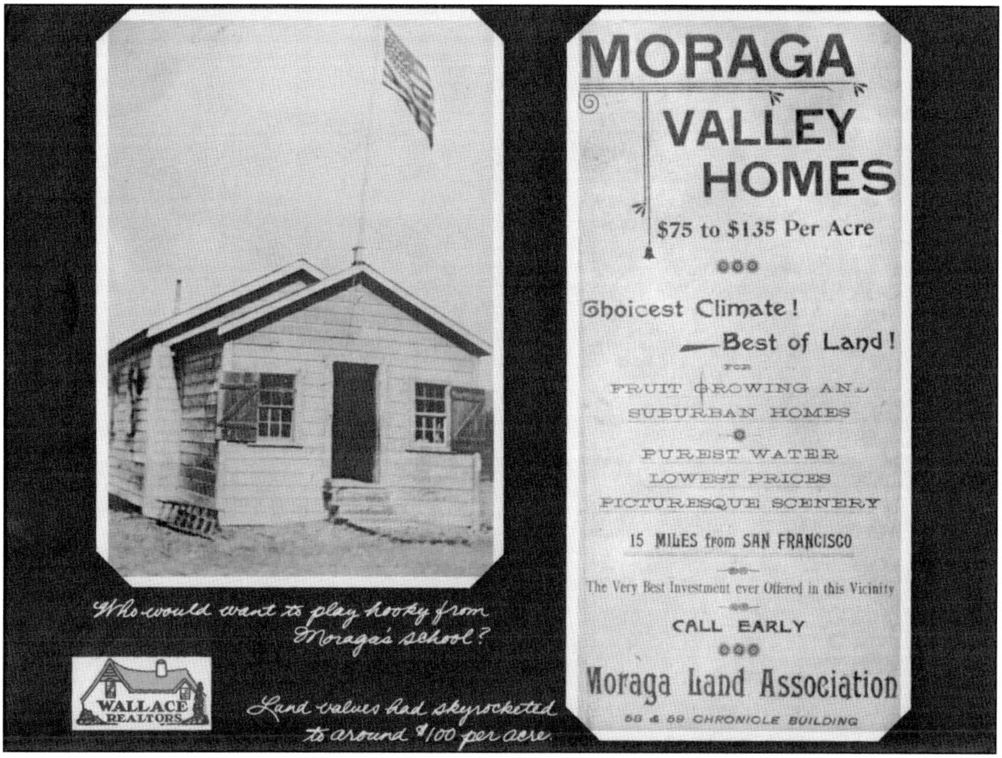

The Moraga Land Association, which existed between 1889 and 1899, published promotional brochures. Wallace Realtors, active in the local real estate business from the early days, provided this display. The large concrete urns pictured below were constructed on Munster Drive (now Country Club Drive) by the Moraga Land Company in 1915. This street was envisioned to be the center of town at the time. Due to the high price of land and the difficulty of obtaining water, this plan was abandoned. While some urns remain in place, others have been moved to public locations, such as the library.

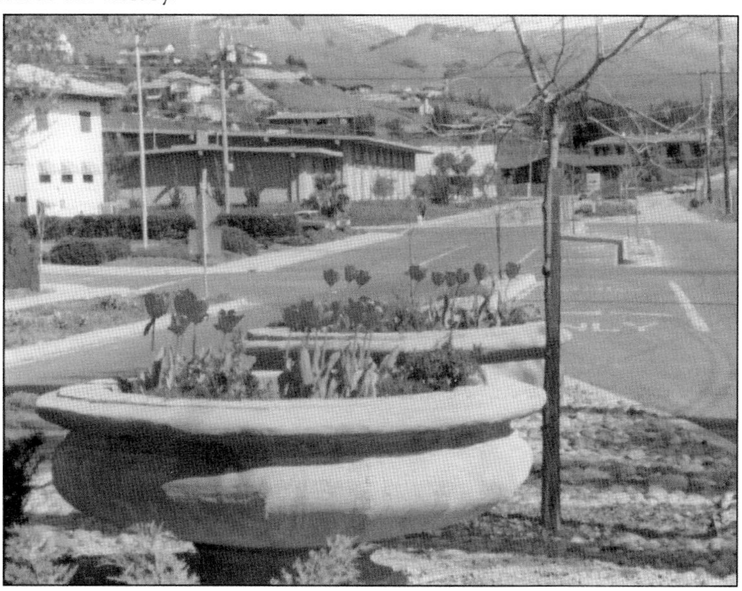

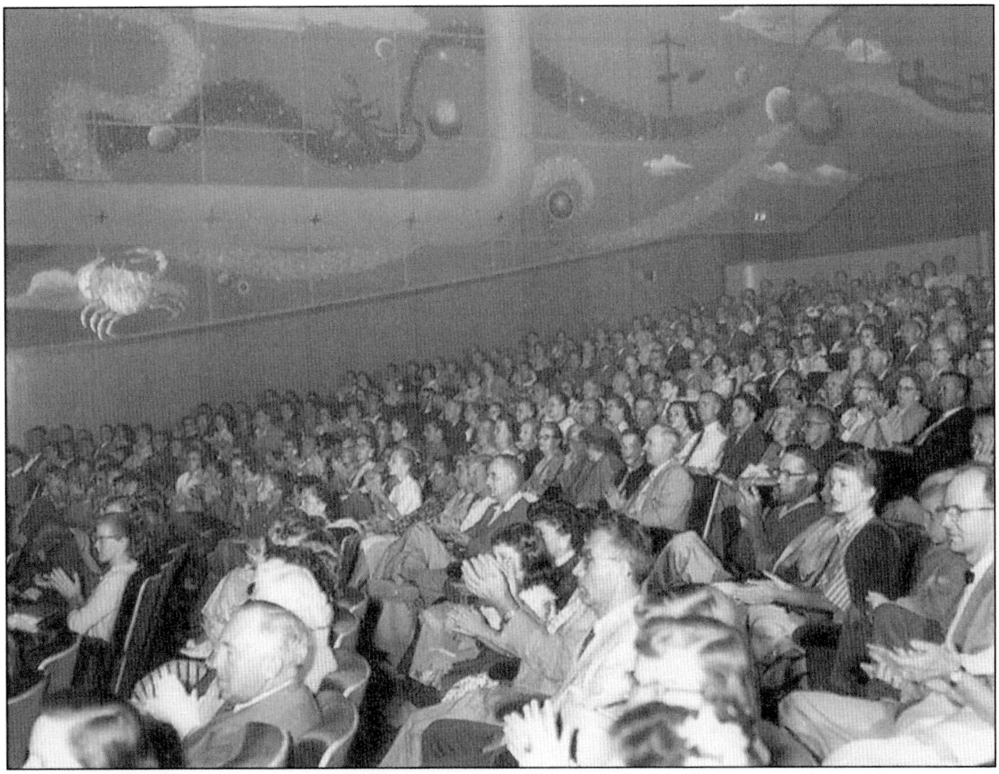

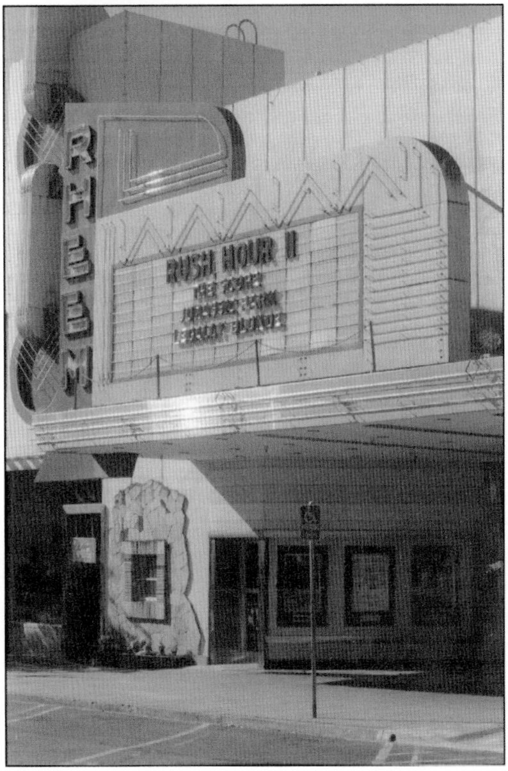

Moraga has had a movie theater since 1959, when the Rheem Theater opened. The image above shows the audience on opening day. At left, the marquee is pictured as it appears today. The theater is flanked by stores and restaurants. Special film presentations and film festivals are commonly featured. Although the future of the theater is uncertain, community efforts are underway to raise funds needed to keep films running here.

Six

Parks, Trails, and Open Space

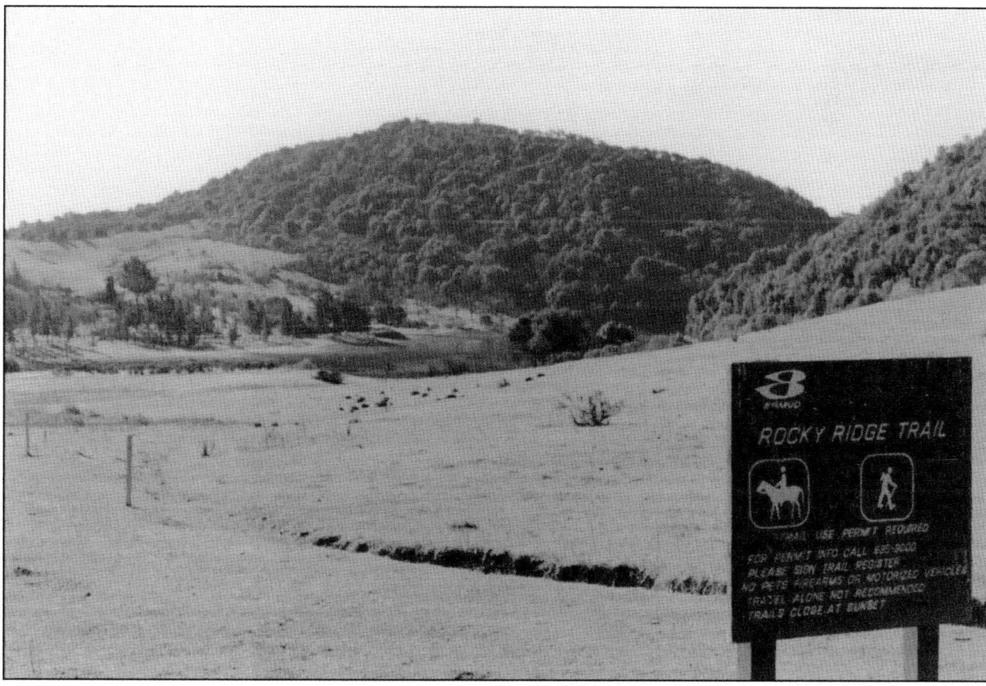

The town of Moraga has been fortunate to have had many advocates who worked hard to create parks and trails and to preserve open space. The grassroots movement to buy and develop land for parks in Moraga began in 1969. After investigating many options for setting up organizations, it was decided to create the Moraga Parks and Recreation Authority, the first of its kind in California. The organization had board members appointed by the county and by the Moraga School Board. In 1972, it purchased the Hacienda de Las Flores grounds and buildings. In 1974, lands were purchased at the end of Camino Pablo to create Rancho Laguna Park. When the town of Moraga was incorporated in 1974, the town took over the responsibility of overseeing the parks and recreation programs. Residents have admired and enjoyed the sights of hills covered with grass and California poppies, trees and shrubs, and local reservoirs and creeks. They can take part in active recreational activities in the open air all around town. Equestrians, joggers, hikers, and bikers find many outlets for their interests within the town limits.

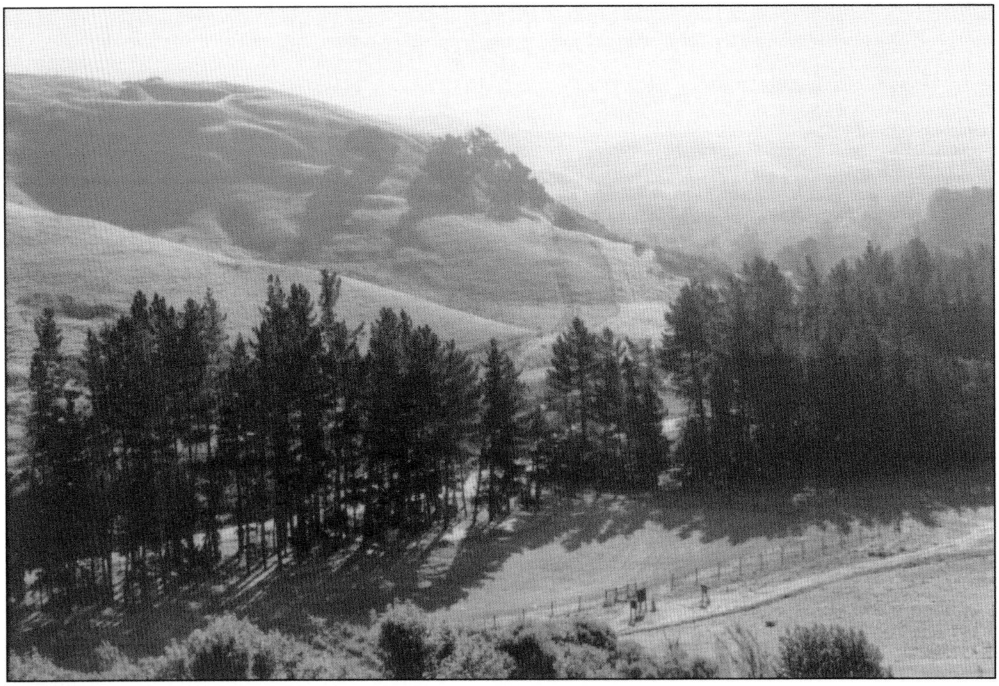

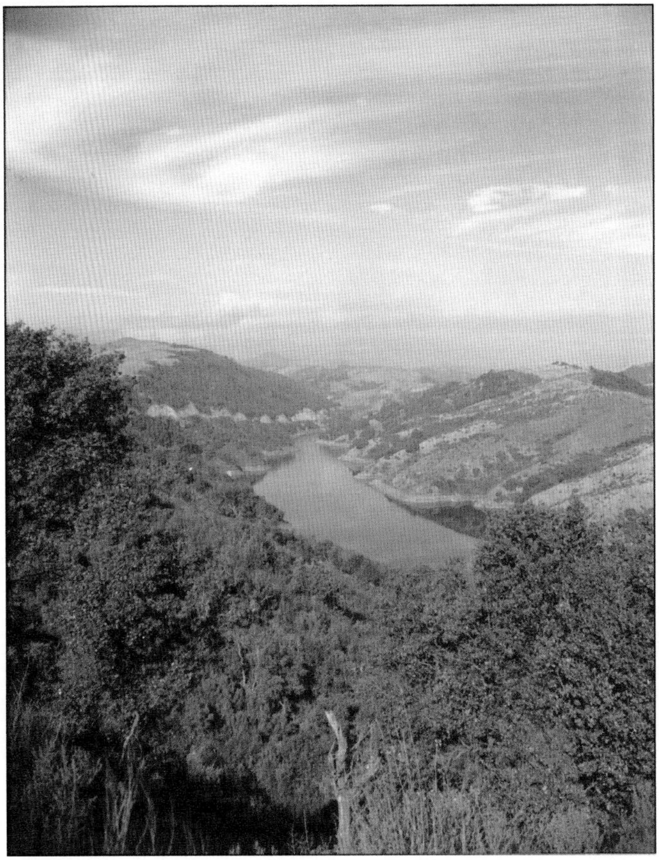

The Valle Vista subdivision was abandoned when the East Bay Municipal Utility District took over the land that borders the San Leandro Reservoir. The land eventually became a staging area for trails that lead in two directions from the parking lot. One trail leads along the San Leandro Reservoir through King Canyon. The trail can be followed to Rancho Laguna or completed as a 6.5-mile loop back to the staging area. The other trail leads down to Canyon Road and then toward Redwood Regional Park with its many trails and picnic areas.

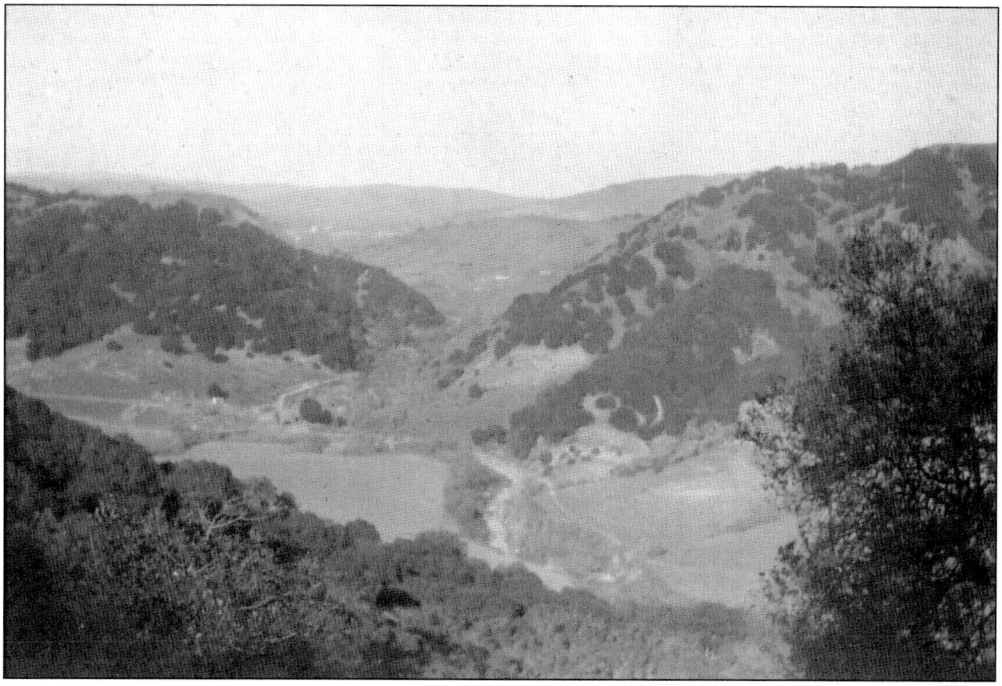

King Canyon is easily visited via hiking trails starting at the Valle Vista staging area. Hikers can follow the trails all the way to Rancho Laguna. The land, now the property of the East Bay Municipal Utility District, borders the Upper San Leandro Reservoir. It may have been named for the King brothers who lived there. Although their residence was in the Redwood area, they ranched in the hills behind Moraga Road on land close to the Sanders Ranch subdivision. The Ranch there was called King Flat.

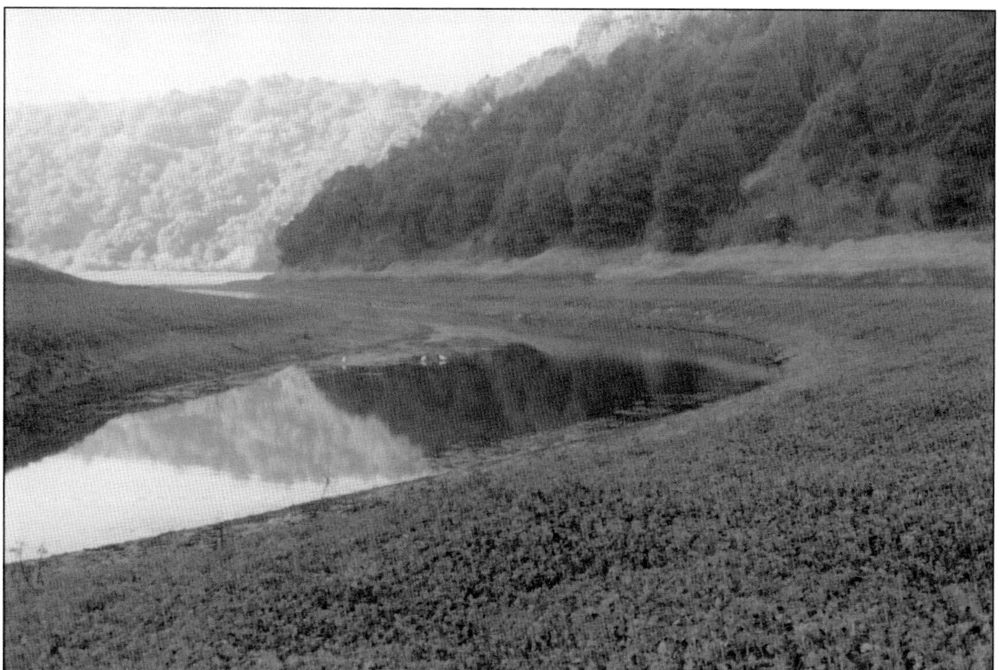

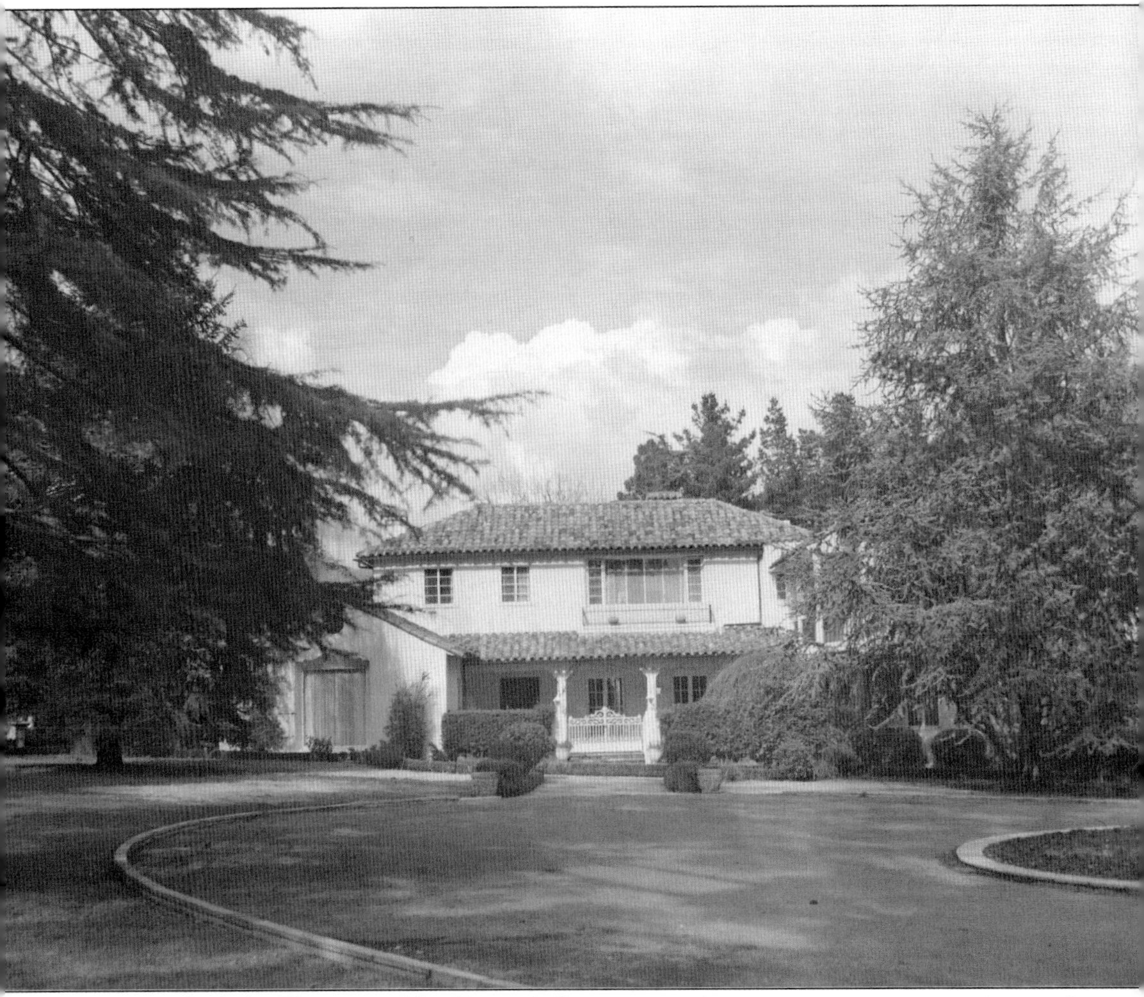

Hacienda de las Flores—or "the Hacienda," as it is now known—was once a mansion on the Donald Rheem Estate. Prior to ownership by Rheem, the buildings constructed in 1916 first served as an orphanage. A 10-acre parcel including the Hacienda buildings was purchased in 1972 from the Christian Brothers of St. Mary's College, who used it as their local headquarters. The land was obtained by the Moraga Parks and Recreation Authority, an organization that existed briefly prior to town incorporation. This photograph is from the days when the mansion was owned by the Christian Brothers. The first park and recreation facility in Moraga, the Hacienda is now used by community organizations for classes and meetings and is rented out for weddings and other celebrations. Other potential uses for the Hacienda are currently being explored, with community input.

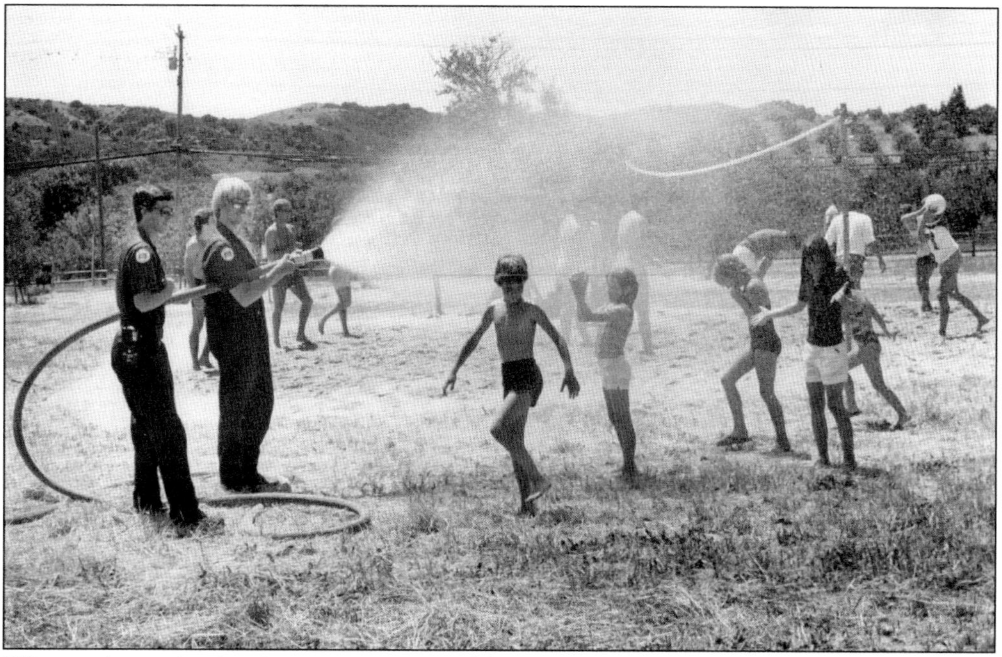

When a plan to develop freeway access to and from Moraga was abandoned, the community saw an opportunity to purchase 20 acres of land at the intersection of St Mary's and Moraga Roads. This land was developed with an emphasis on open space. The park was dedicated in 1982. It is connected to the Lafayette-Moraga recreation trail and has play structures, a giant chess board, bocce ball, barbecues, a skate park, and Frisbee golf facilities. There is also a bandstand that features bands every Thursday evening in summer months. Above, firemen spray children with a fire hose, while in the background, locals play volleyball in the sand. Below, musicians play to listeners on the grass.

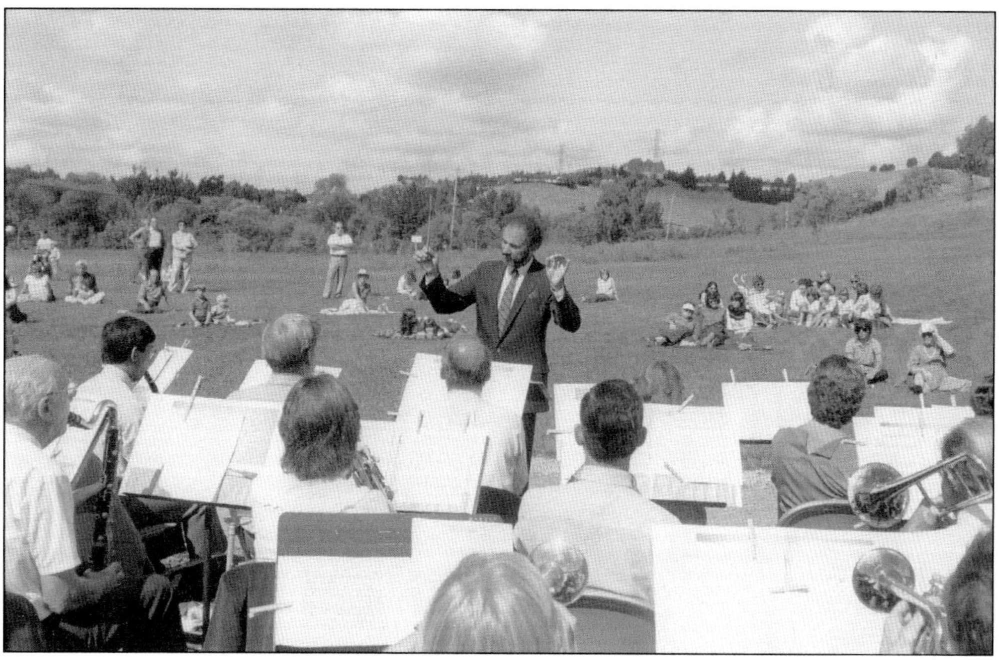

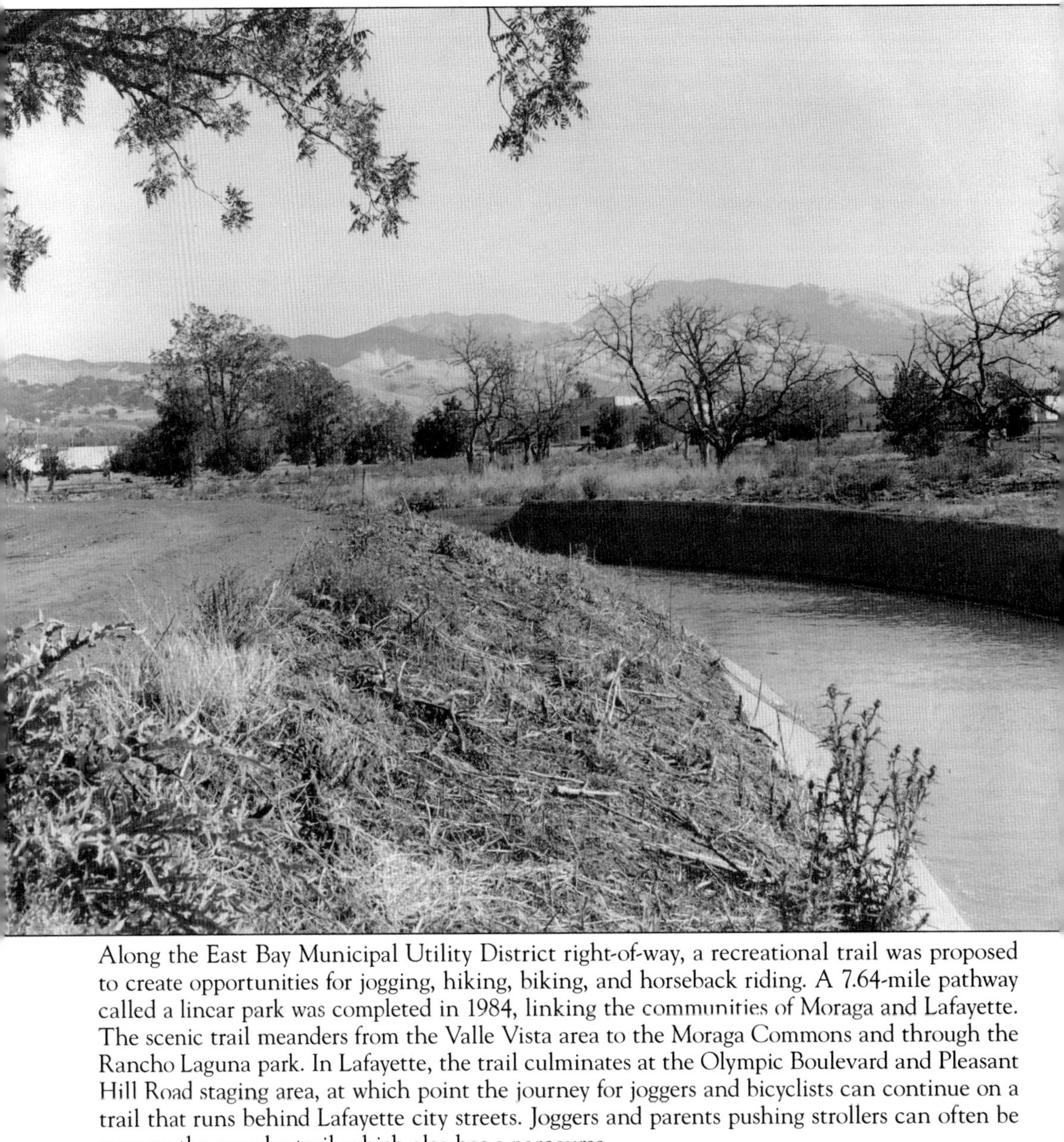

Along the East Bay Municipal Utility District right-of-way, a recreational trail was proposed to create opportunities for jogging, hiking, biking, and horseback riding. A 7.64-mile pathway called a linear park was completed in 1984, linking the communities of Moraga and Lafayette. The scenic trail meanders from the Valle Vista area to the Moraga Commons and through the Rancho Laguna park. In Lafayette, the trail culminates at the Olympic Boulevard and Pleasant Hill Road staging area, at which point the journey for joggers and bicyclists can continue on a trail that runs behind Lafayette city streets. Joggers and parents pushing strollers can often be seen on the popular trail, which also has a parcourse.

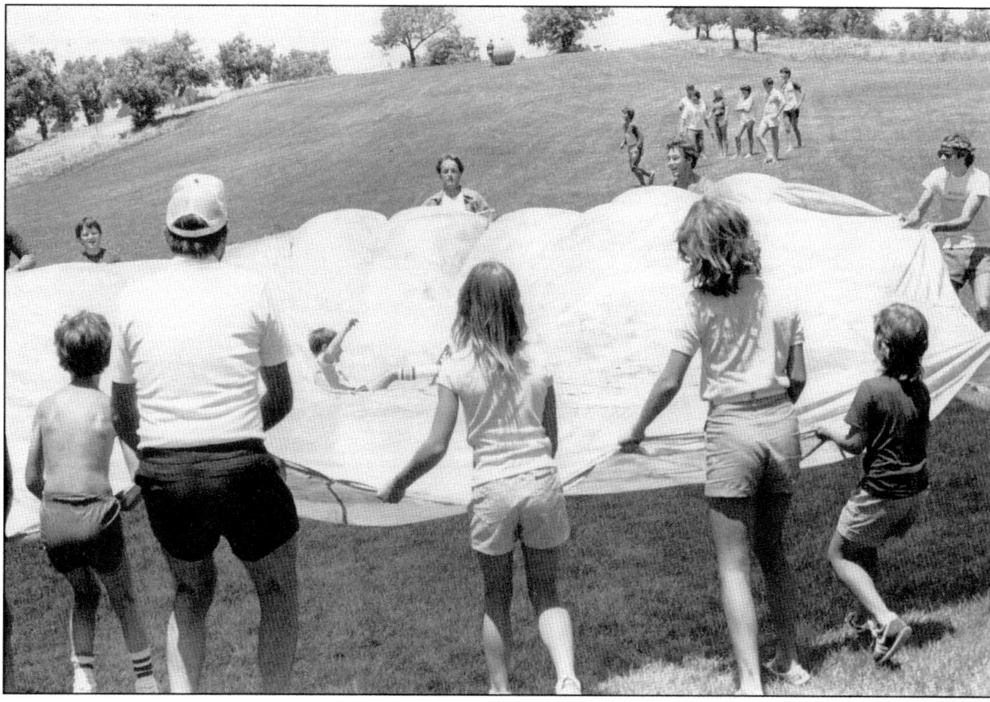

The Lafayette-Moraga Trail runs by the Moraga Commons, which is a popular place for children to play. The hilly area has been used for grass skiing, picnicking, and fireworks-watching, while the excellent weather in Moraga makes the Moraga Commons a good outdoor setting for community activities such as the Pear and Wine Festival and Fourth of July celebrations.

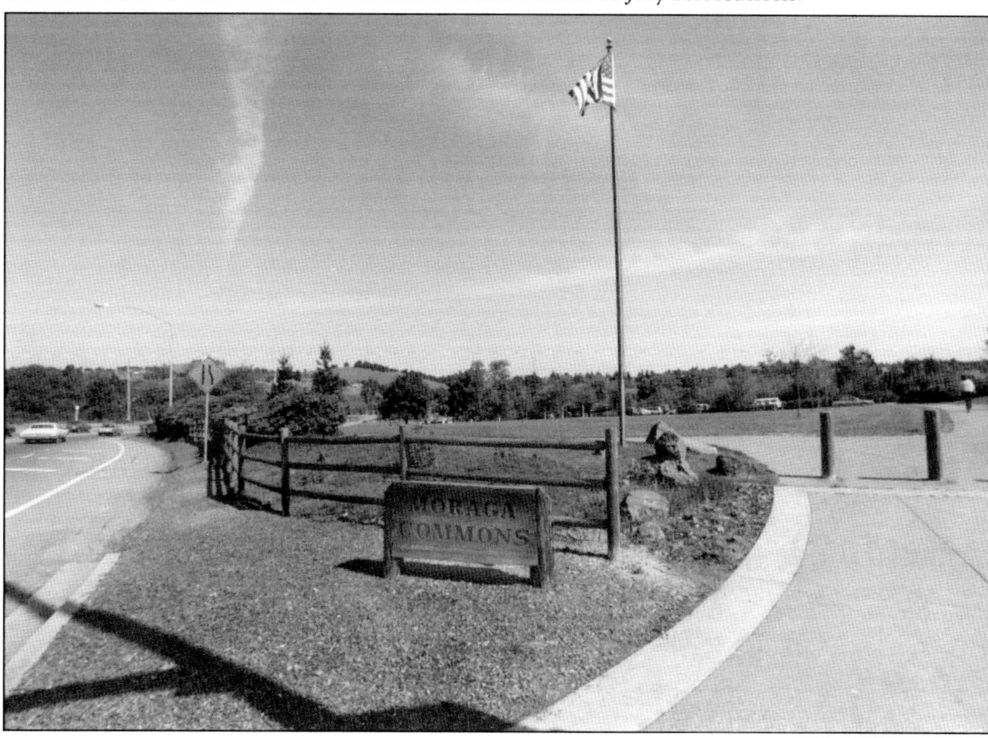

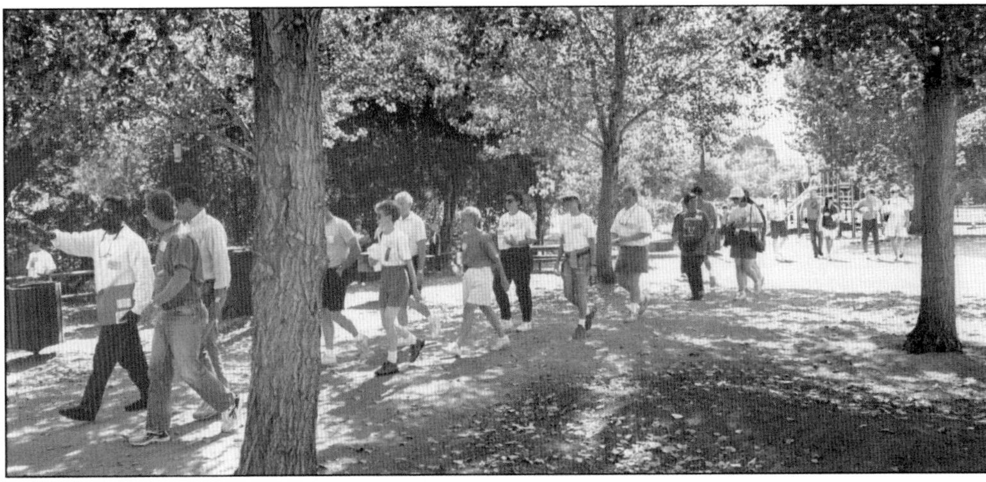

Residents of the Moraga area put together a petition that resulted in Measure A, devoted to protecting open space with more specific language regarding areas to be developed or protected than had previously been recorded. The language of Measure A addressed the protection of hillsides and ridges from development. Below, the measure is discussed at a town council meeting. The measure passed in 1986 and gave impetus to the efforts to preserve the beauty of the hills around town.

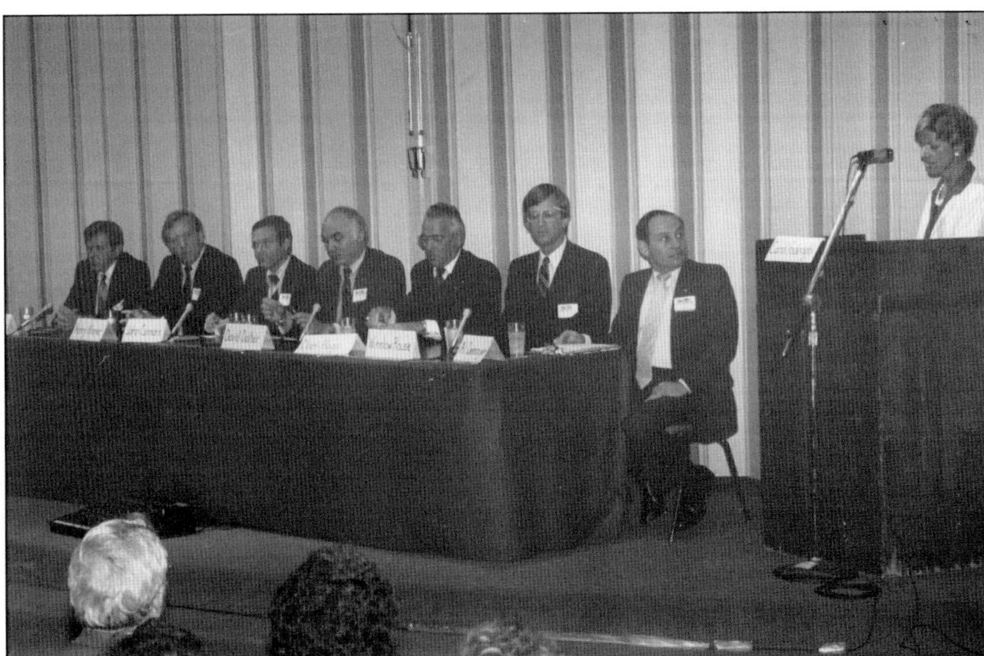

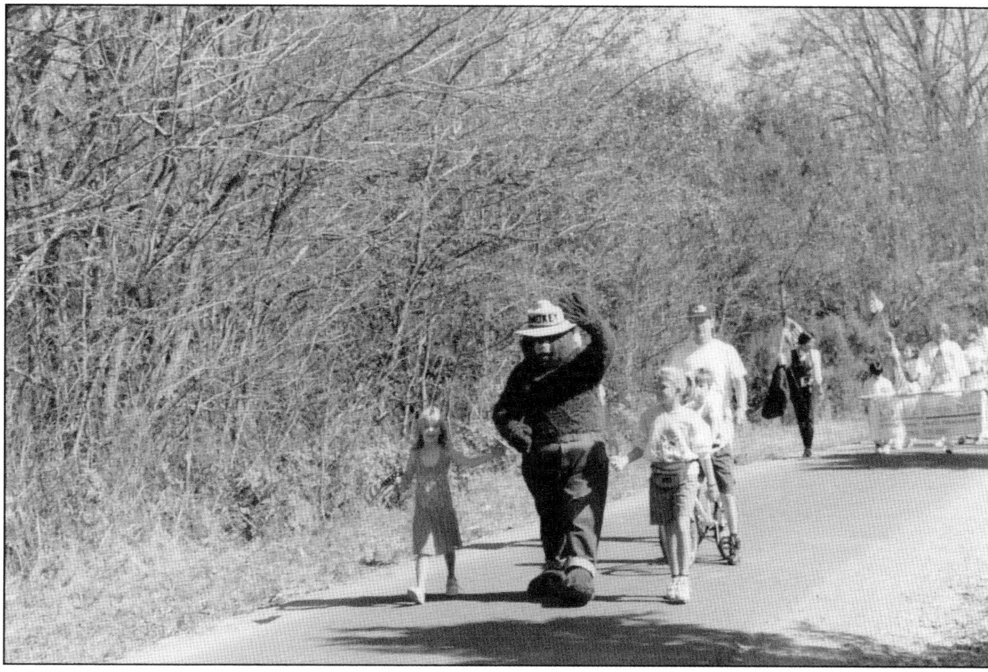

The legacy of the railroad in Moraga is preserved by the dramatic transformation of the railroad beds into trails for hiking, biking, and horseback riding. The efforts of Measure A to preserve open space culminated in a Rails to Trails Convention, pictured here, as the Lafayette-Moraga Trail was celebrated as part of the national Rails-to-Trails Conservancy. This parade, part of the festivities, took place in October 1992.

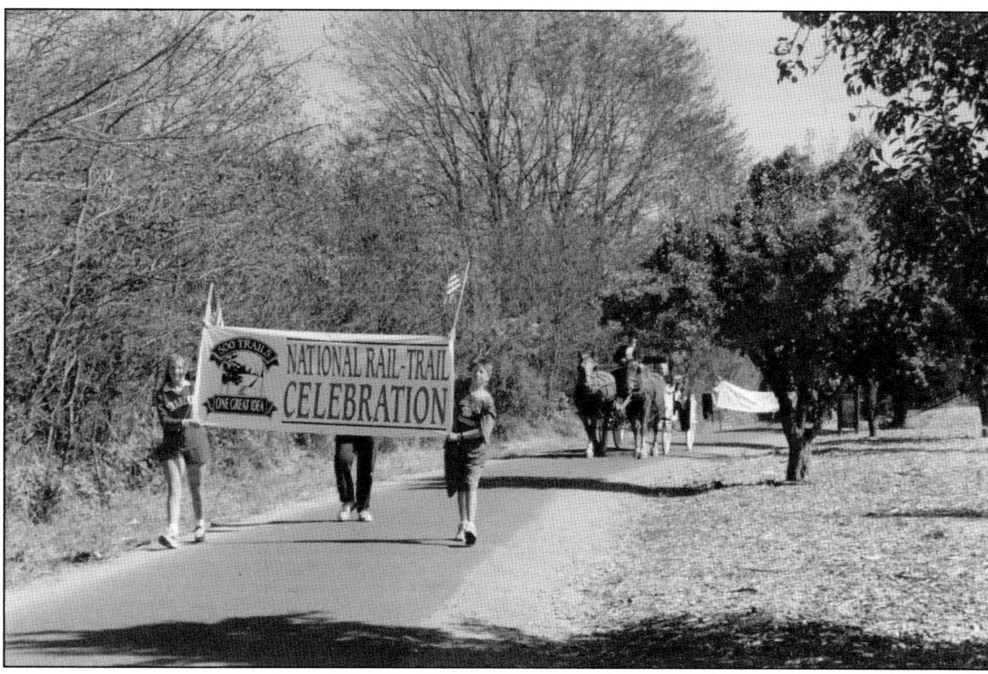

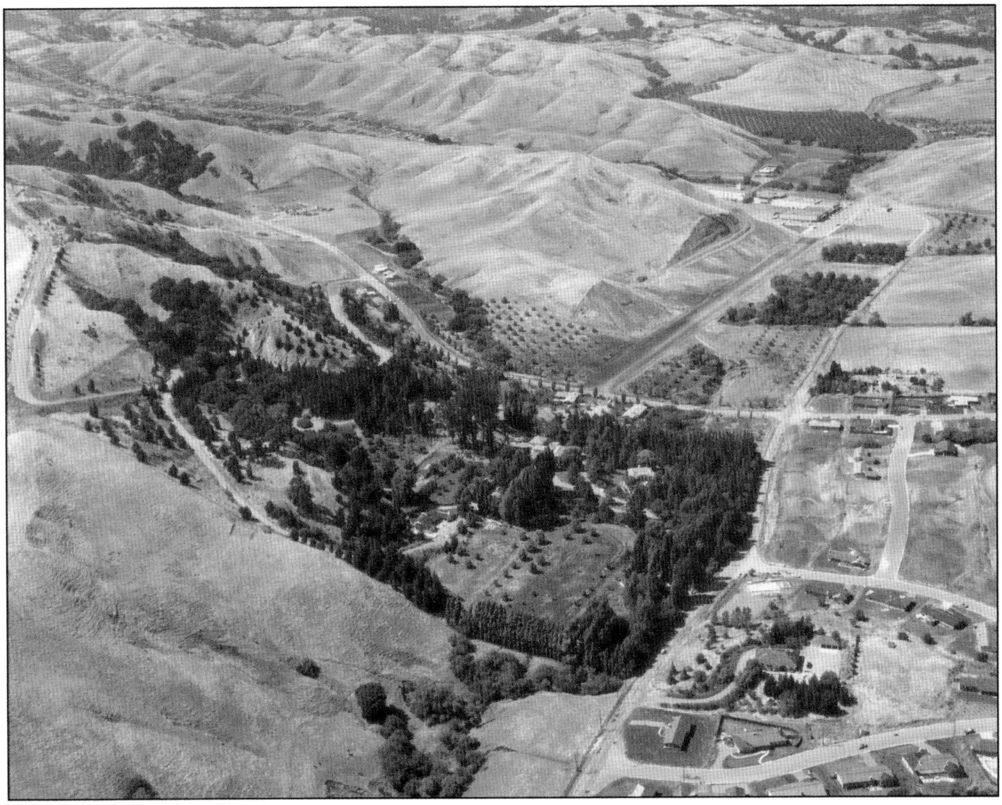

The Mulholland Hill Open Space Preserve, now a protected ridge off of Laird Drive behind the Donald Rheem School site, has a long history. Along with ancient geologic formations, fossils of prehistoric animals and plants have been found in this area. Open space at the top of the hill has been preserved as a walking path, which can be accessed via a trail from the Hacienda. At the top, hikers can take in the excellent views. The surrounding area has been developed into residential subdivisions. (Both photographs by R.L. Copeland).

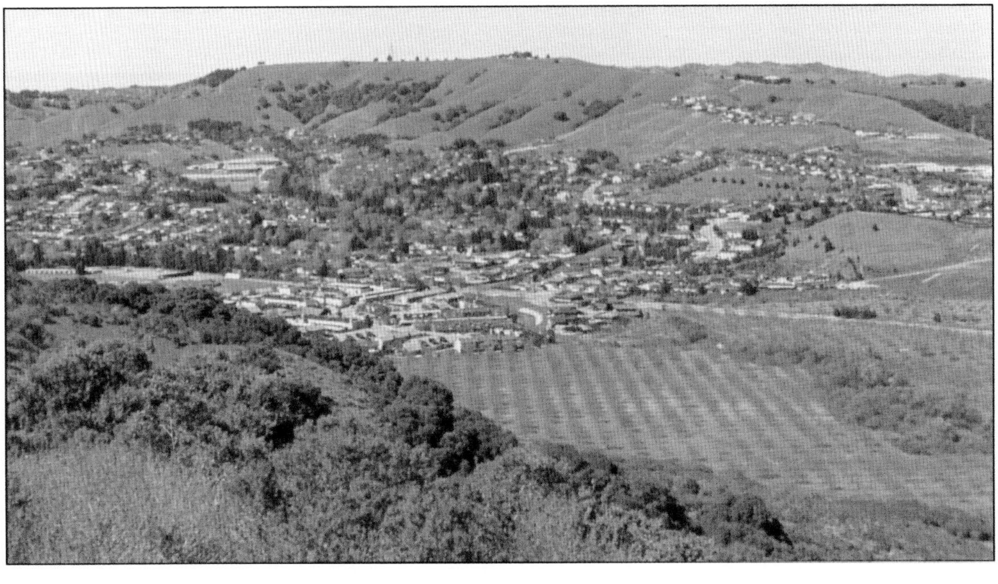

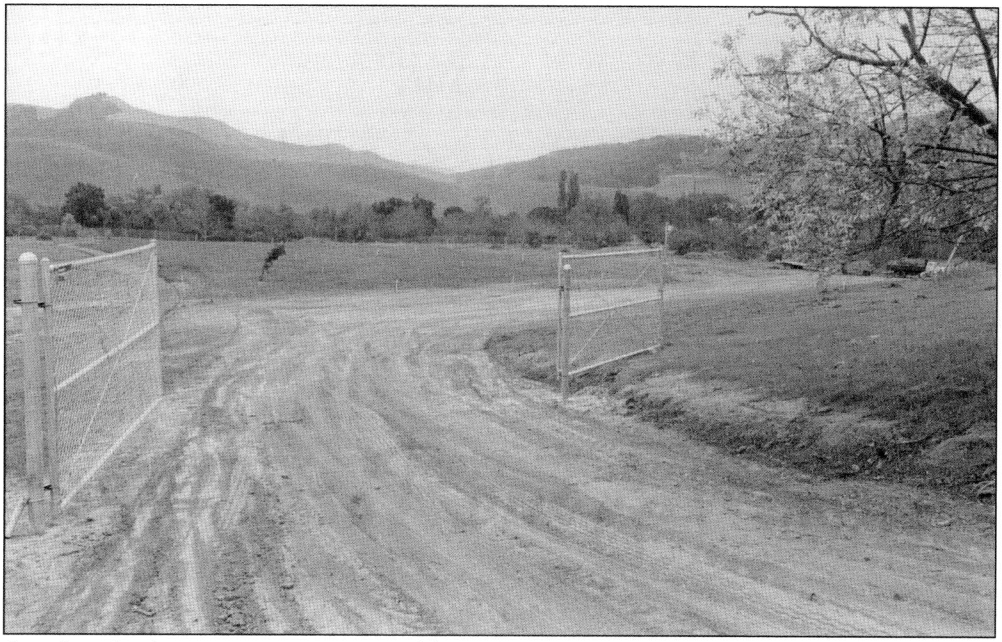

A park with a large grassy area, picnic tables, a playground, a small biking circle for children, and trail access, Rancho Laguna covers over eight acres and is situated at the end of Camino Pablo Road. A small train play structure for children and a plaque are dedicated to the historical presence of trains and train stations in Moraga. The town of Moraga organized a highly successful family camp out, which included storytelling and professionally led stargazing, at Rancho Laguna in July 2014. The event was followed a year later in the summer of 2015 with a sellout family camp out under the stars. Rancho Laguna is one of the parks annually weeded and fixed up by volunteers in the Moraga Beautiful campaign organized by the town.

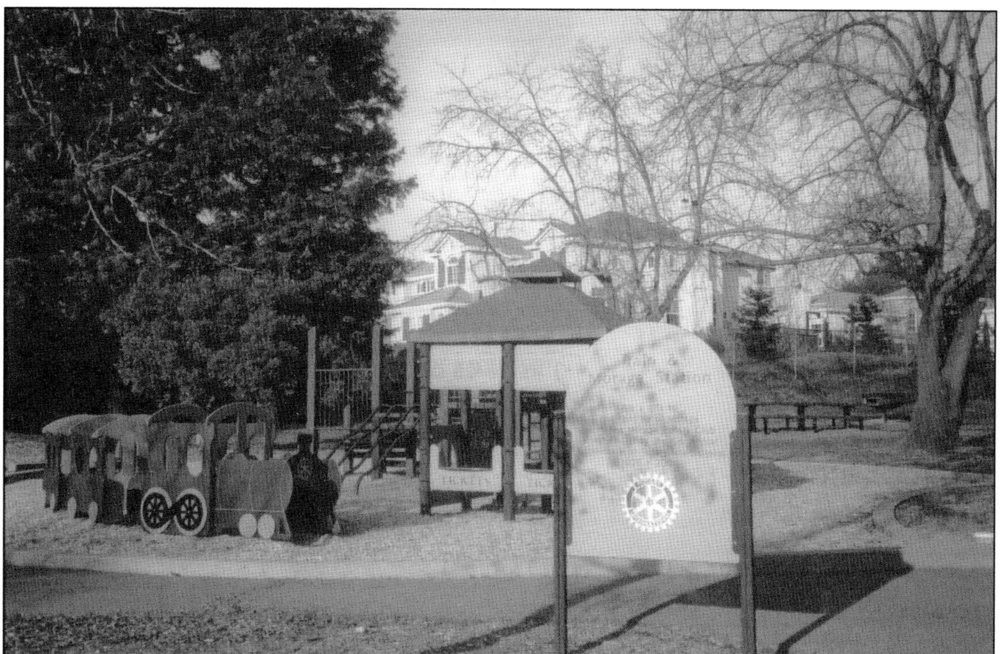

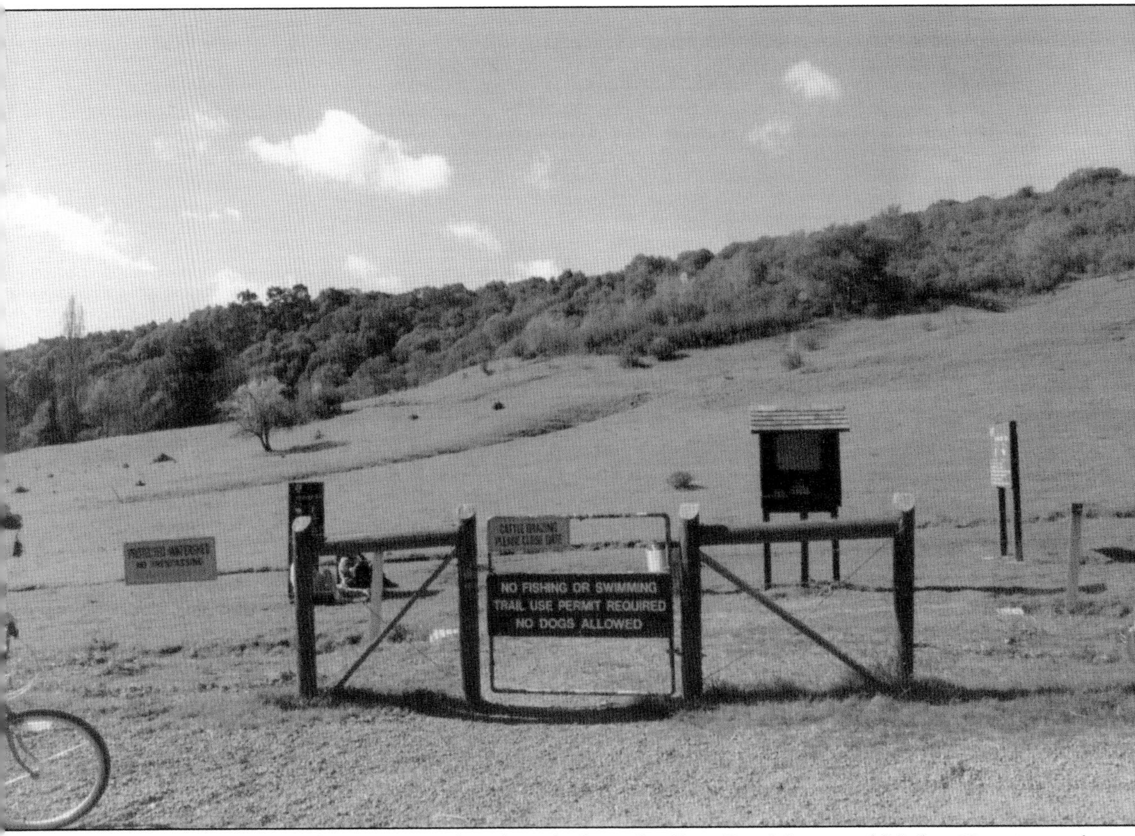

The Valle Vista subdivision was abandoned when the East Bay Municipal Utility District took over the land that borders the San Leandro Reservoir. The land eventually became a staging area for trails that lead in two directions from the parking lot. One trail leads along the San Leandro Reservoir through King Canyon. The trail can be followed to Rancho Laguna or completed as a 6.5-mile loop back to the staging area. The other trail leads down to Canyon Road and then toward Redwood Regional Park, with its many trails and picnic areas.

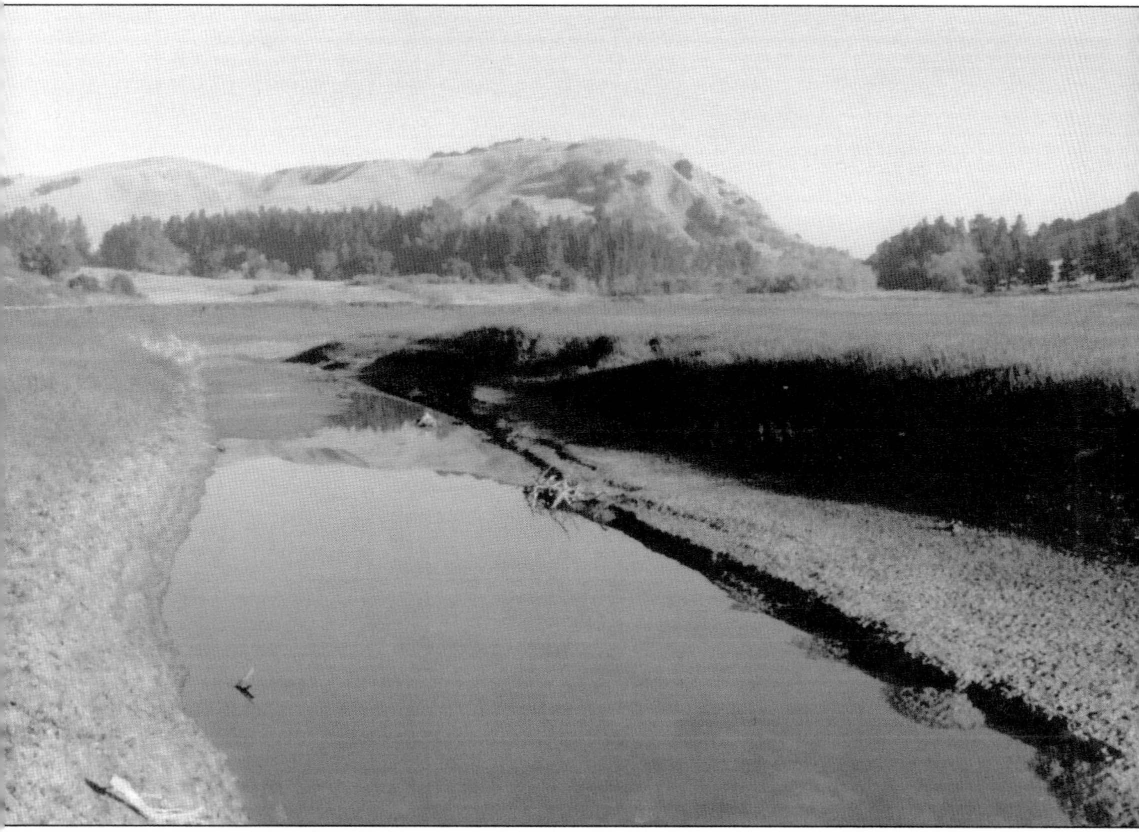

The town of Moraga has been fortunate to have had many advocates who worked hard to create parks and trails and to preserve open space. Residents can take part in active recreational activities in the open air all around town. Views of the San Leandro Reservoir are spectacular from the King Canyon Trail. Across from the staging area, the Lafayette-Moraga Trail can be accessed. (Photograph by Don Falconer.)

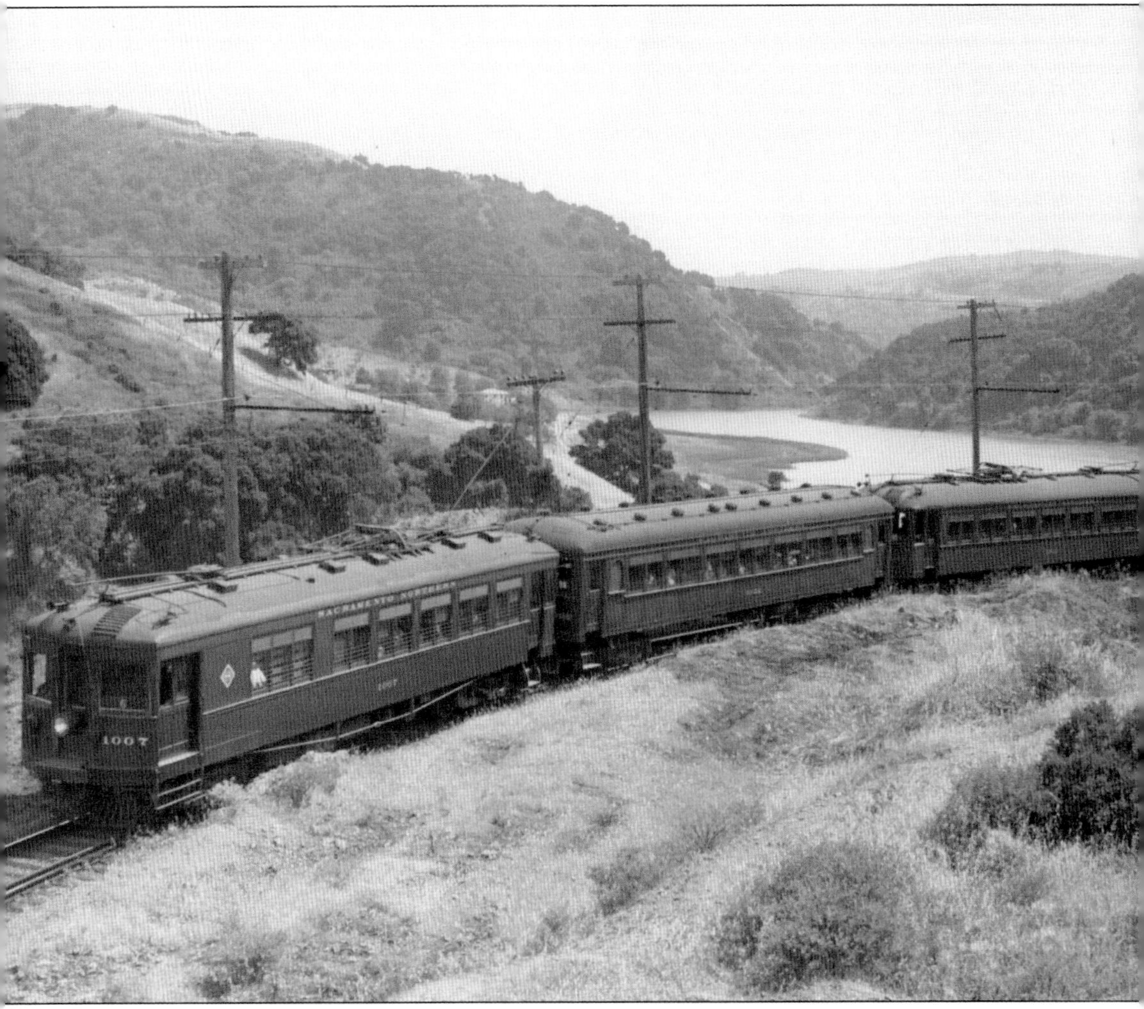

In this photograph of a Sacramento Northern passenger train at Valle Vista, the San Leandro Reservoir, which belongs to the San Leandro Creek Watershed, can be seen in the background. This area, once an excellent hunting and fishing venue, is still known to hikers and birders for its wildlife and natural beauty. Following the tenor of the Rails to Trails slogan, the beautiful vistas seen once by passengers on trains are now accessible, thanks to the efforts of many individuals and organizations, by locals and visitors who tramp and bike the trails. (Photograph by Wilbur C. Whittaker).

Seven

ST. MARY'S COLLEGE

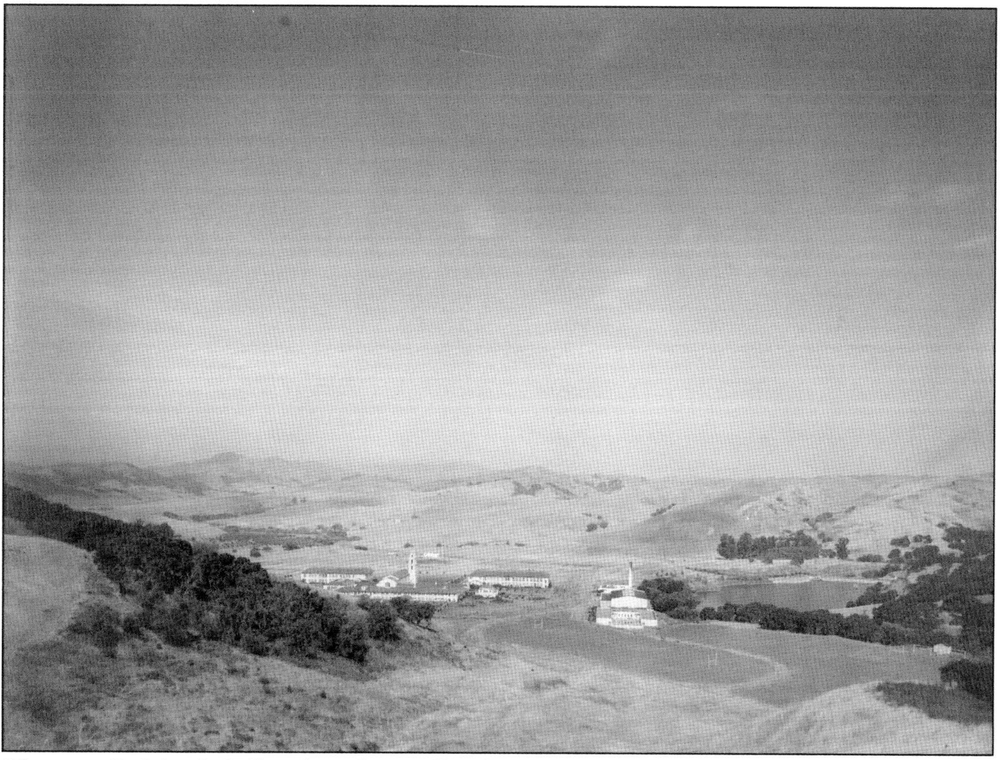

Classes at St. Mary's College have been offered in Moraga since 1928. St. Mary's was established as a four-year college by the Christian Brothers in 1868. Originally located in San Francisco, the school moved to Oakland and then came to Moraga after 100 acres of land were donated by the Moraga Company. It has been a coed institution since 1970. Located on St. Mary's Road, the campus is visible from the Lafayette-Moraga Trail.

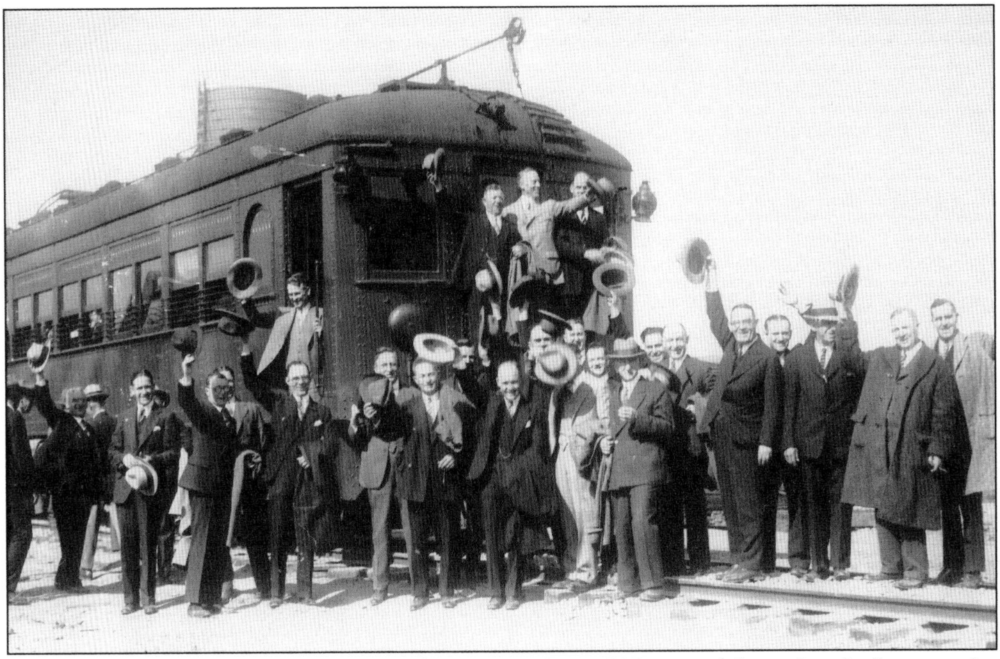

The moment of laying the cornerstone for St. Mary's in 1928 was celebrated with cheers at the Sacramento Northern "Short Line" tracks at the college library. The campus was smaller at that time than it is today, but some of the buildings have endured the decades. The buildings used then that are still in service today are Dante Hall, Galileo Hall, and the chapel. (Both photographs from Vernon Sappers collection.)

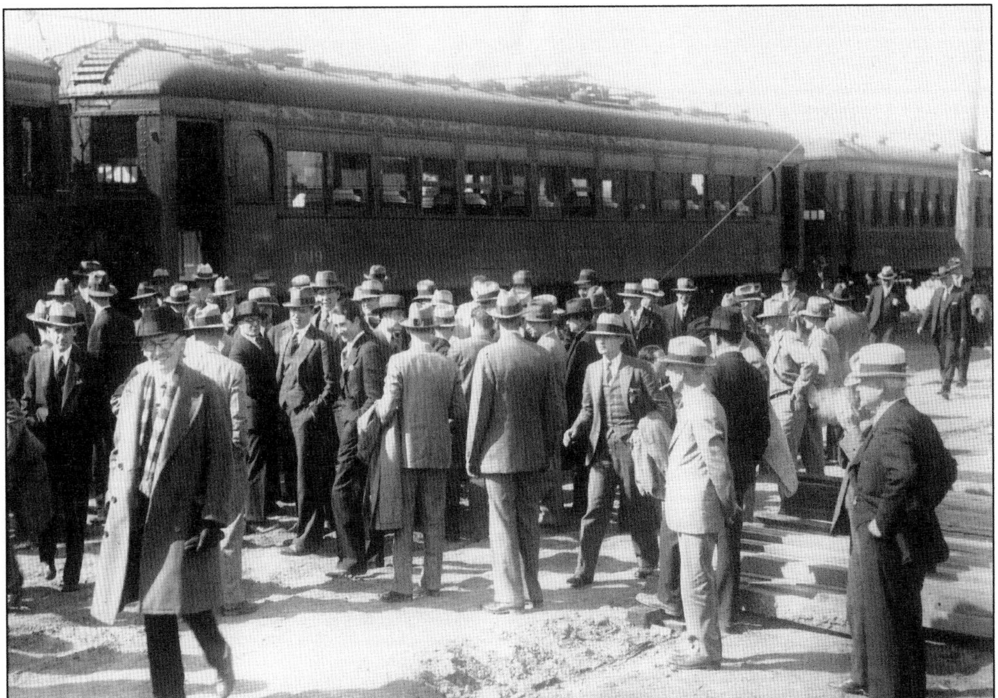

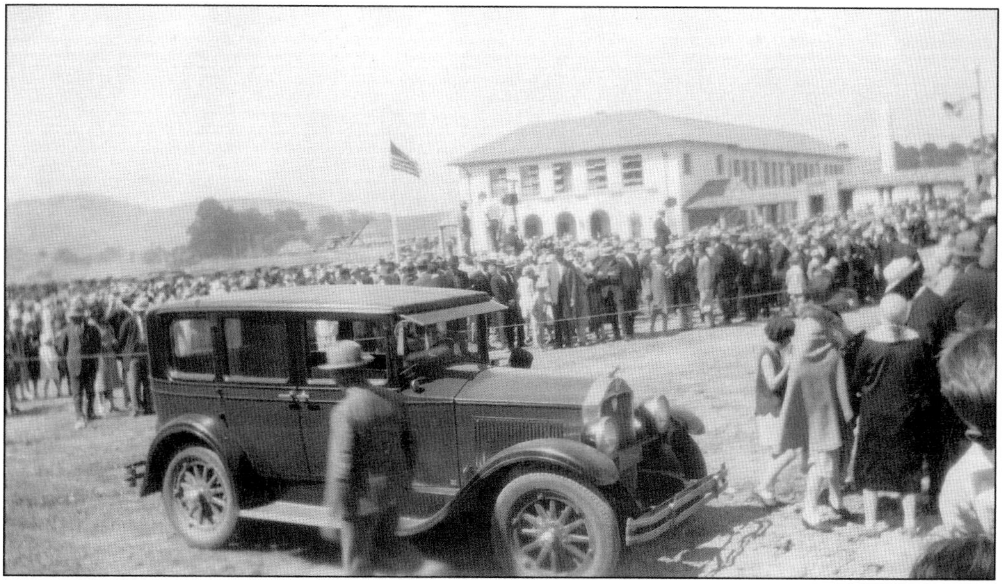

When construction on the chapel, designed in Mission Renaissance style, was finished in 1928, Archbishop Edward J. Hanna presided over the dedication ceremony. The bell tower of the chapel was modeled after that of the Cathedral of Cuernavaca. The photograph below shows students lounging on the lawn in front of the chapel, enjoying a concert.

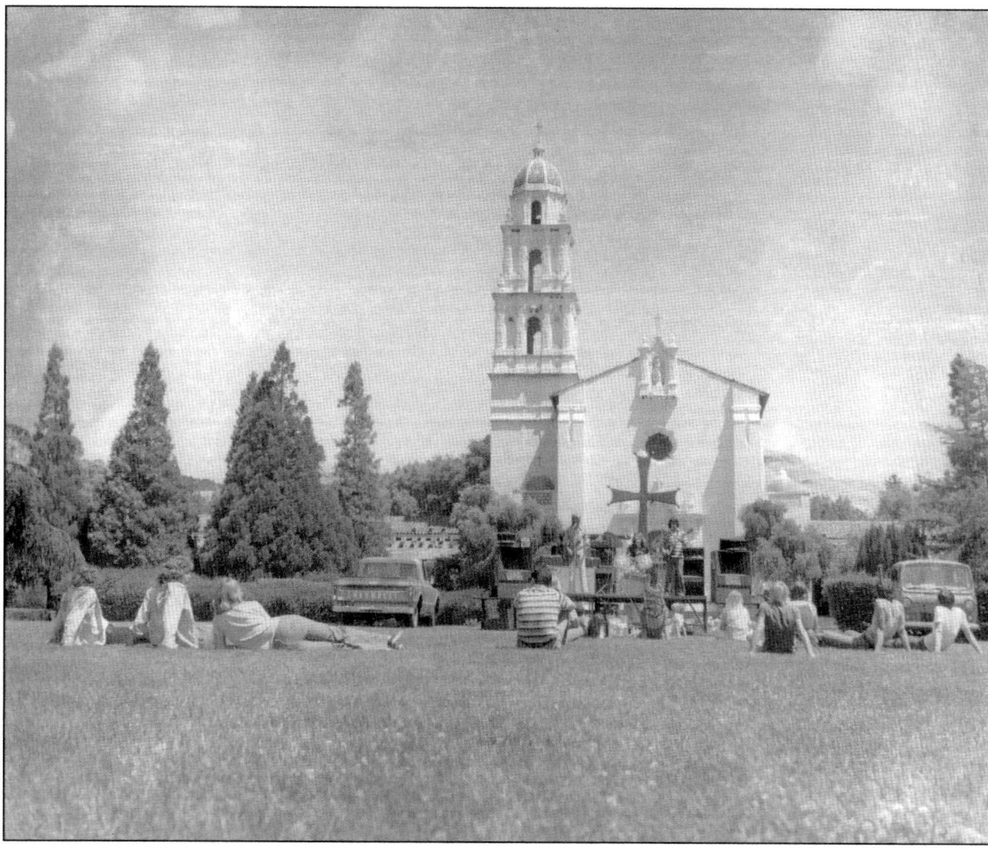

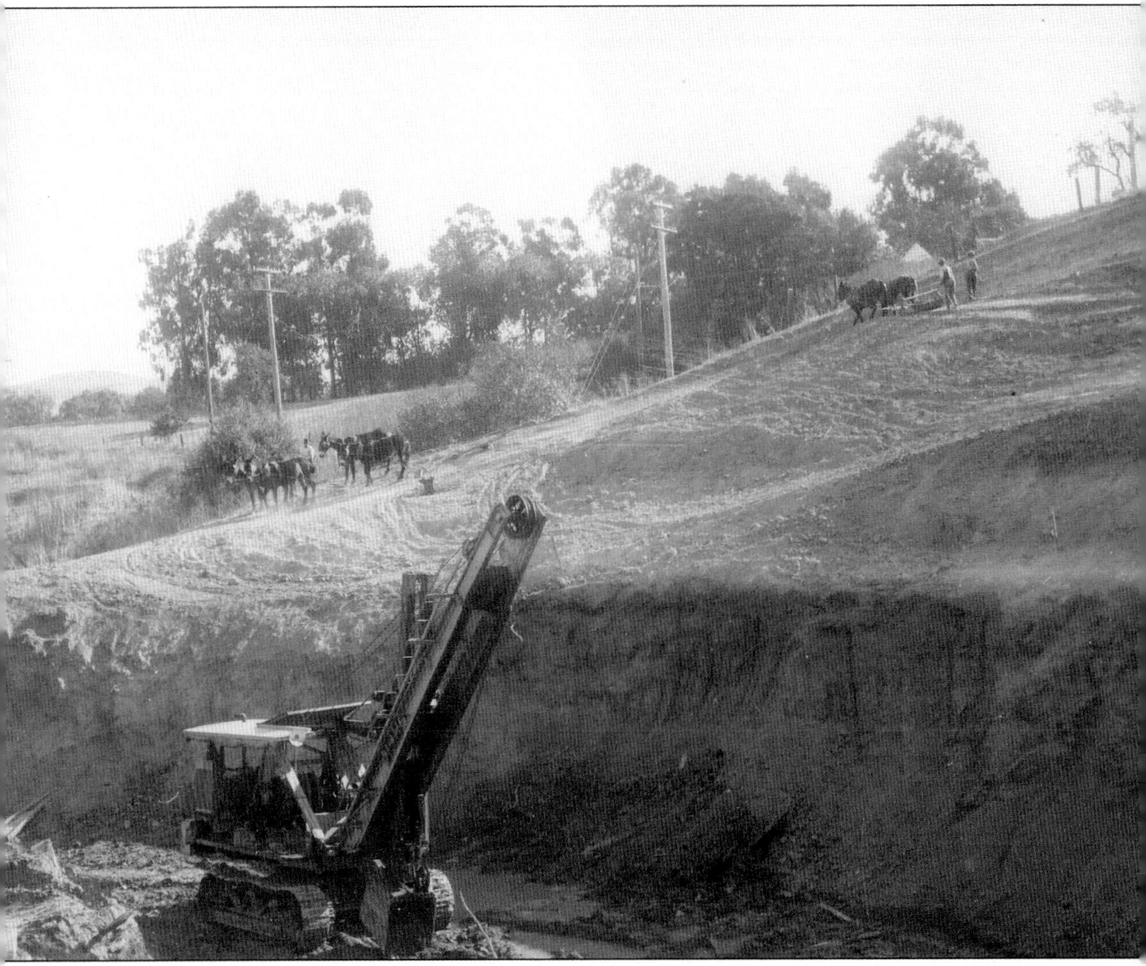

Lake La Salle was dredged with Fresno scrapers drawn by horses and by machinery as the Moraga Valley used old and new methods of land development. The reservoir was created in 1927 when the water from Las Trampas Creek was dammed. While some water for the college came from wells, the artificial lake was the main water supply for many years. When the US Navy established a pre-flight school at St. Mary's in 1942, it also persuaded The East Bay Municipal Utility District to pipe freshwater to the college. This added a much more certain supply of water to the campus.

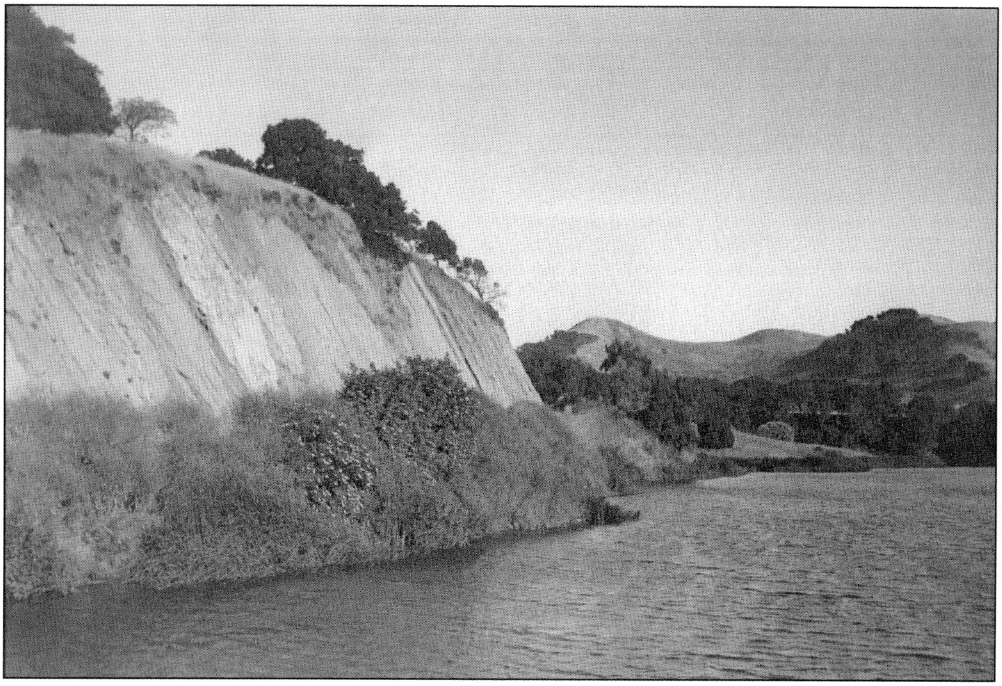

In 1935, when these photographs were taken, Lake La Salle still existed. The dam was placed on the former Manuel Rose Ranch. Since then, the lake has been filled in. When the pre-flight school occupied the campus, silt was pumped out of Lake La Salle, and the foundation for playing fields at the front of the school was created.

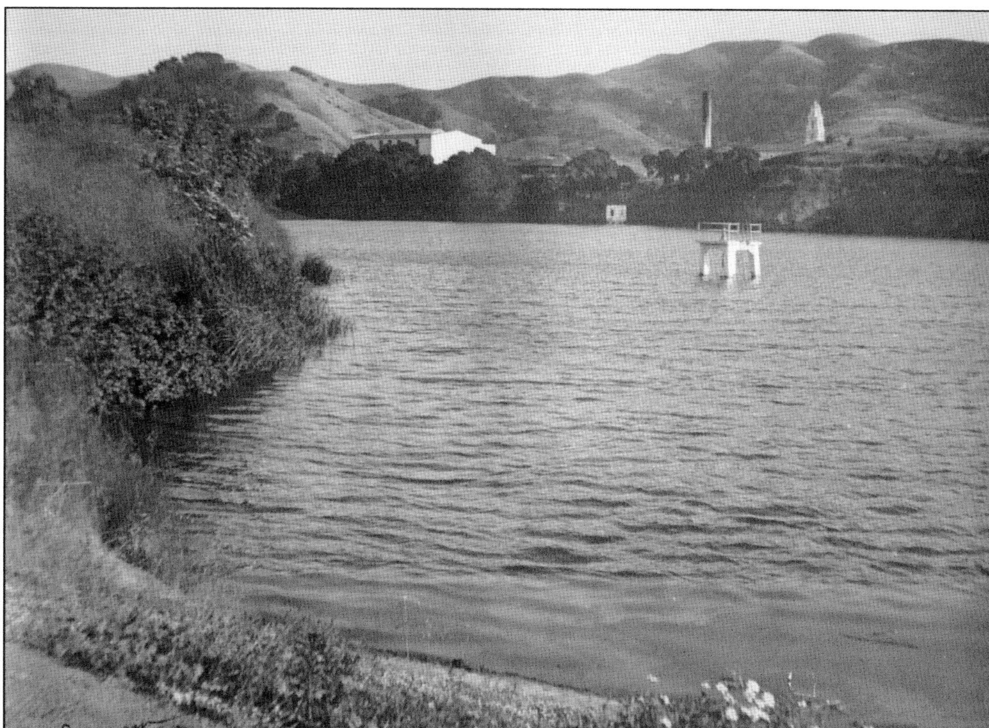

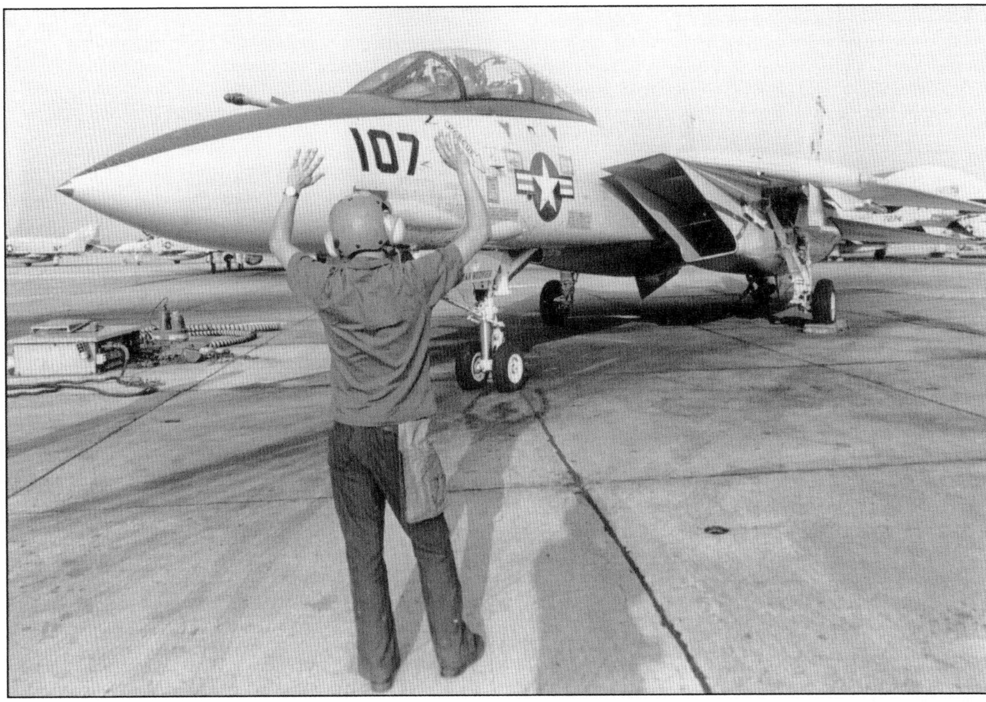

The photograph above was taken in 1942, the year the US Navy set up a pre-flight school at St. Mary's College. The Naval pre-flight school was conducted until 1946. Former US president Gerald Ford was at one time an instructor at the school. Below, mail sorting at the pre-flight campus post office involves the cheerful contribution of clergy and servicemen alike.

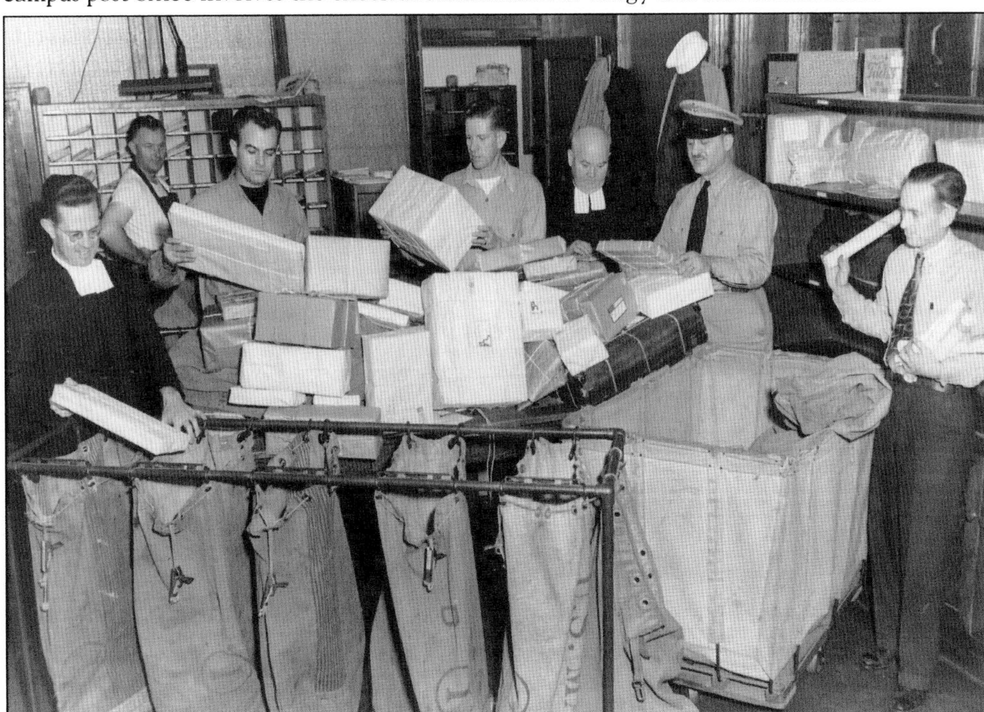

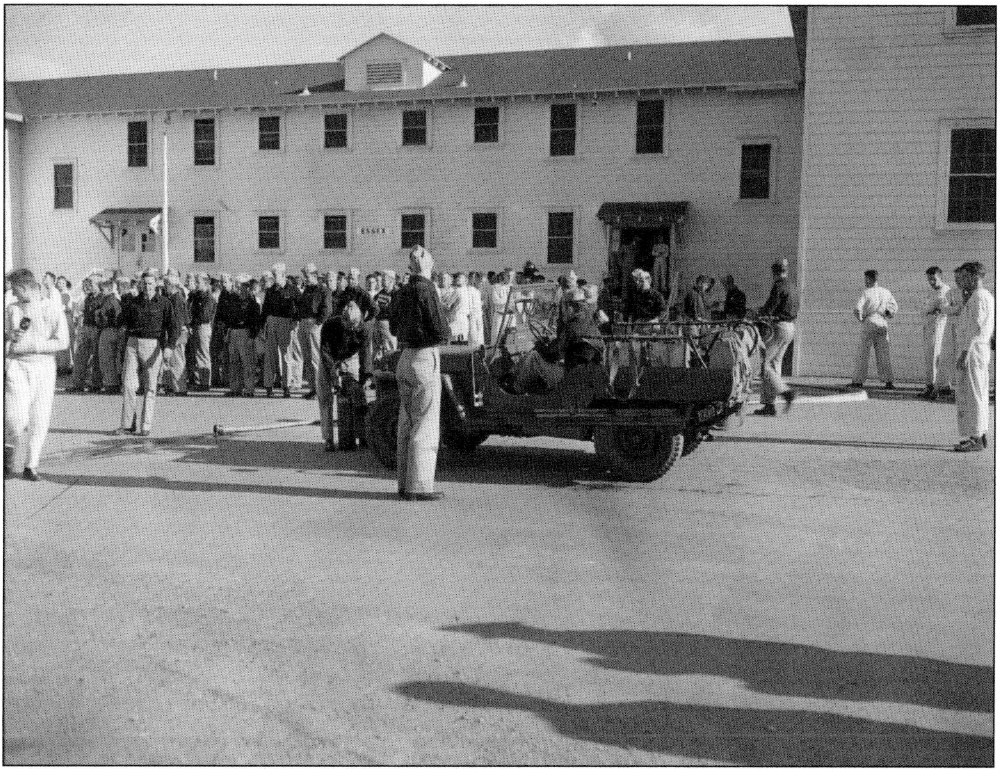

During the time that St. Mary's was the location for a Naval pre-flight school, it underwent many transformations. Buildings were constructed for use for the new school and later removed. The teaching was done by Navy personnel, who graduated the first pre-flight class on September 9, 1942. At final count, 14,959 cadets were trained there.

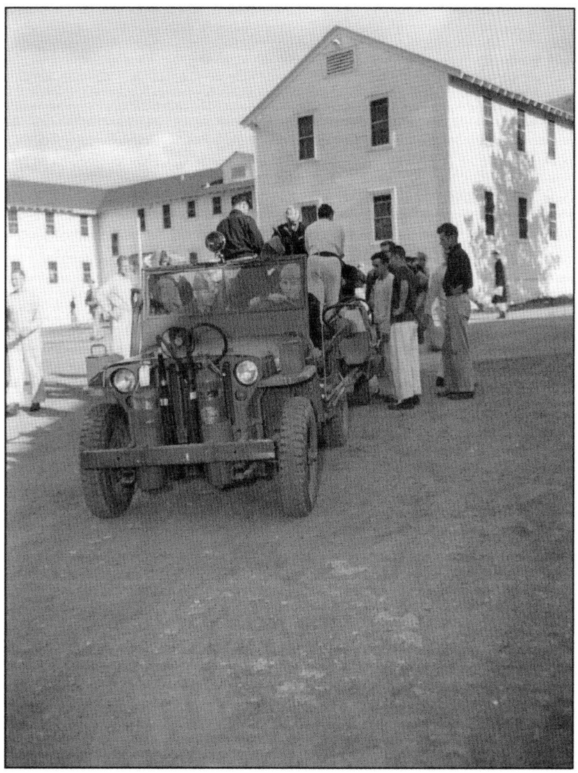

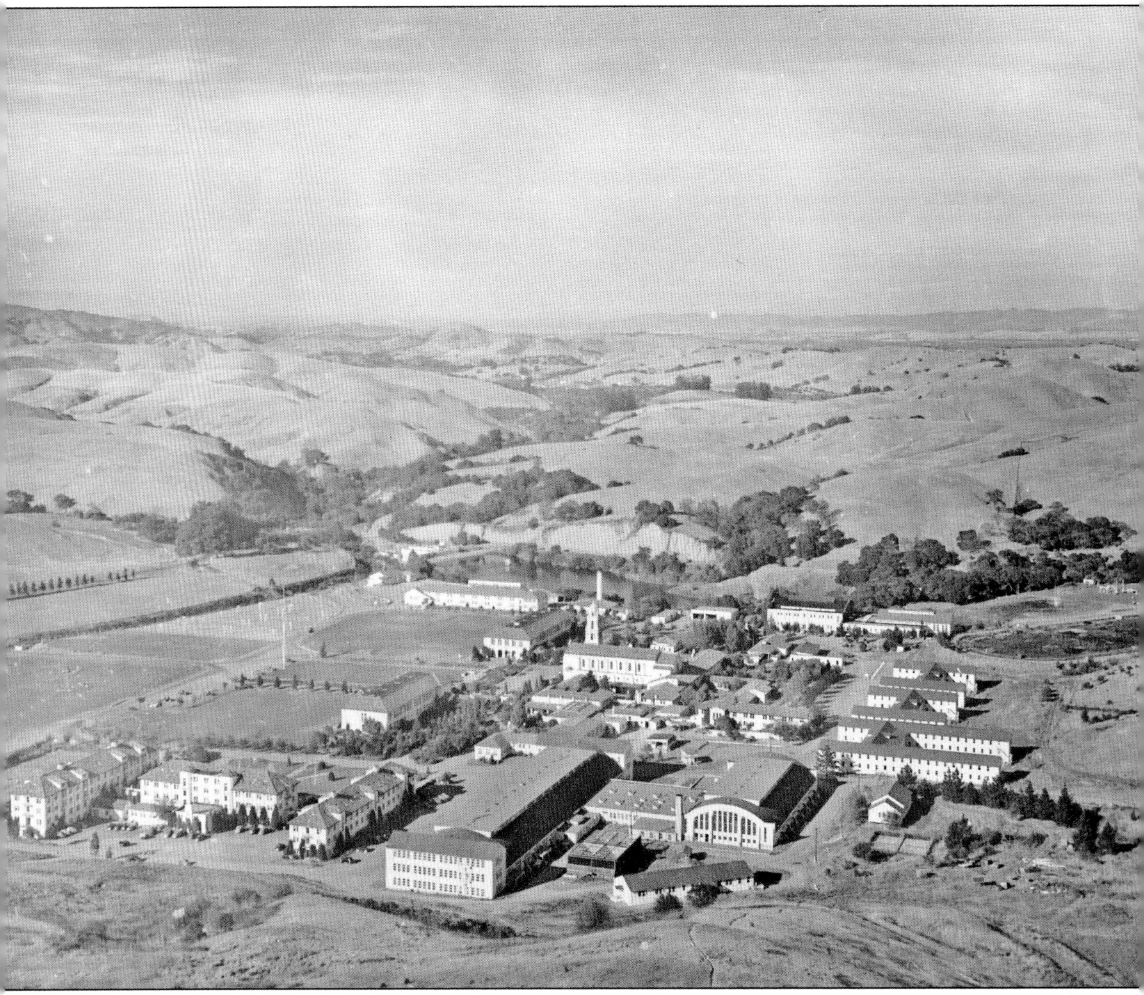

This 1946 aerial view of the campus during pre-flight training days shows how different things looked. The Navy built many buildings, including barracks and a field house. A rifle range was set up. One former cadet recently recalled that the cadets had a large workload that included more than just military drills. They studied academics, including meteorology and astronomy. They played sports of all kinds. Their military training included pistol and rifle practice and physical and mental challenges. For some cadets, one of the challenges was a hike carrying plenty of gear to the top of nearby Mount Diablo. (Photograph by US Navy, courtesy Moraga Historical Society).

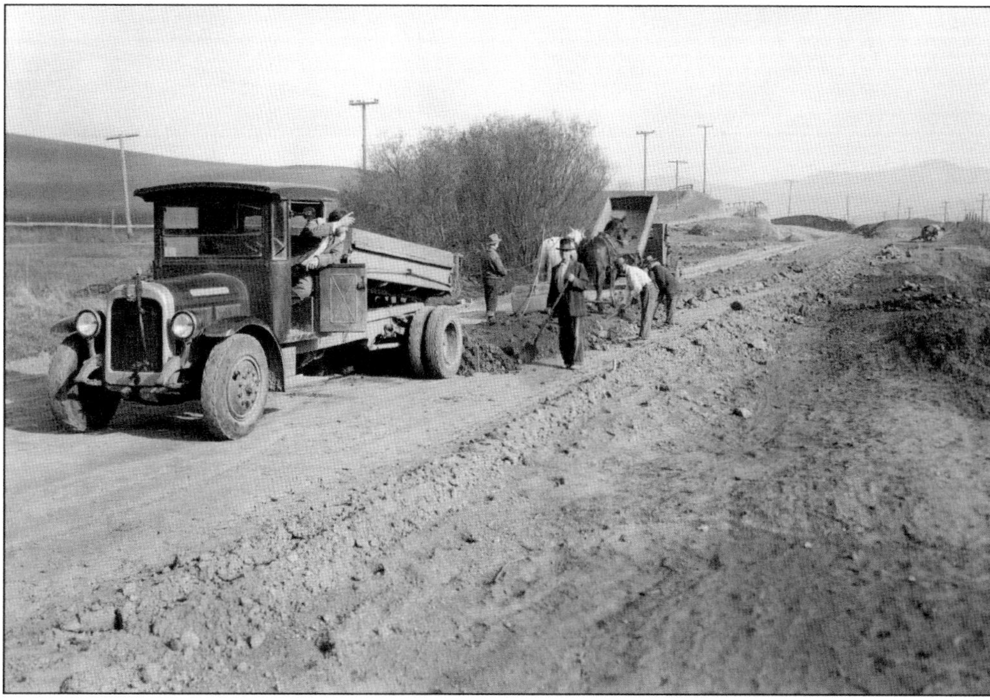

St. Mary's Road was constructed by the Moraga Company in 1929. The photograph above shows the dirt road with a view towards St. Mary's College, while below is the road at the western boundary of the college. The Moraga Company wanted to attract a college campus to the local area. The company offered to donate land to Holy Names College and to St. Mary's. Holy Names was not interested, but St. Mary's College, at the time located in Oakland, took up the offer.

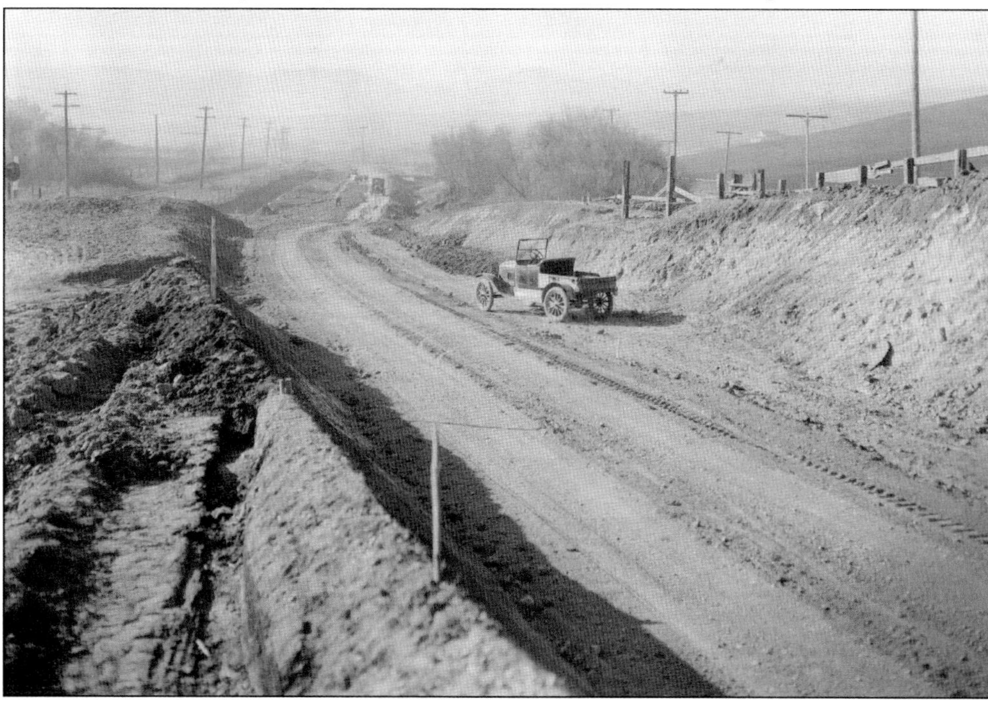

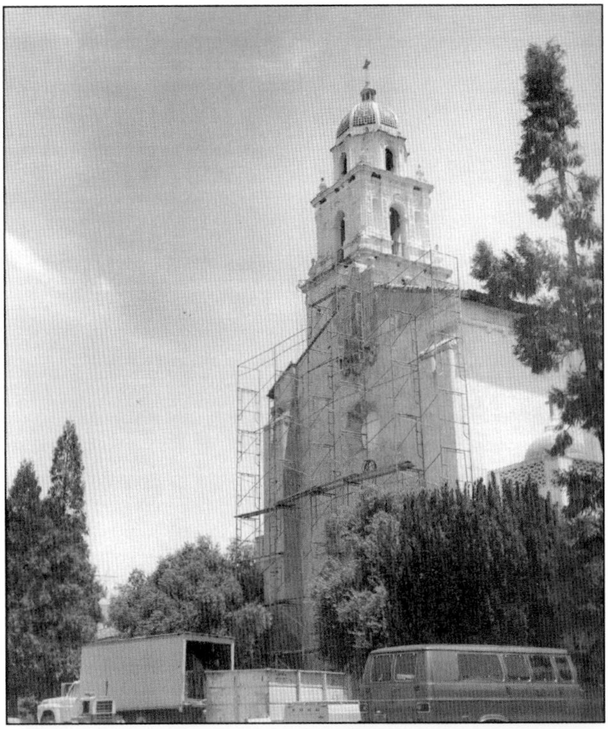

The chapel at St. Mary's was designed in the Mission Renaissance style by John J. Donovan of Oakland. The chapel received a facelift in 1998 after damage from the Loma Prieta earthquake. At that time, the statue of John the Baptist fell and damaged the steps. The whole chapel structure was strengthened for earthquake safety, and interior design changes were made, such as adding a Spanish-tile floor. The pews, fashioned in 1928, were refinished, and a new organ was installed. Dedicated in 1928, the chapel is easily visible to those entering the campus from the front, and serves as a central focal point. Below, cadets march past the chapel during Navy pre-flight training days.

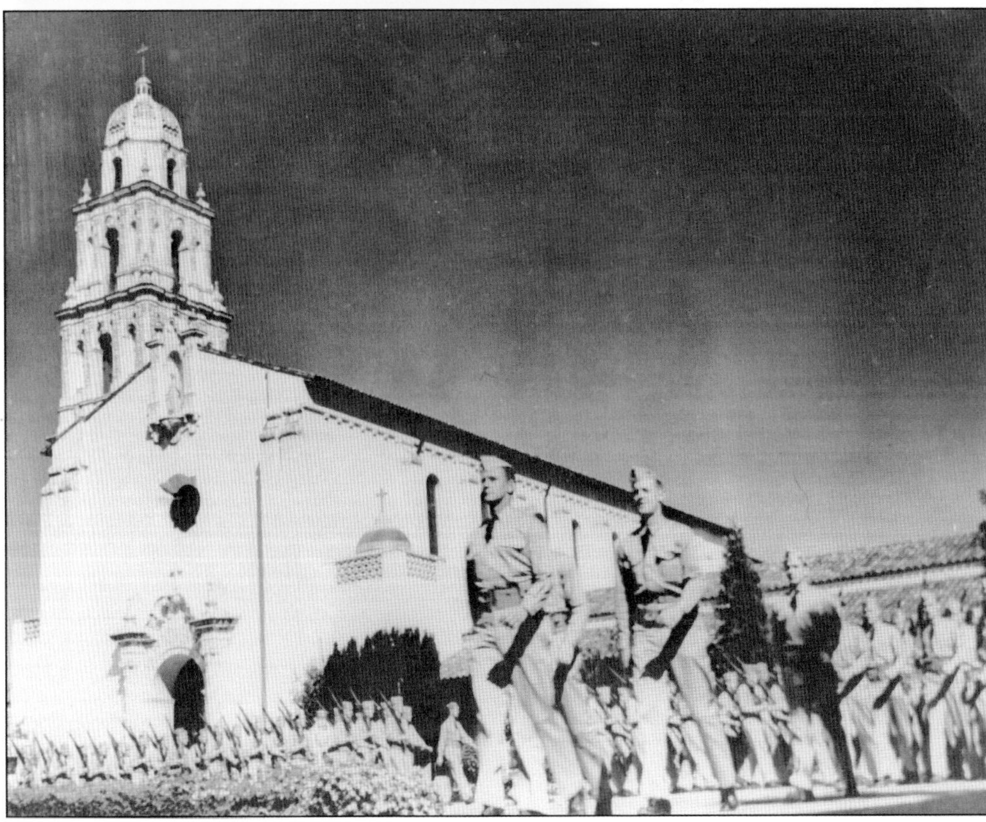

Eight

A Small Town with a Large Sense of Community

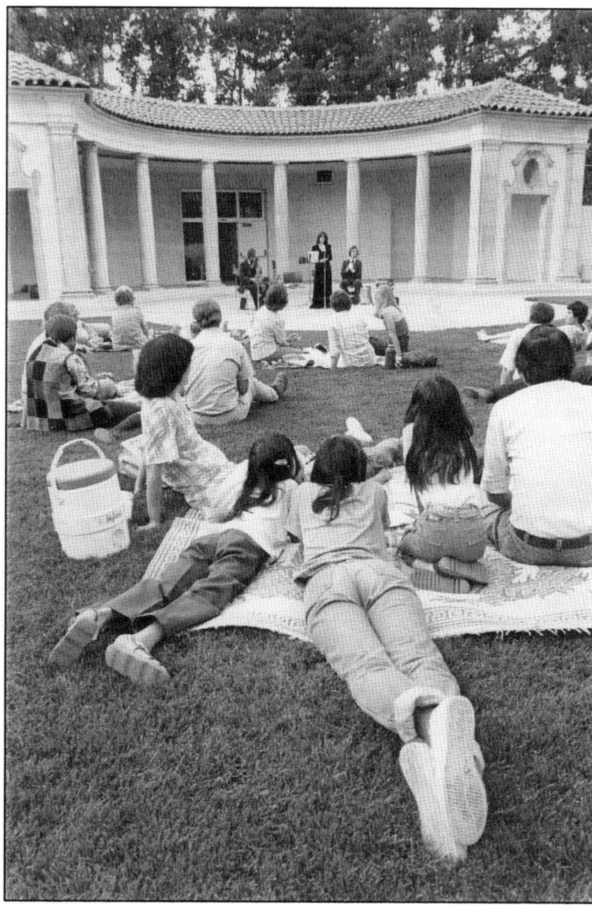

The excellent suburban location near San Francisco and Oakland and the natural beauty of the town of Moraga are features that have long attracted capable, vital, and committed community residents. The shared skill set in this town is enormous, and there is always a lot going on. Residential areas are diverse and attractive, and surrounded by landscaping or open space. The centrally located Hacienda serves as a gathering place for locals to take classes, hold meetings, or enjoy outdoor events, such as this concert in 1979.

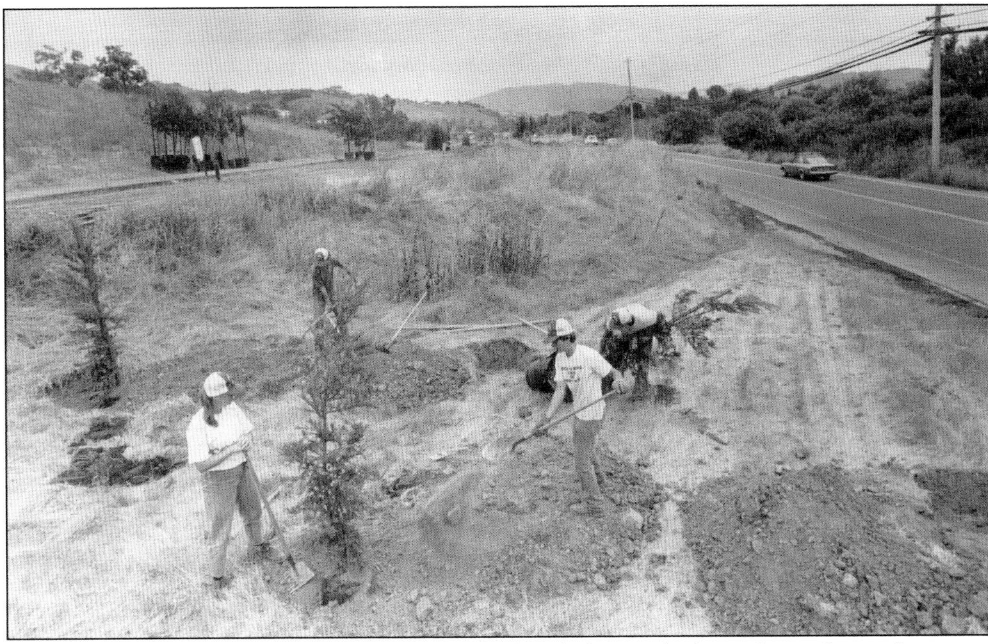

At and near Moraga Commons, locals pitch in to break the tough clay soil in order to plant trees. In 2008, Moraga joined Tree City USA, which inspires towns and cities to plant trees in the spirit begun with the first Arbor Day in 1872. Since joining Tree City USA, the Town of Moraga has been committed to planting at least one tree a year, but community groups were planting long before that. The photograph below is from 1983.

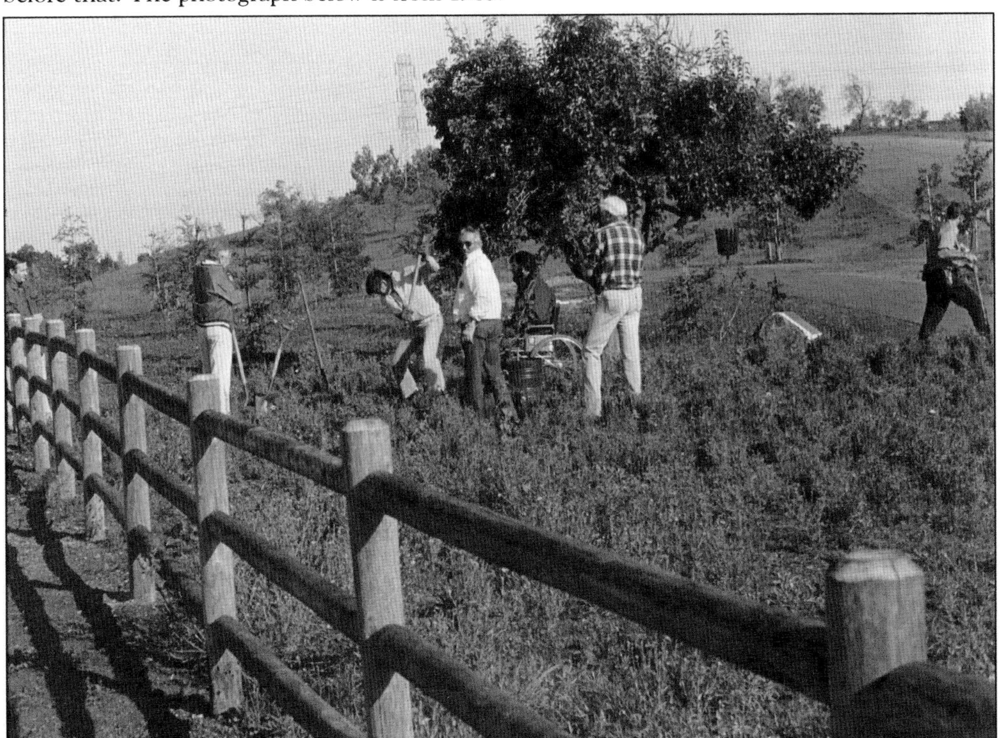

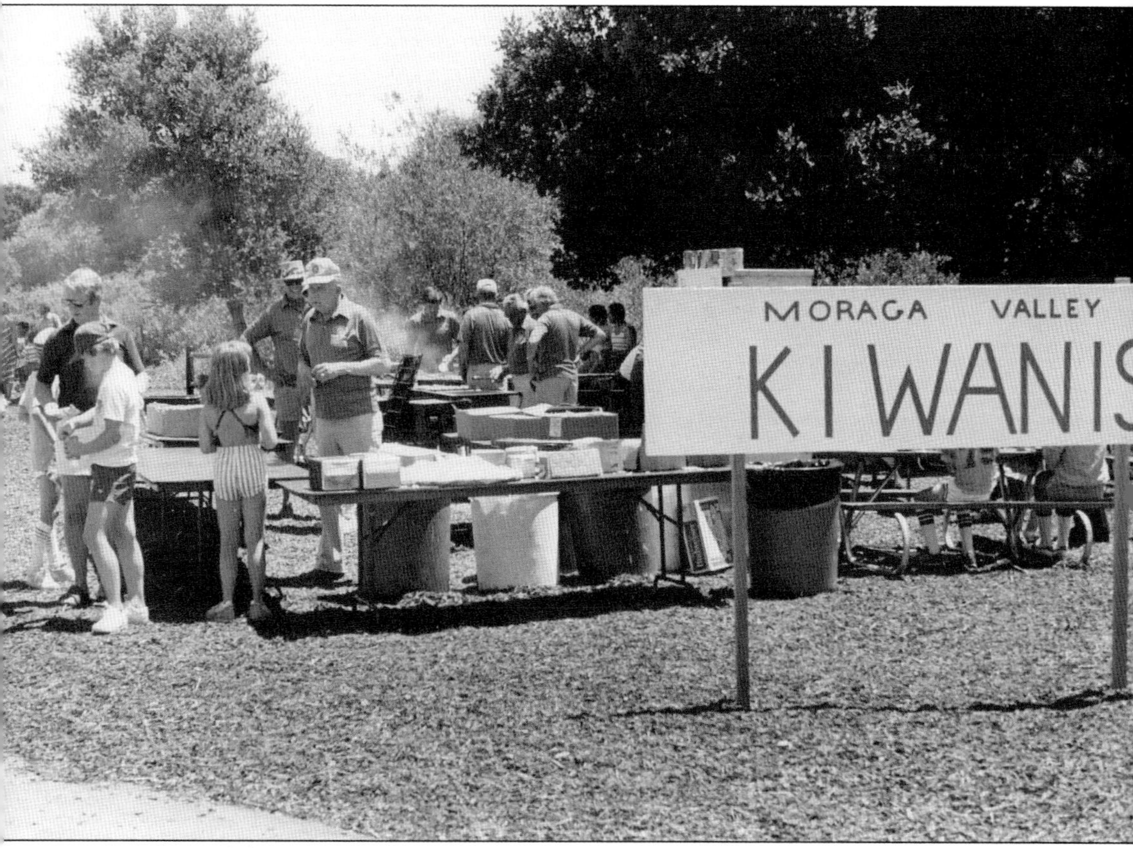

Kiwanis is one of the many active organizations in Moraga. Here, the Moraga Valley Kiwanis Club hosts a barbecue at the Moraga Commons. The club sells See's candy during the winter holidays to raise money for its causes. In recent years, the Kiwanis members worked with St. Mary's Catholic Institute for Lasallian Social Action to repair the bandstand shell at the Commons. The Kiwanis Club also replaced deteriorated wooden steps of an exterior staircase at the Hacienda de Las Flores with new masonry steps.

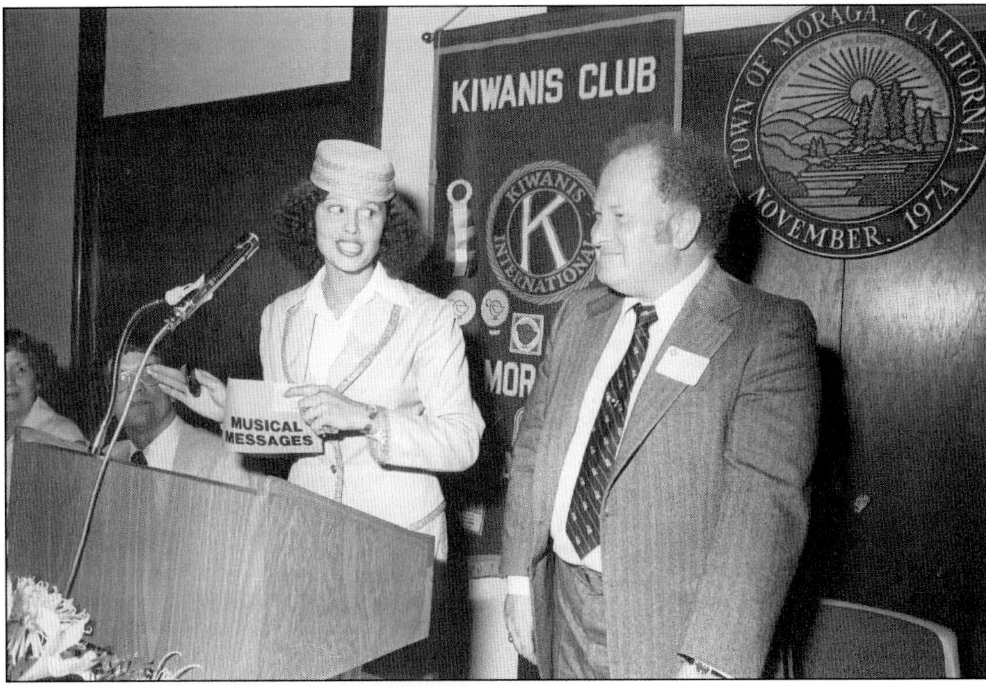

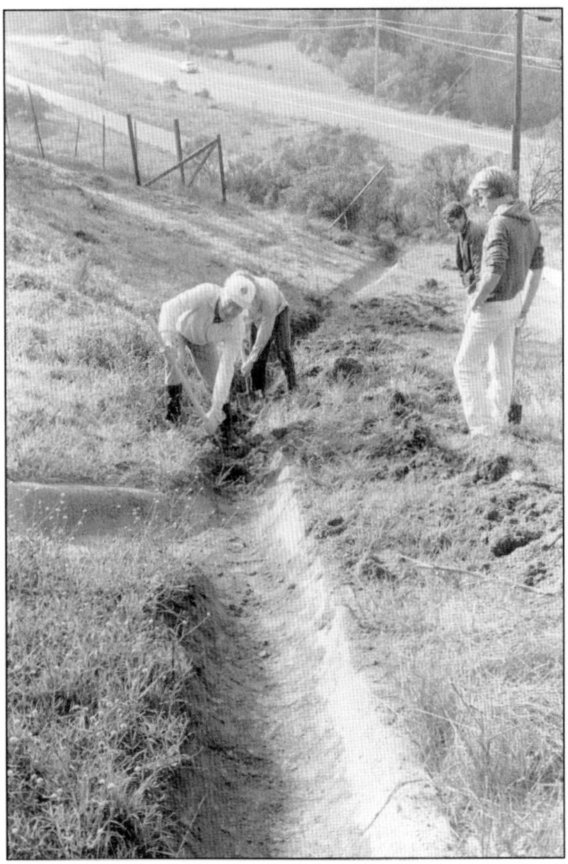

Barry Gross, mayor of Moraga, was honored by Kiwanis club representatives as citizen of the year in 1979. Gross, an attorney, was on the Moraga Town Council in its inaugural year of 1974. In 1977, he was appointed to draft the framework for the Parks and Recreation Commission in Moraga. Moraga has no shortage of help when need arises. At left, volunteers from the Moraga Lions Club work on drainage and hillside erosion challenges. The Moraga Lions Club is still active. Recent projects include e-cycling and shredding. Their annual crab feed raises funds to help many local nonprofit organizations, including those which help the visually impaired.

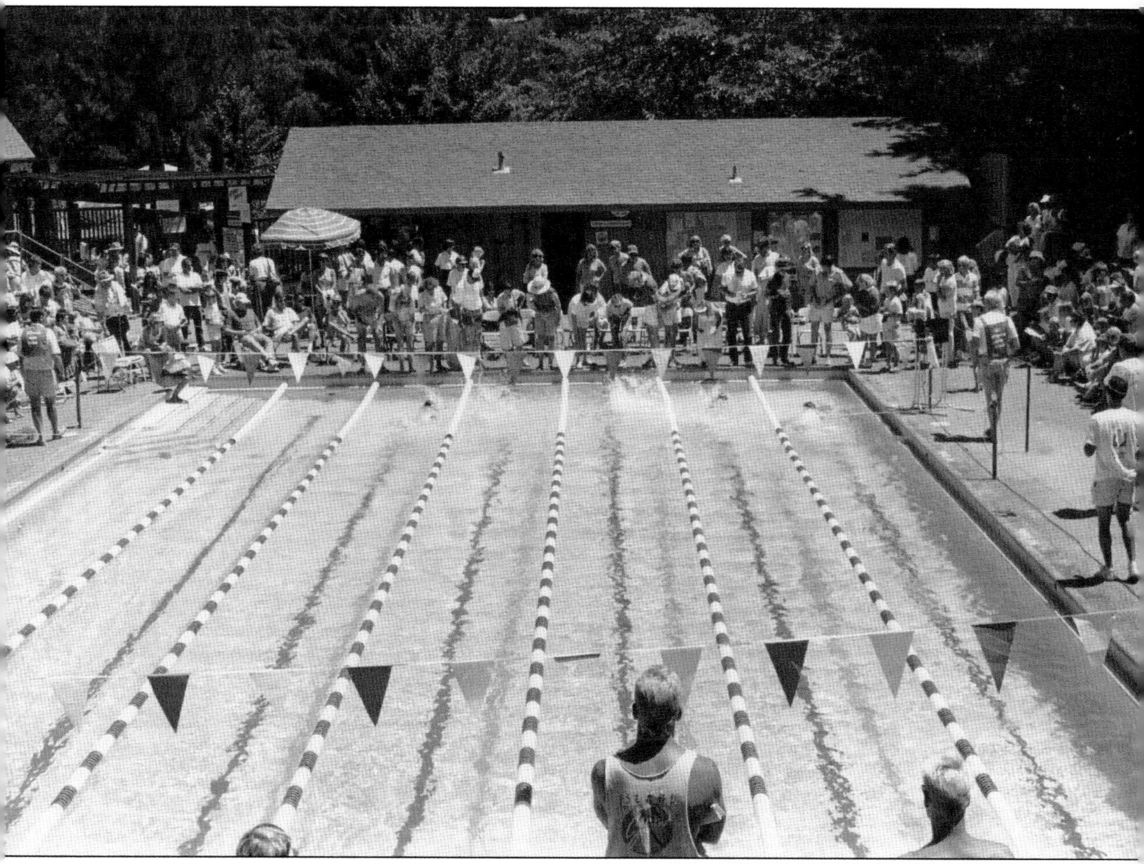

There are several recreational swim clubs in Moraga. Throughout the summer on Saturday mornings and Wednesday evenings, the air is filled with the sounds of splashing water and cheering parents as the teams hold their meets. Young swimmers compete mainly within the Orinda-Moraga Pool Association, although other teams in Lafayette and Walnut Creek are also sometimes welcome opponents. The culmination of the swim season is the Orinda-Moraga Pool Association competition, an annual three-day league meet in early August held at the Soda Aquatic Center at Campolindo High School, a competition pool that has bleacher seating for up to 1,000 people. Parents, coaches, and children devote an enormous amount of time, energy, and creativity to make this event, and the whole swim season, a success every year.

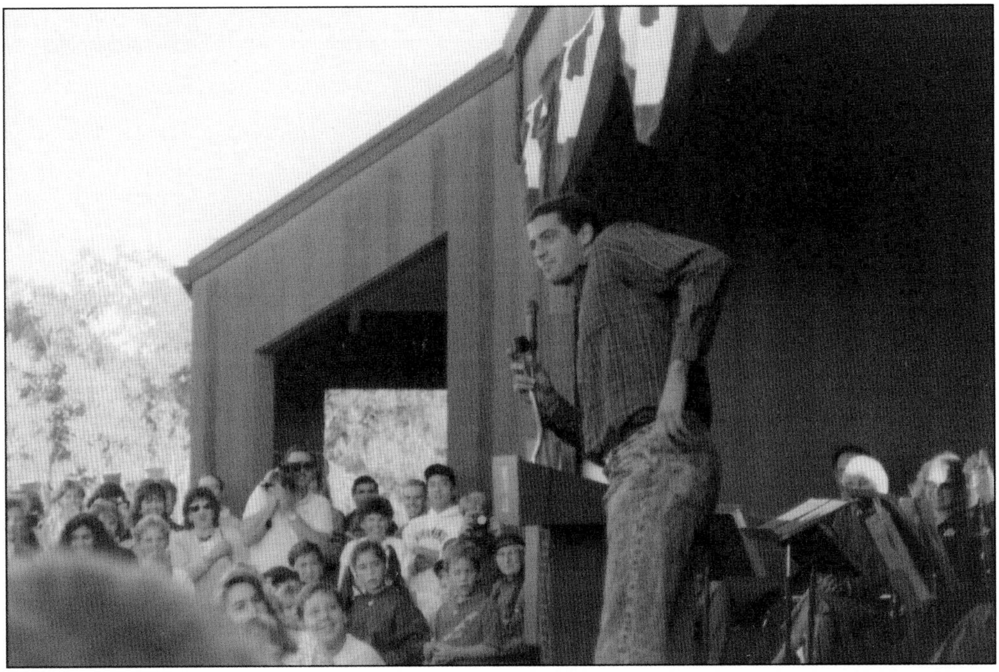

Moraga has produced a number of Olympians, of which the town is very proud. Kim Vandenberg, a graduate of Campolindo high School, won a bronze medal in 2008 swimming the 800-meter freestyle relay. Peter Varellas played for the US water polo team in the 2008 Olympics, when the team won the silver medal. He also played on the US Olympic team in 2012, when the team made it to the quarter finals. Matt Biondi, pictured here in 1988, won 11 Olympic medals in his career from 1984 to 1992, including five gold. At the Moraga Commons bandstand, Al Dessayer, then mayor, gave Biondi the key to the town.

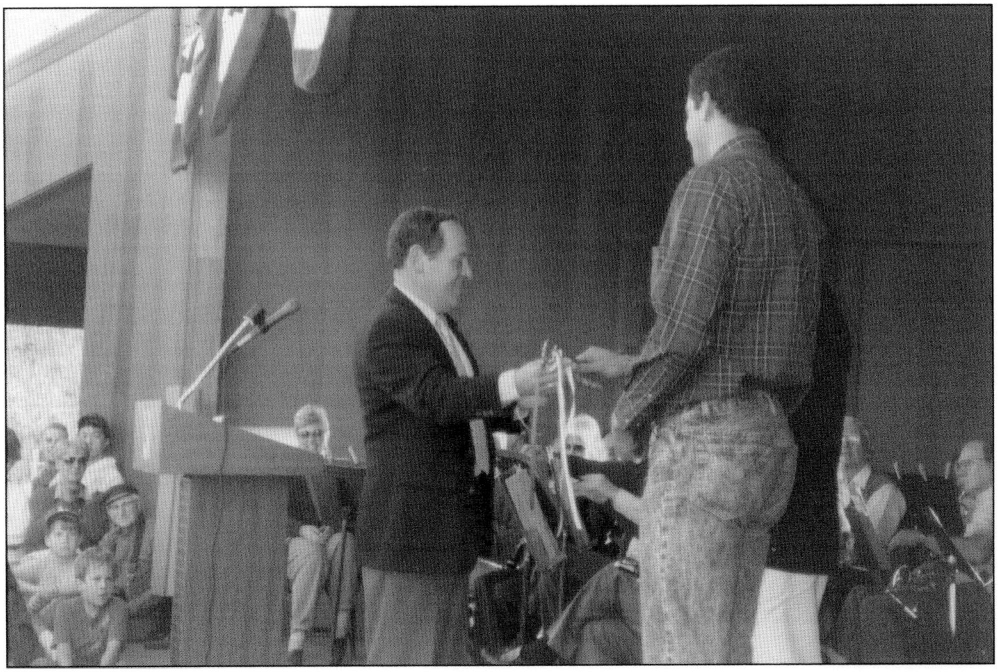

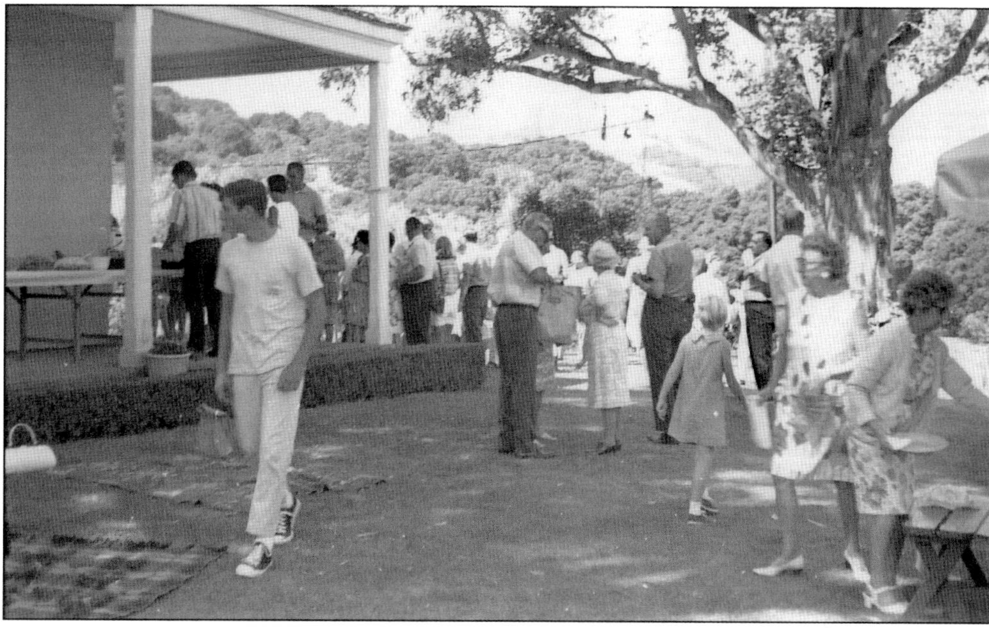

The Moraga Historical Society, founded in 1965, preserves the history of the town of Moraga and the Moraga Valley. Volunteers maintain the archives at the Moraga History Center. In addition to an annual banquet, an annual potluck at the Hacienda, and several speaker presentations, the society arranges for historically informative field trips that, following Spanish tradition, are called *romerías*. This photograph shows a romería that celebrates the Moraga family heritage with a picnic at the Moraga adobe. The cake pictured below features the Moraga family crest.

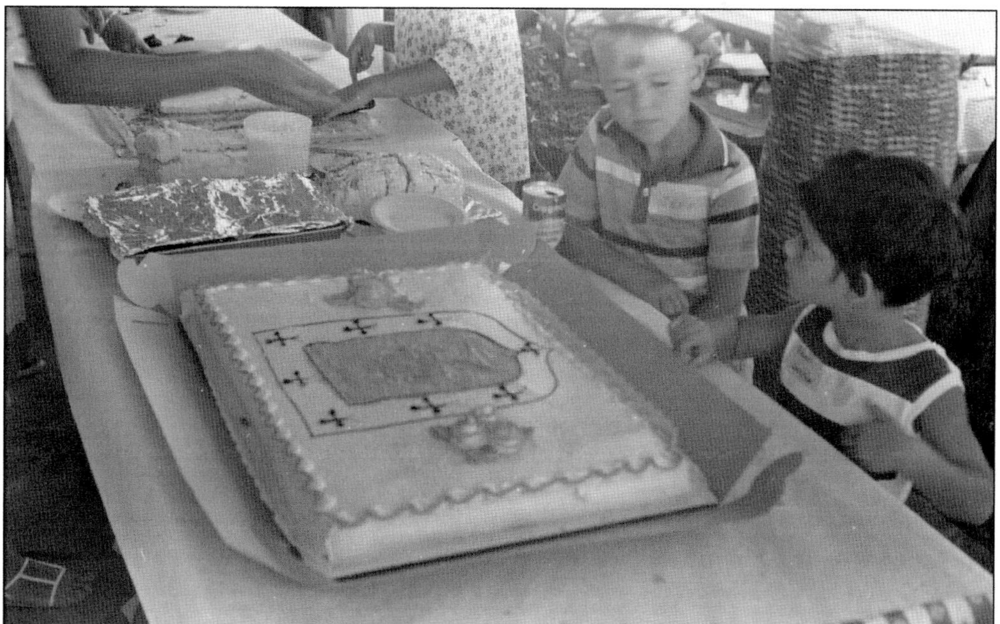

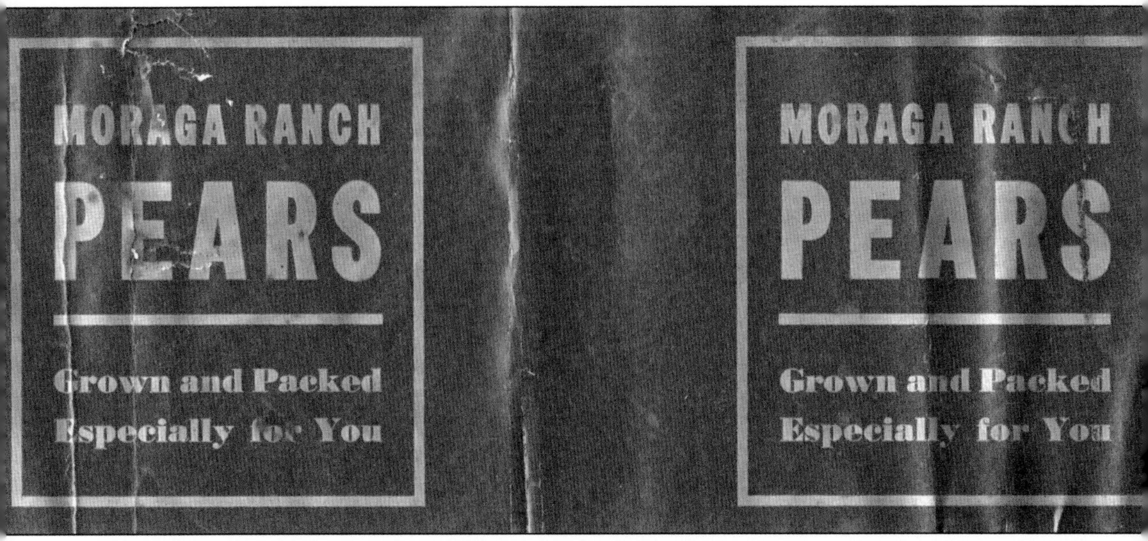

The Moraga Park Foundation regularly organizes volunteer events to support the local parks and trails. Honoring the tradition of the pear harvest from days gone by, represented here with a photograph of the historical local label, the organization oversees an annual pear harvest from local trees, donating the pears to the Contra Costa County and Solano County food banks. Moraga donates about 10,000 pounds of pears each year. Pears in Moraga go way back. Two packinghouses were constructed by the Stewart Fruit Company, which operated in the 1920s in the Moraga Valley, and they were used at that time to capacity. Conducting their business statewide, the company packed and shipped pears by train to canneries and eastern destinations, making the Moraga-grown pear well known.

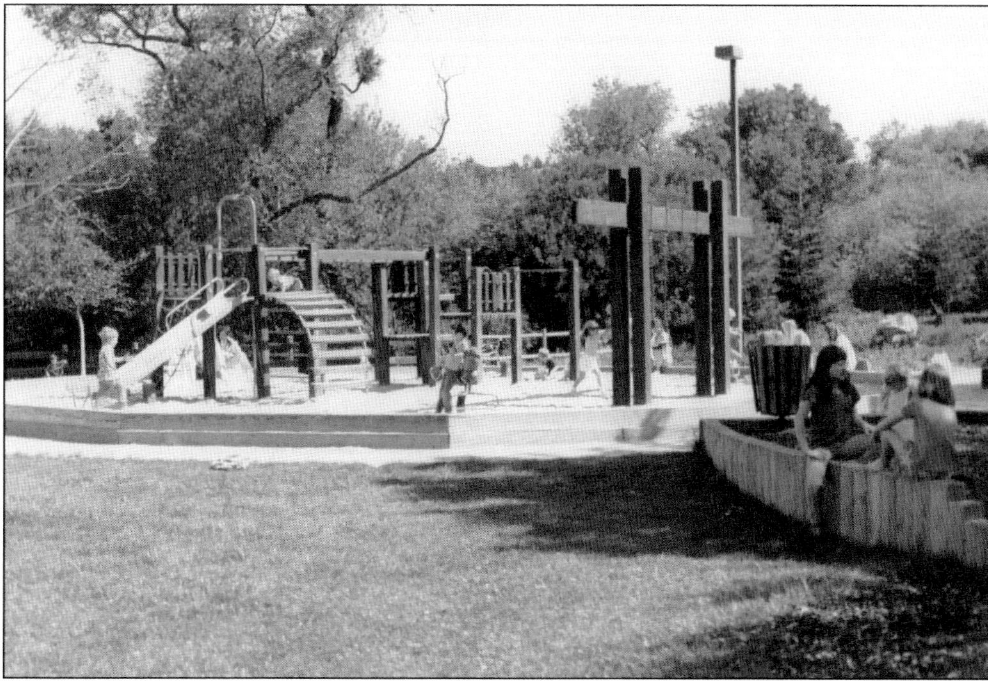

The Moraga Commons is a favorite place for parents to bring youngsters. Children can run, play, and bike safely away from street traffic within the confines of the park. Fourth of July at the Moraga Commons begins with two main events: a race through city streets finishing with a pancake breakfast and a bicycle parade for children conducted within the park on an asphalt pathway supervised by local police officers who lead the parade. Tricycles and wagons, well decorated with red, white, and blue streamers, also get into the mix, and the event is always a great success.

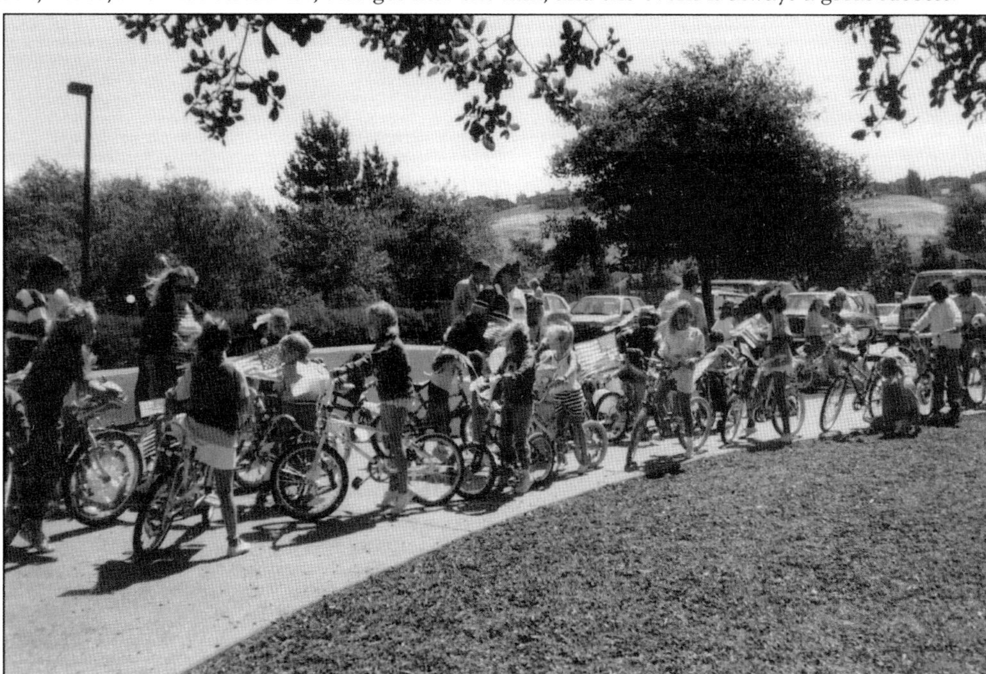

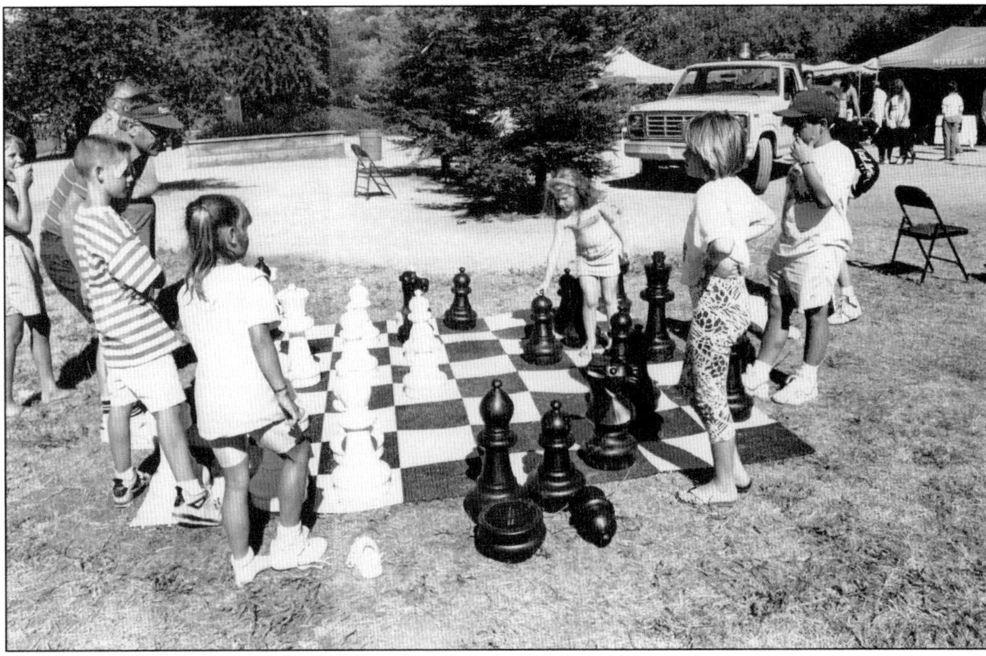

Many residents converge at the Moraga Commons for the celebration of the Fourth of July. These photographs from 1990 (above) and 1987 show the lively ambiance. A variety of activities, from giant chess games to barbecue lunches, may be enjoyed. In addition, local organizations share information from booths. The weather is usually very warm, and the festivities can be enjoyed outside all day long. At night, the fog may roll in, so locals might dash home to grab a jacket before returning to the hills at the Commons to watch the fireworks set off from the country club golf course and enjoy the live music from the bandstand.

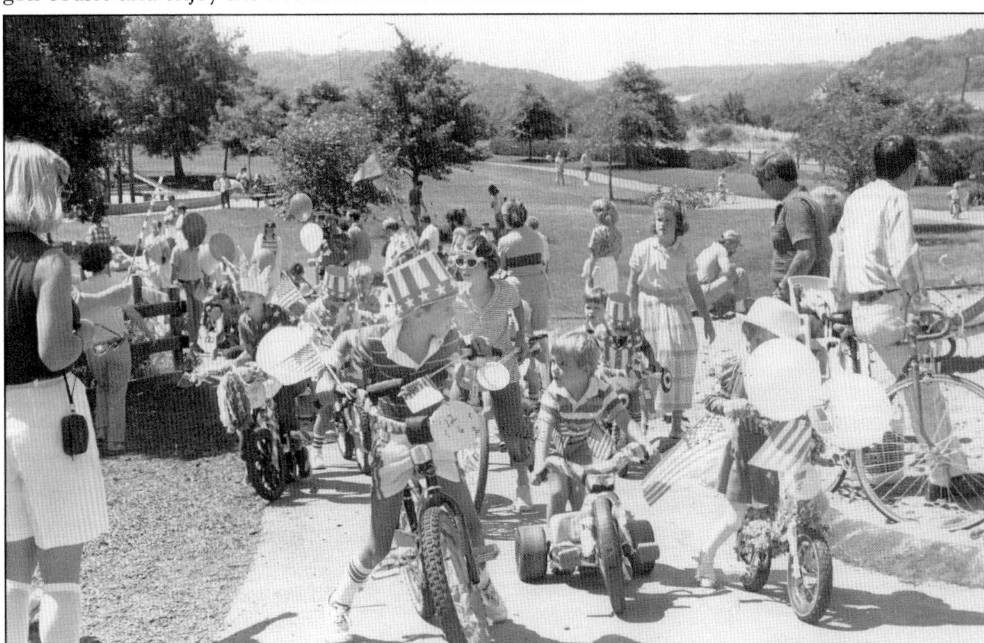

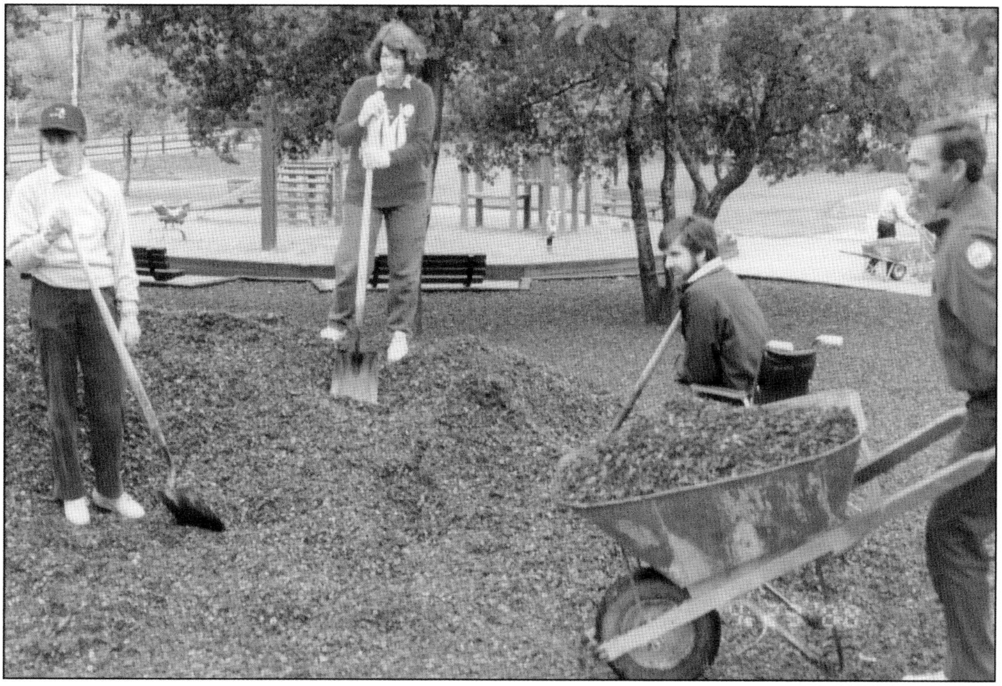

For over 25 years, the Town of Moraga has paired with the Moraga Chamber of Commerce to sponsor annual days of volunteer work called Moraga Beautiful. This effort has put many local volunteers to work over the years creating and maintaining important community projects. At the Moraga Commons, they have shoveled tan bark, stained the play structures and benches, and weeded. Work has also been done at Rancho Laguna, another park. Former mayor Margaret DePriester was one of the original event coordinators. The idea was to have local residents spruce up the local parks. It has become a tradition and a way to bring people together for a good cause.

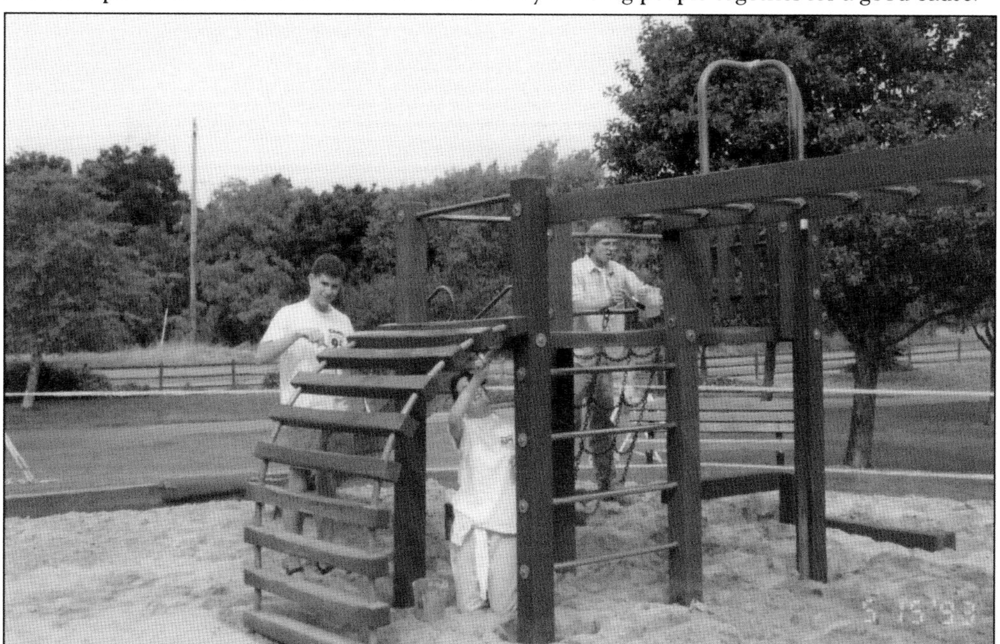

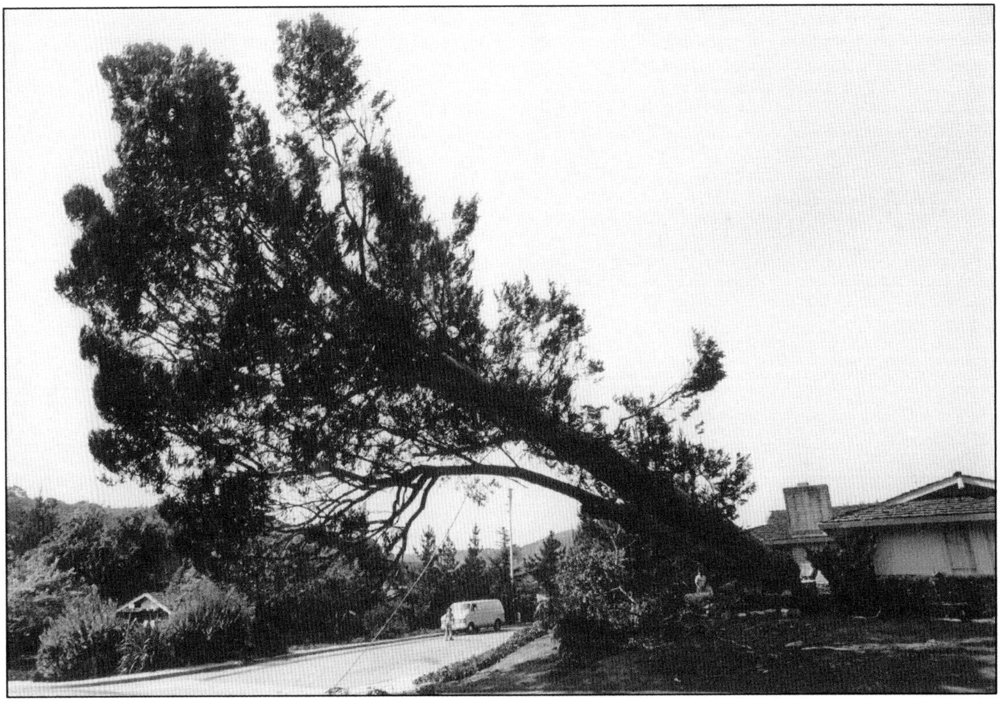

Also featured on the cover of the book, this large eucalyptus stood at the intersection of Camino Pablo and Oxford Street until it came down in 1980. The attractive residential area took over much of the farm and ranch land. Camino Pablo, seen below, is one of the original roads that went through the ranches of the Moraga Valley. Remnants of the orchards that once lined Camino Pablo add to the beauty of the drive down this road. The road serves as a residential gateway to two schools, several swim and tennis clubs, and Rancho Laguna park.

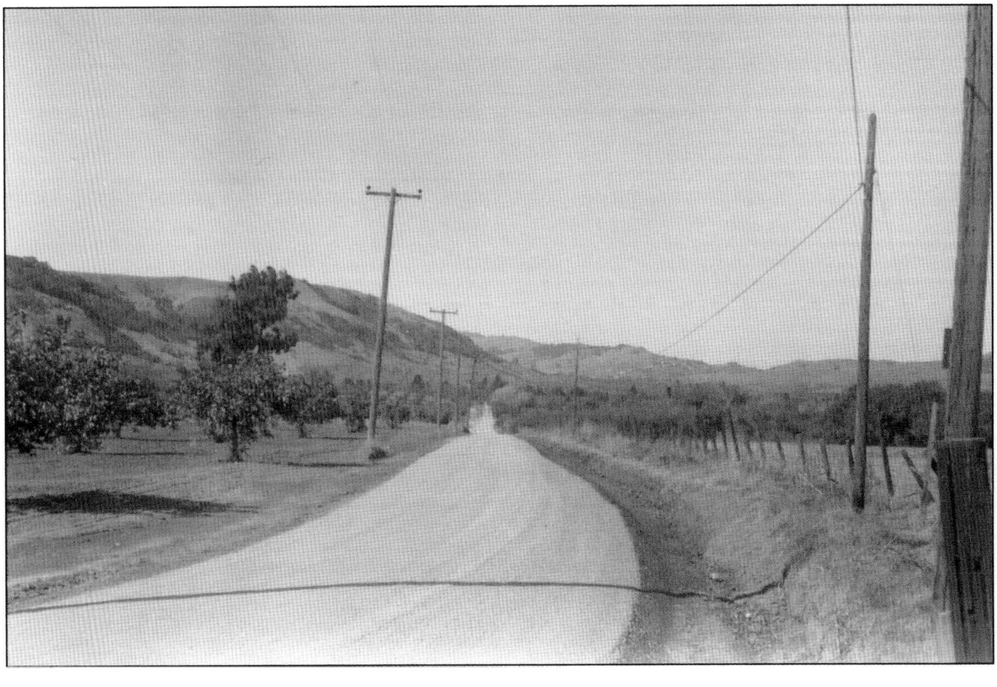

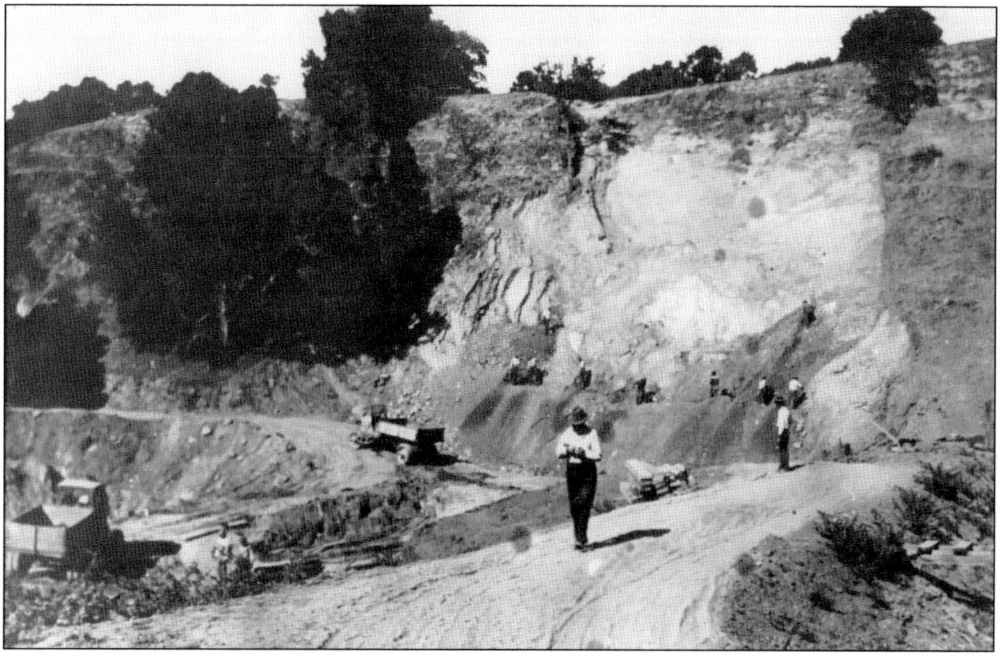

Construction on Bollinger Canyon Road took place in 1927–1928. This road leads through "the Bluffs," a somewhat rural area of town, with dirt roads and working ranches. The area is a remnant from the very distant past. Prehistoric fossils have been found at the base of the hill. In decades past, motorists could also see the prints of mastodon hooves, stamped into the side of the hill, which had tilted due to the geologic shifting that is so common in California. The hill has now eroded to the point that it is almost impossible to see anything but a glimpse of what was once a heavy footprint. The photograph below, taken by Don Falconer in 1967, shows the etching once evident on the Bluffs of the ripples of an ancient sea.

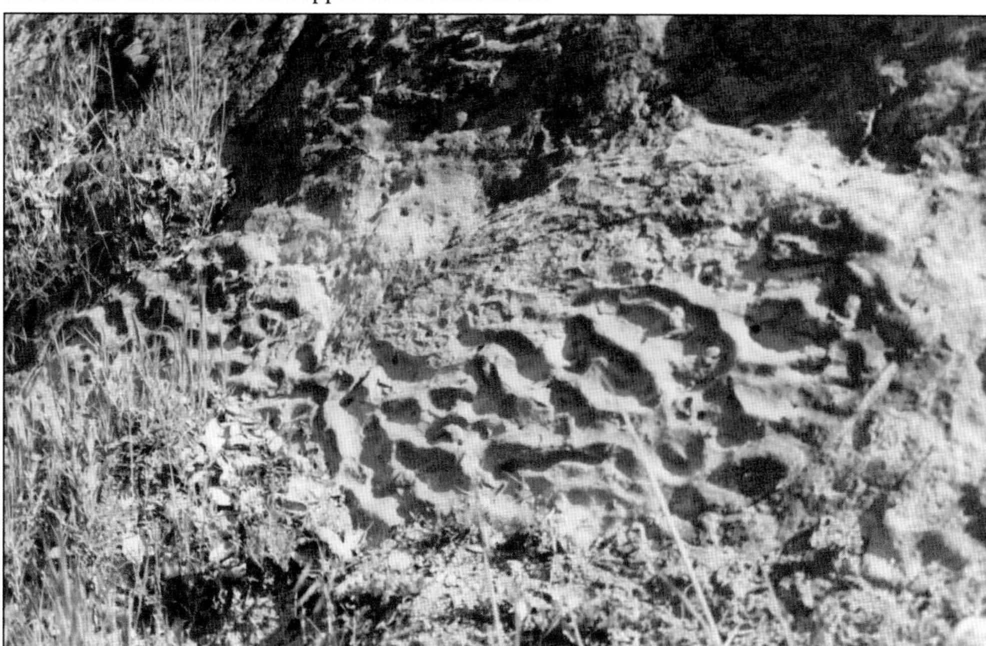

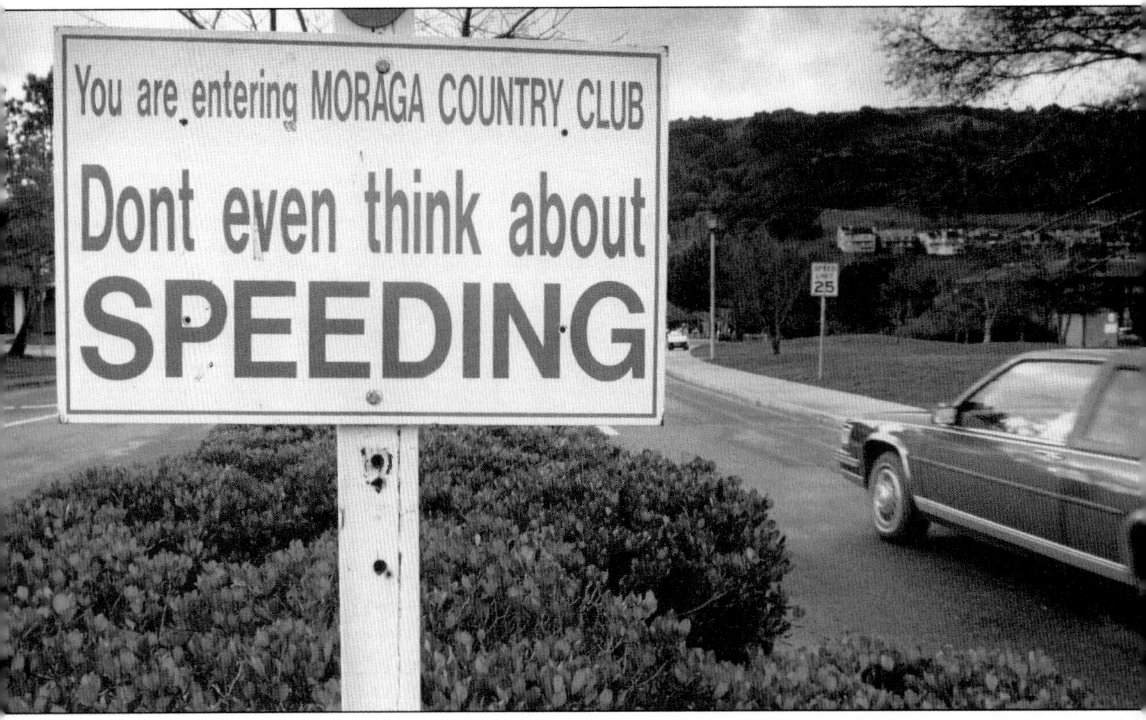

Country Club Drive was once named Munster Drive, for Otto Munsterer of the Moraga Company. Munsterer managed the pear orchards. The street was intended to be part of the main part of town but now sits on the outskirts. County Club Drive now leads, naturally enough, to the Moraga Country Club and to the subdivision of the same name. The country club has swimming, tennis, and golf. The golf course is used not only for playing, but also does double duty on the Fourth of July, when the town fireworks are set off from there. The Moraga Country Club subdivision was developed by Moraga Enterprises Inc., which purchased the land from Russell Bruzzone in 1972.

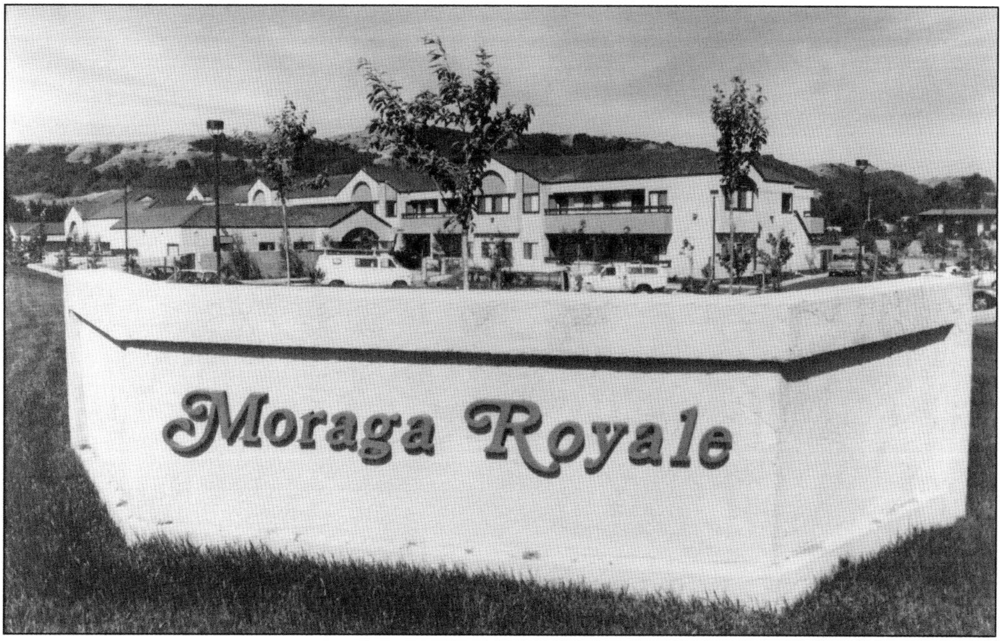

Seniors have a place in Moraga. There are several assisted living facilities, including Moraga Royale, seen here under construction in 1986. It is situated on Canyon Road. In addition, the popular group Moraga Movers, originally organized in 1975 under the name Moraga Hacienda Seniors, hosts monthly luncheons and dinners, and plans interesting excursions. Transportation is provided in a van owned by the group. Retired Moragans are often very active in community volunteer efforts, contributing valuable skills to many local organizations.

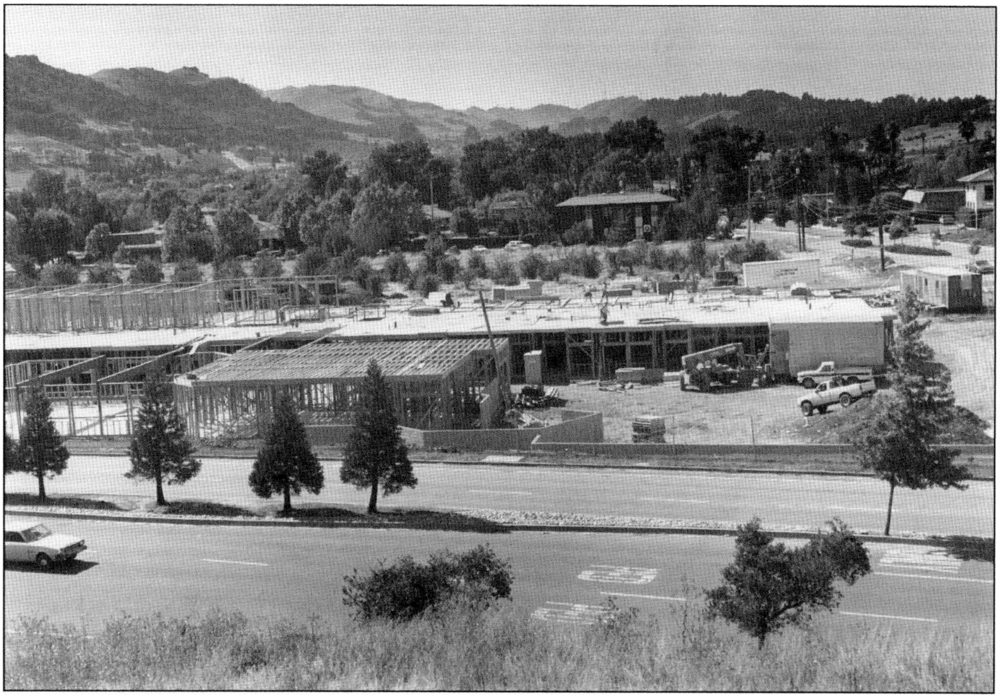

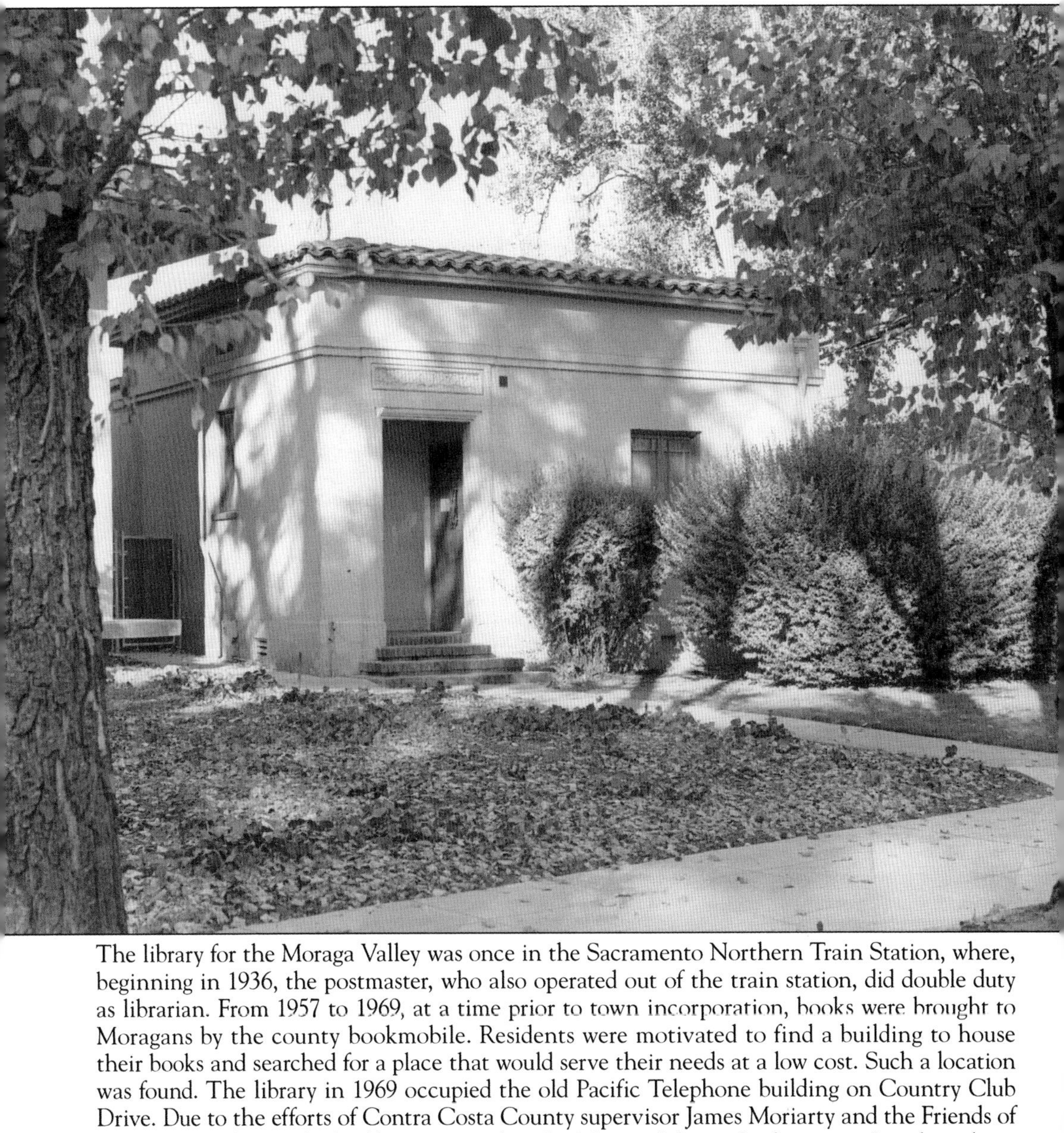

The library for the Moraga Valley was once in the Sacramento Northern Train Station, where, beginning in 1936, the postmaster, who also operated out of the train station, did double duty as librarian. From 1957 to 1969, at a time prior to town incorporation, books were brought to Moragans by the county bookmobile. Residents were motivated to find a building to house their books and searched for a place that would serve their needs at a low cost. Such a location was found. The library in 1969 occupied the old Pacific Telephone building on Country Club Drive. Due to the efforts of Contra Costa County supervisor James Moriarty and the Friends of the Moraga Library, the building was used as the Moraga Library for five years. Local residents provided the funds and labor needed to renovate the building.

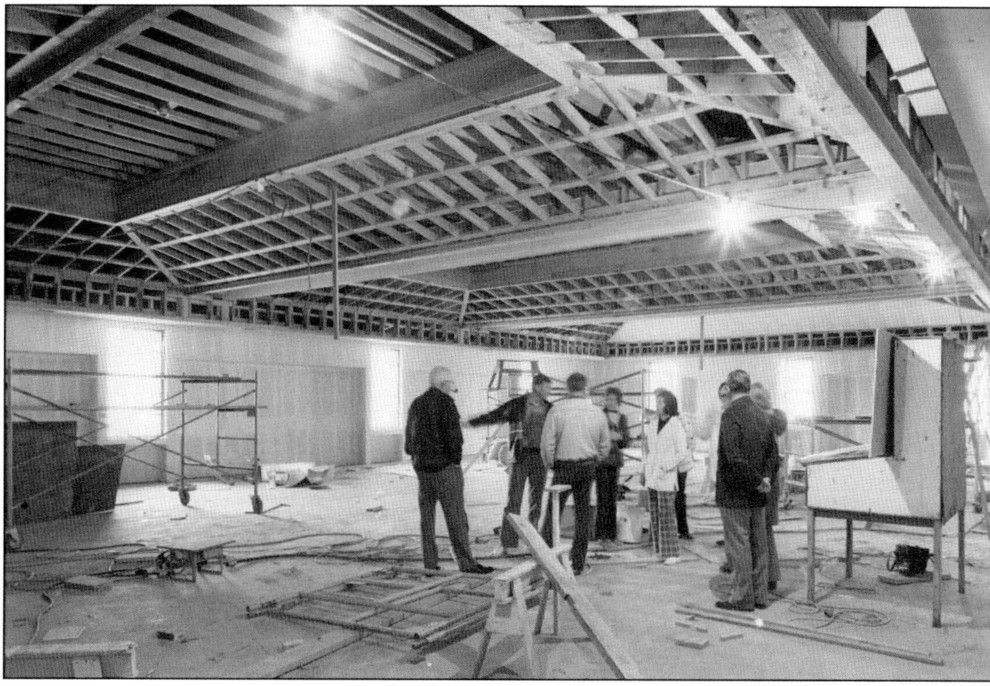

Taken in 1979, the above photograph shows the construction of the new library. Friends of the Moraga Library inspect the progress of construction. When finished, the front of the library was landscaped by the Moraga Garden Club, an organization that actively plants and tends flowers all over town. As seen below, on the front steps of the new library stands one of the original urns from the old townsite. The library is on St. Mary's Road, across from the Lafayette-Moraga Trail and the Moraga Commons. The efforts of the Friends of the Moraga Library, formed in 1968, resulted in the purchase of the site for the building, and fundraising by the Moraga Service League, the Moraga Rotary, and other groups provided funding to furnish the building.

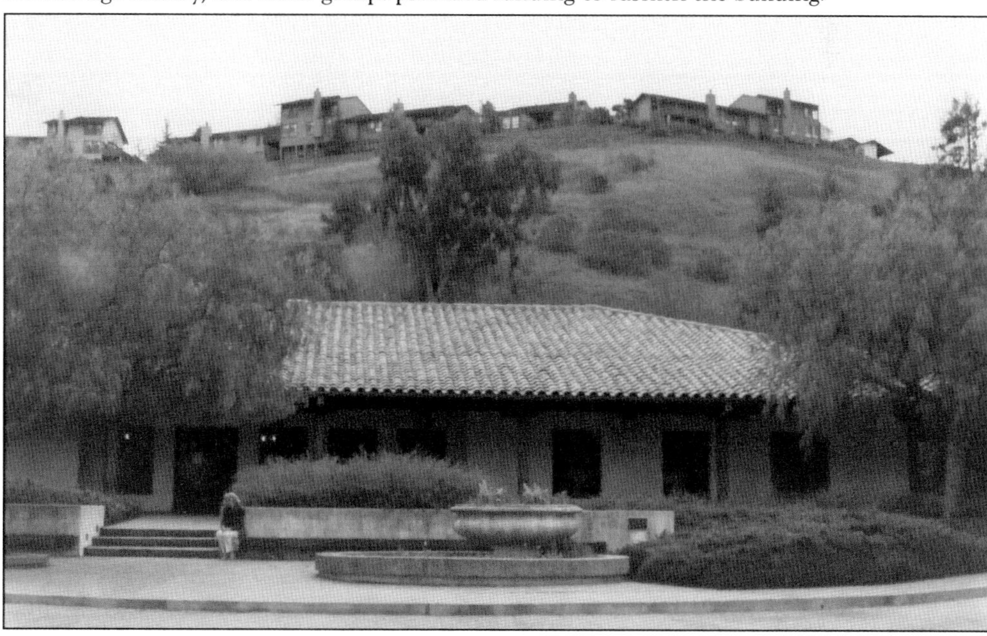

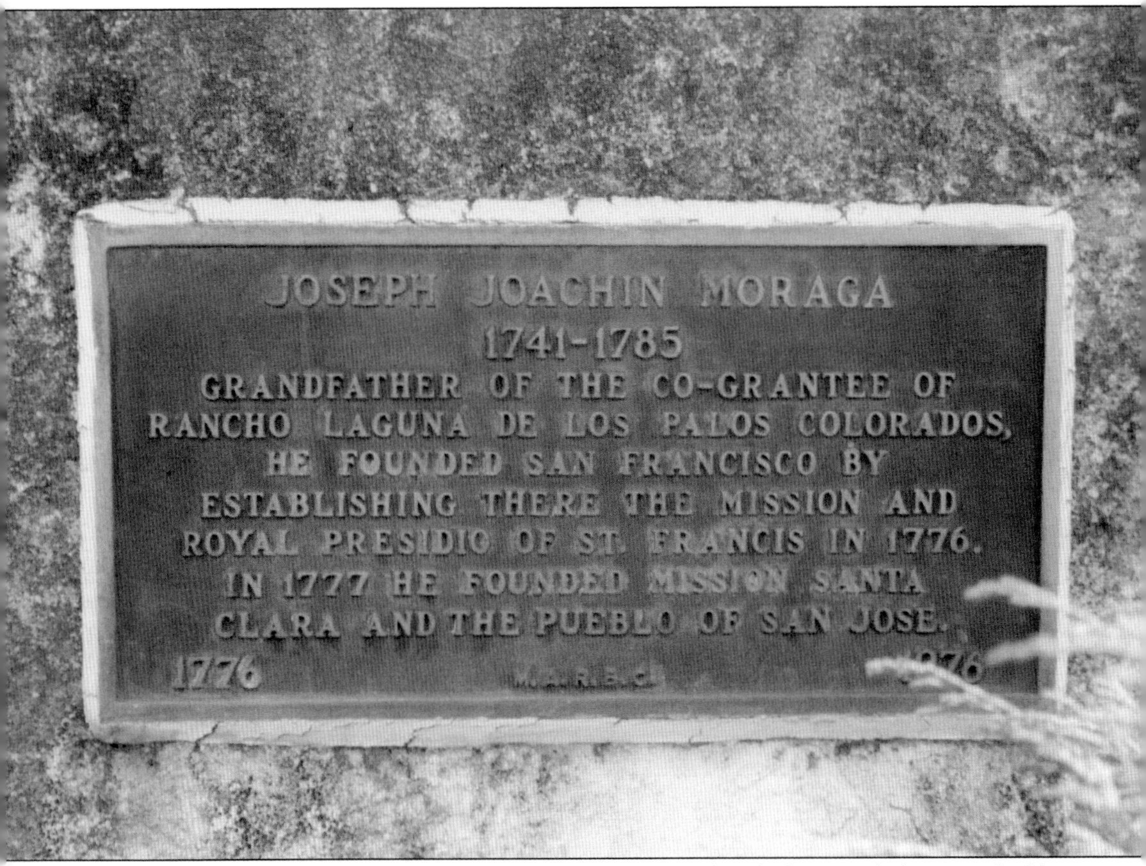

In 1976, the Moraga American Bicentennial Commission placed a historical plaque at the library building to commemorate the bicentennial of the founding of San Francisco. As proudly stated on the plaque, the origins of San Francisco are connected to the heritage of the town of Moraga. The land in Moraga was once part of the land grant from the Mexican government to Juan Bernal and Joaquin Moraga. Moraga was grandson of Lt. Joseph Joaquin Moraga. As second in command in the De Anza expedition, Moraga established the San Francisco Presidio and Mission Dolores. The mission was officially dedicated by Fr. Junipero Serra under the name Mission San Francisco de Assisi in October 1776. The land grant that was given jointly to Moraga's grandson and his cousin Juan Bernal was gifted in recognition of the service of Moraga. (Photograph by Les Krames.)

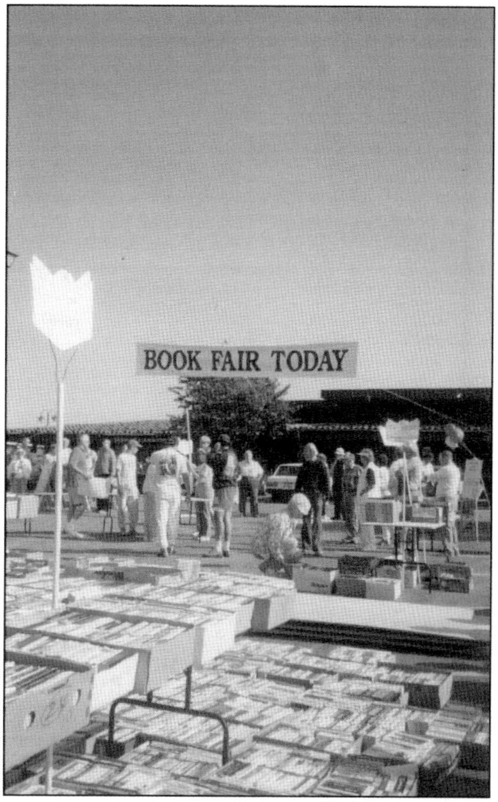

Book fairs are held regularly by the Friends of the Moraga Library. In addition, there is a small book shop where some of the more interesting used books donated regularly by local residents can be bought for a few dollars apiece. The photograph below shows, on the right, active community members Elsie and the late Dewey Mastick at one of the lively book fairs. The book fairs are enjoyable community events where residents meet and chat, find interesting books at a good price, and help support the local library. Toward the end of the event, the remaining books are often gathered into large shopping bags and sold for a dollar a bag.

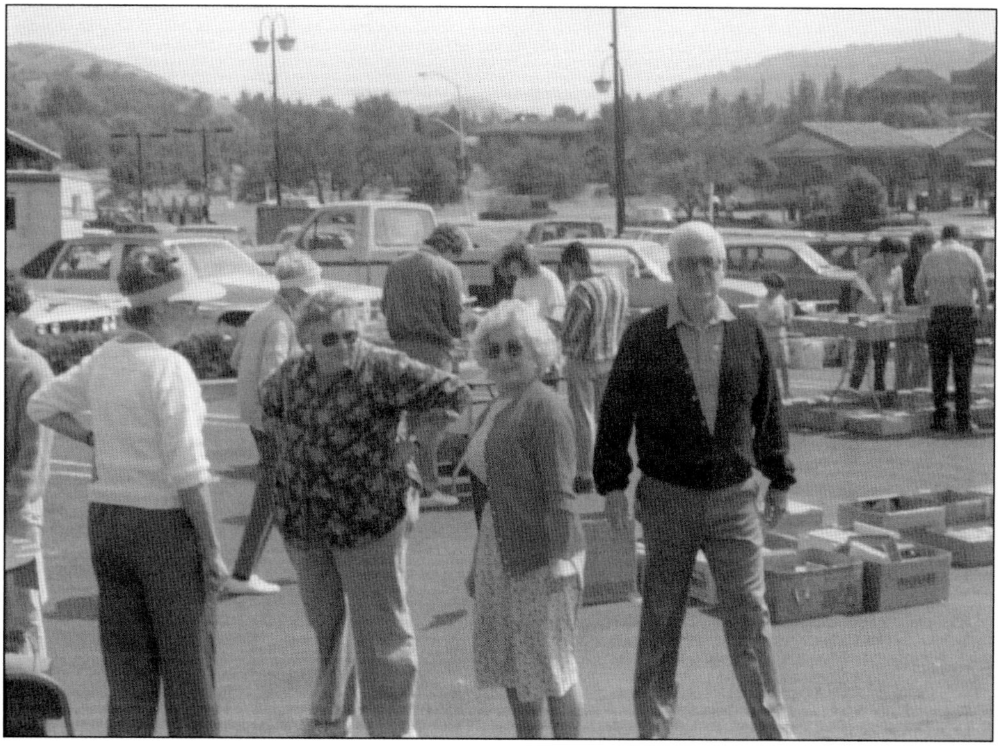

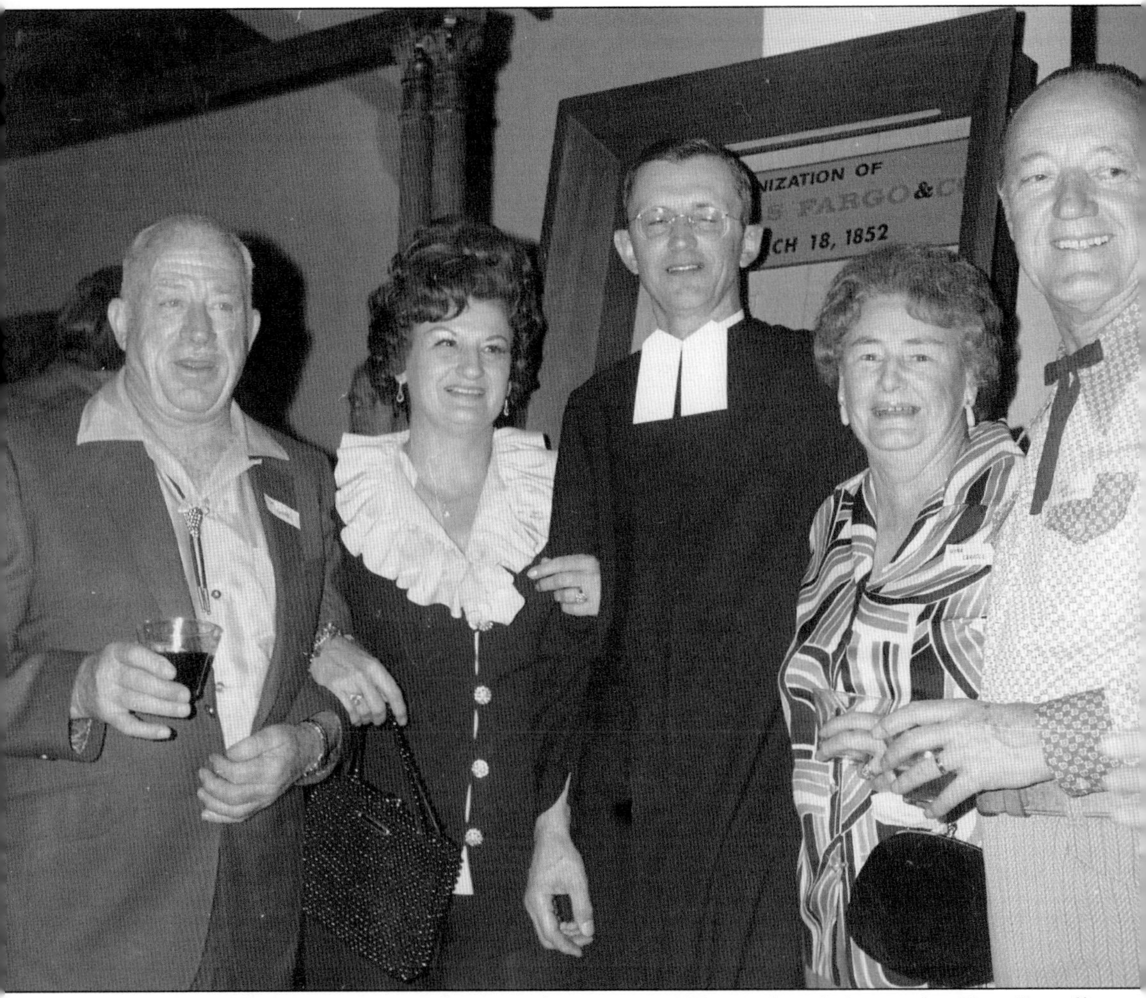

Attending the Moraga Historical Society banquet in 1971 are, from left to right, Tom Carroll, Kay Moriarty, Brother Dennis Goodman, and Contra Costa County supervisor Jim Moriarty. The organization, which has now celebrated 50 years since its founding in 1965, continues to host a banquet every fall. The highlight of the banquet is always a presentation by a speaker with expertise on history. The Moraga Historical Society also provides lectures open to the public on historical topics several times a year. Since 1999, the Moraga Historical Society has maintained archives at the Moraga History Center, located at the Moraga Library. The center is open on several days each week when visitors are welcome to bring their questions and research interests to the archives staff. This organization also produces a quarterly newsletter with articles on local history.

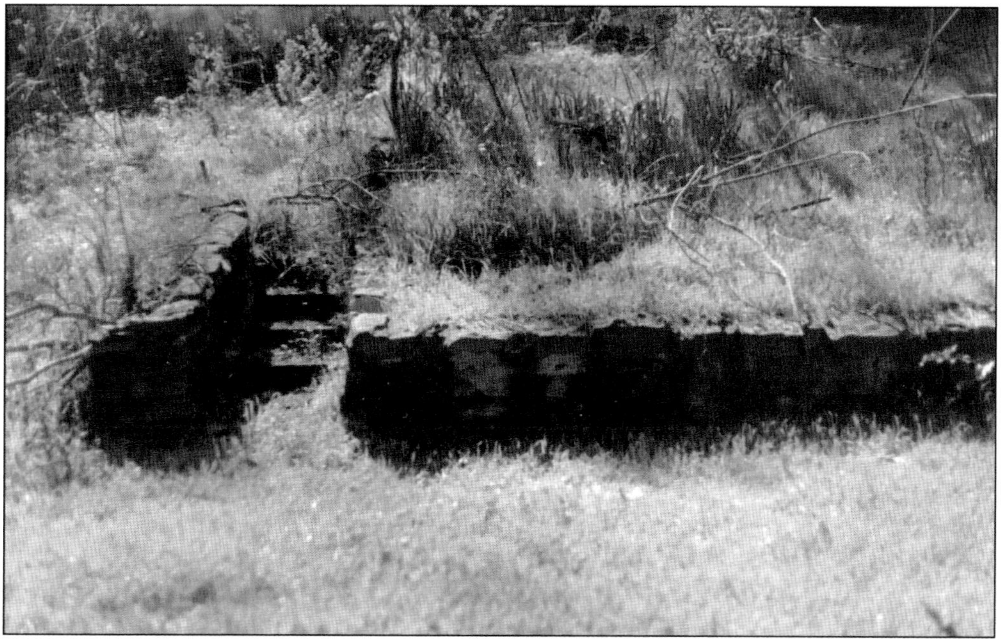

These "steps to nowhere" are remnants of the Valle Vista subdivision. Here and there, bits of foundation remain, and this one is just off the Riche Loop Trail near the staging area. Hikers can amble up the steps, brushing away the encroaching shrubbery, and imagine how it may have been to live in Moraga in years past. Valle Vista was taken by eminent domain to become watershed, but signs of the former commuter subdivision remain.

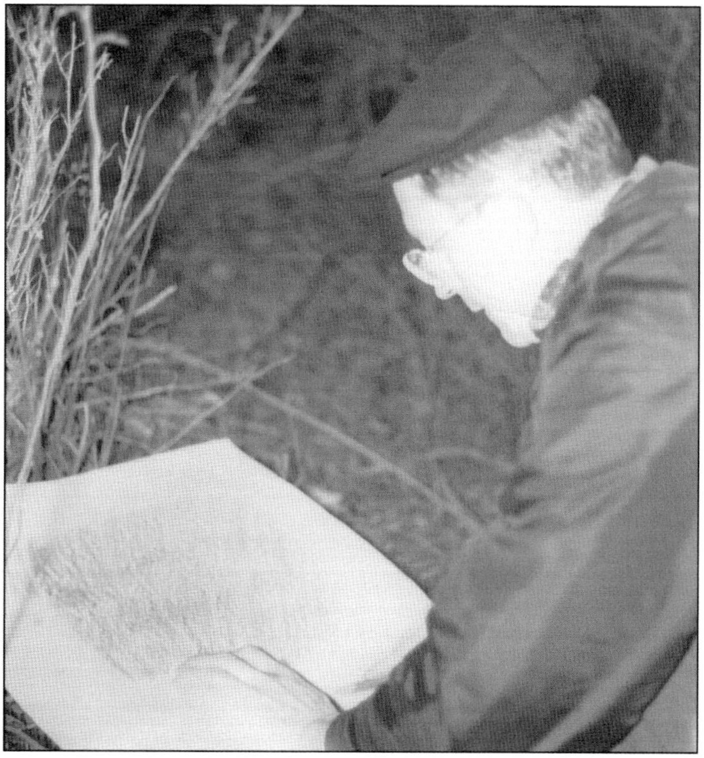

Brother Dennis Goodman, well known for his many contributions to researching and preserving Moraga history, brushes a gravestone in 1968 in the old Valle Vista commuter subdivision, now protected watershed managed by the East Bay Municipal Utility District. The gravestone of Elisa J. Berry now sits outside the Moraga History Center. Preserving an important marker of past life in Moraga, Brother Goodman has connected a distant past with the present.

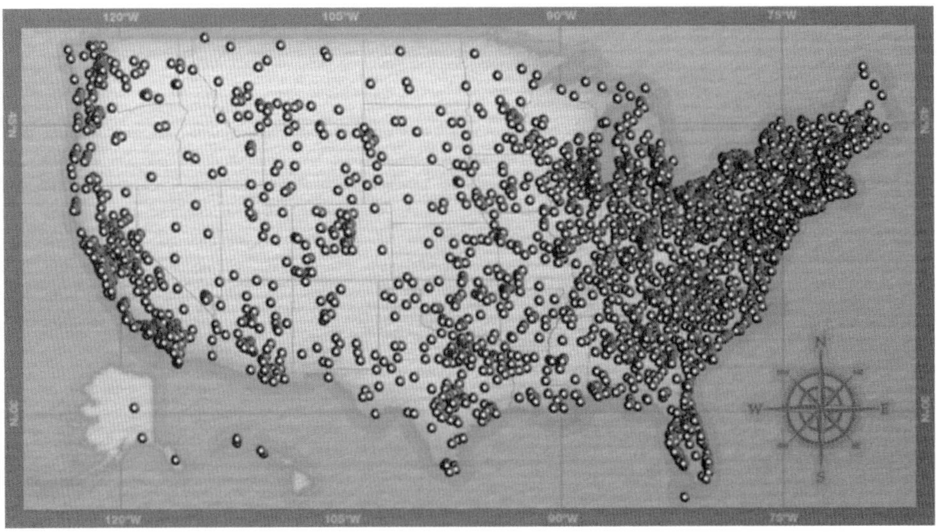

Consistent with our mission to preserve history on a local level, this book was printed in South Carolina on American-made paper and manufactured entirely in the United States. Products carrying the accredited Forest Stewardship Council (FSC) label are printed on 100 percent FSC-certified paper.

MADE IN THE USA